HOME RUN

Other Books by David Vincent

*The Midsummer Classic:
The Complete History of Baseball's All-Star Game,*
with Lyle Spatz and David W. Smith

SABR Presents the Home Run Encyclopedia,
with Robert McConnell

Home Runs in the Old Ballparks

HOME RUN

The Definitive History of Baseball's Ultimate Weapon

DAVID VINCENT

Potomac Books
An imprint of the University of Nebraska Press

Copyright © 2007 David Vincent

Published in the United States by Potomac Books, Inc. All rights reserved. No part of this book may be reproduced in any manner whatsoever without written permission from the publisher, except in the case of brief quotations embodied in critical articles and reviews.

Library of Congress Cataloging-in-Publication Data
Vincent, David, 1949 July 26-
 Home run : the definitive history of baseball's ultimate weapon / David Vincent. — 1st ed.
   p. cm.
 Includes bibliographical references and index.
 ISBN-13: 978-1-59797-035-8 (alk. paper)
 ISBN-10: 1-59797-035-2 (alk. paper)
 1. Home runs (Baseball)—History. I. Title.
 GV868.4.V56 2007
 796.357'26—dc22
                                2006023385
ISBN 978-1-59797-036-5 (paperback)

(alk. paper)

First Edition

*For JoLynne
Who Makes Everything Worthwhile*

CONTENTS

List of Illustrations		ix
List of Figures		xi
List of Tables		xiii
Foreword		xv
Acknowledgments		xix
Preface		xxi
1	The Nineteenth Century	1
2	The Deadball Era	20
3	Rules Changes in 1920	35
4	Babe Ruth	43
5	The Roaring Twenties	57
6	The Golden Age of Baseball	72
7	Integration	90
8	Expansion	108
9	Post-Season Home Runs	136
10	The Designated Hitter Era	158
11	The All-Star Game	182
12	The Ultimate Weapon	197
13	Conclusion	230
14	Postscript: The 2006 Season	234

Appendix A. Career Home Run Milestones	239
Appendix B. Single-Season Home Run Milestones	241
Appendix C. Single-Game Home Run Milestones	244
Appendix D. Yearly Home Run Leaders by League	245
Appendix E. Hollywood Homers	254
Bibliography	257
Index	259
About the Author	279

ILLUSTRATIONS

Brotherhood Park, Cleveland	5
Harry Stovey	15
Frank "Home Run" Baker	28
Babe Ruth	45
Ralph Kiner	92
Bobby Thomson and "The Shot Heard 'Round the World"	96
Roger Maris hitting number 61	112
Mark McGwire	175
Ted Williams	183
Barry Bonds	209

FIGURES

1.1	Home Run Production Rate (1876–2005)	4
1.2	Home Run Production Rate (1876–1900)	5
2.1	Home Run Production Rate (1901–19)	21
2.2	Breakdown of Home Runs by Type (1901–19)	22
5.1	Home Run Production Rate (1920–30)	58
5.2	The 1927 Home Run Race	65
6.1	Home Run Production Rate (1931–46)	73
7.1	Home Run Production Rate (1947–60)	91
8.1	Home Run Production Rate (1961–72)	109
8.2	The 1961 Home Run Race	113
10.1	Home Run Production Rate (1973–93)	161
12.1	Home Run Production Rate (1994–2005)	197
12.2	The 1998 Home Run Race	213
13.1	Home Run Production Rate with Trend Line (1876–2005)	232

TABLES

1.1	Progression of the Season Record	10
1.2	Progression of the Season Record without 1884	10
1.3	Progression of the Season Surrendered Record	12
1.4	Progression of the Career Record	14
1.5	Progression of the National League Career Record	19
2.1	Progression of the American League Season Record	25
2.2	Progression of the American League Career Record	26
3.1	Game-Ending Hits Before 1920	36
4.1	Progression of the Left-Handed Season Record	47
5.1	Progression of the American League Season Surrendered Record	60
5.2	Progression of the National League Season Record	62
5.3	Brothers Homering in the Same Game	67
5.4	Dates of Each 25,000 Home Runs	69
6.1	Progression of the Right-Handed Season Record	75
6.2	Progression of the Career-Surrendered Record	83
7.1	Progression of the Switch-Hitters Season Record	101
10.1	Home Run Production Rate by Position (1973–2005)	159
10.2	Players Who Homered with No Defensive Position	160
11.1	Home Run Derby (1959) Results	193

FOREWORD

Jayson Stark, Senior Writer, ESPN.com

I didn't have to read this book to know that David Vincent didn't invent the home run. He also never hit a home run, not counting Wiffle Ball. And he has never belted out a home-run call into any microphone near you, at least not into any microphones that were actually plugged in.

But in my lifetime, I can't recall a single human being whom I would associate more closely with the home run than David Vincent. He's a man with a real life and a real job and a real wife. But there's a whole segment of society that knows him only for his tireless, passionate, unparalleled devotion to the study of the long ball. In fact, there's a pretty good chunk of that society that doesn't even know his name. But that's only because he has become, truly, the Sultan of Swat Stats. And it's hard to imagine how much less we'd know about those swat stats if he didn't have his laptop surgically attached to his fingertips, ready to instantly research how many times in history a player named Homer has hit (what else?) a homer. Or something like that.

A lot of this is my fault. I'll confess to that right at the top. I'm the one who coined that nickname (now engraved for posterity on his business cards). And I'm the one who first started asking this guy every goofy home run trivia question my relentless brain could manufacture. To my amazement, he had an answer for every darned one of them. And he always will, because he loves finding all those answers the way the rest of us love watching baseballs disappear over all those fences.

I first came across David in August 1992. I was a baseball columnist at the *Philadelphia Inquirer* then. He was just a name, as far as I knew, on the Society for American Baseball Research's member list. But I soon found out he was much more than that. My question back then concerned Gary Sheffield and Fred McGriff, then of the Padres. They had just hit back-to-back home runs twice in the same game. I wanted to know—okay, make that: I *needed* to know—just how rare that feat was. Someone referred me to him as a guy who might know. *Might*? One whir of the hard drive, and poof. We had our answer. The first of a never-ending (literally) series of answers.

Pretty soon, I found myself calling David just about every week—because, well, he knew *everything*. Okay, he knew how to look up everything. But just as good. By 1993, I was referring to him in print as "brilliant." By the next year, he was a "genius" and a "magician." Then, for a while there, I was calling him "Professor Longball." Finally, in 1998, when home runs seemed to burst into the news for some reason, I realized just what he was—the Sultan of Swat Stats.

We all knew back then that the home run record book was being rewritten before our eyes. We needed David, however, to keep us filled in on just how dramatic and sweeping that rewrite campaign truly was. So he might not have had quite the impact on the American sports scene that year that Mark McGwire and Sammy Sosa had. But for those of us trying to chronicle it—not to mention grasp it—David Vincent was our lifeline, the man who could always put the events of the day in staggering perspective.

Who knows how many home run factoids he has looked up over the last decade and a half. A million? A billion? A gazillion? Whatever, it has eaten up so many hours of his life, he could have walked from here to the moon in about the same time. But he has always been there for us. All of us. Sportswriters. Broadcasters. Authors. Teams. Players. Or just his fellow SABR members. He has become The Man To Call—for anyone who ever had a home run question, just because there was always another one worth asking. And he has never asked for one penny from any of us.

He finds a way to help all of us, whether he has the time or not. And he does it with such relentless joy and good humor, he never makes us feel as though we've imposed on him in any way. That, of course, is because he's more immersed in this pursuit, and more curious about the answers that lie just over the horizon, than anyone else on earth.

So if anyone is uniquely qualified to chronicle the history of the home run, to lay out exactly how much it has changed both the landscape of baseball and all of us who care so much about baseball, it is David Vincent. The home run defines him, just as he defines the home run. He has chased more homers than any outfielder who ever lived. He just chases them with a keyboard instead of a glove. So if you have ever wondered how we arrived at this juncture in baseball time, where Home Run Derbies and home run highlights have become the focal point of our sporting attention spans, you have come to the right place. David Vincent has been waiting all his life to write this book. Now we all owe it to him to read it.

ACKNOWLEDGMENTS

David Smith, my friend and colleague on many projects, has helped immensely with his baseball and science knowledge. In addition, Dave served as an early reader and helped me focus on the important facts. I could not have written this without his help.

Lyle Spatz, another friend and colleague, also served as an early reader and made this volume readable with his comments and suggestions. Lyle, who was a freshman in high school on October 3, 1951, and heard the Bobby Thomson home run in his tenth period Biology class, has never recovered.

Clem Comly served as fact checker and final reader, a pair of tasks that should not be given to a friend. He performed his duties with his usual good humor and attention to detail.

Many members of the Society for American Baseball Research (SABR) have contributed time to make the Tattersall/McConnell Home Run Log a much better data collection. Among those volunteers is Ron Selter, who has also offered his help to me in two areas of expertise: ballparks and advanced mathematics.

Retrosheet (www.retrosheet.org) has been an invaluable resource while writing this book. Thanks to those volunteers for their efforts to improve the quantity and quality of baseball history on the Internet.

Thanks to all the folks at Potomac Books, especially Kevin Cuddihy and Laura Hymes, for shepherding this book through the process.

No effort on my part could be complete without mentioning the late Bob Davids, who founded SABR. I still value the friendship I shared with Bob and all that I learned from him about baseball and life. Another founding member of SABR, Bob McConnell, has taught me a lot about home run history through conversations and his writing.

My wife, JoLynne, who prepared the index for this volume, has been by my side every step of the way with editorial and moral support. They are both appreciated.

Thanks to all these folks for their help in preparing this volume.

PREFACE

__Home run__ n. A four-base hit on which the batter scores. It is usually accomplished by driving the ball out of the playing area but into fair territory. . . . The home run provides baseball with much of its excitement and drama. Home runs routinely change the course of a game and are instrumental in putting fans in the seats.
—The Dickson Baseball Dictionary

Home run. Four-bagger. Circuit clout. Round-tripper. There are many terms used for the event and, whatever name is used, it is one of the most electrifying plays in baseball. It is also one of the most difficult feats to accomplish in all of sports. Approximately one-third of a second after the pitcher releases the ball it enters the hitting zone. In that amount of time the batter must recognize the pitch type and placement (high or low? curve or fastball?) and make the barrel of the bat meet the ball at the optimum angle. If the batter performs this act perfectly and strikes the ball with the best part of the bat at the perfect spot on the ball, the result may be a home run.

And when it happens, the crack of the bat on the ball signals a moment to remember—the high, arching flight of a five-ounce, nine-inches-in-circumference sphere beyond the outfield barrier. That flight always draws a noisy, physical response from fans and the media, and, in contrast, often causes all motion on the field to stop as the ball flies over the heads of the fielders.

Fans often jump to their feet en masse when a slugger crushes a ball. Sometimes it seems as if all the air is sucked out of the ballpark by the collective intake of thousands of breaths as animated people watch the flight of the ball. This is always followed by an immediate expelling of all that air accompanied by amazed shouts that are either joyous or sad, depending on the rooting preference of the person.

This fascination is not restricted to the ballpark. Homers get more air time on televised baseball highlight shows than any other event in the game. Some shows even run a collection of those long balls together in a package—one dinger after another.

For most broadcasters, the home run call is their signature moment. It is the phrase that is remembered long after that person is no longer on the air. Harry Carey's call ("It could be . . . it might be . . . it is! A home run!") is one of the most memorable of all time because of his style of delivery and because a nationwide audience heard it repeated for many, many years. The call by Dave Niehaus ("Fly Away!"), while perhaps not as widely known, is certainly one of the most elegant and simple of all homer calls. Regardless of the style, home run calls are usually memorable, mostly owing to the event they are describing.

Sports analogies have found their way into every day language but perhaps none more so than the home run. People use the homer as a metaphor for success in business, the entertainment industry, and personal life. A phrase such as "This product has been a home run for us!" is common. "You really hit a homer with *that* presentation!" or "We need you to hit a walk-off homer here." are other examples of long balls in every day life. Announcers in other sports often use the homer as analogy, too. More than one football announcer has described a long touchdown pass as "throwing a home run."

But why this fascination? In most sporting events, fans are attracted to the athlete who can run the fastest or jump the highest or throw a piece of equipment the farthest. In baseball, this maximum event is certainly hitting the ball out of the park. Most fans usually are not awestruck by hit and run plays or sacrifice bunts; they do not jump to their feet because a batter hits a ground ball to the second baseman. But almost every fly ball that approaches the outfield fence draws the physical responses, even when that ball is caught on the warning track.

One of the funniest moments in the long history of homer fascination came from a television commercial for Nike shoes that ran in 1999. It featured Atlanta Braves pitchers Tom Glavine and Greg Maddux talking about how "chicks dig the long ball." They attempt to transform themselves from Cy Young Award winners to sluggers with humorous results. This entertaining commercial had a clear underlying message: home runs are very popular with the fans.

This book will track the home run, its usage, and how it has changed the game through the years. Although the National Association (1871–1875) is recognized as the first professional league, that circuit will not be discussed here. Baseball historians differ on the major league status of the National Association because of its uneven schedule and constantly changing collection of teams. Here, we will start all statistics and discussion with the beginning of the National League in 1876.

The following leagues are covered in this volume:

National League, 1876–2006
American Association, 1882–91
Union Association, 1884
Players League, 1890
American League, 1901–2006
Federal League, 1914–15

All home run statistics used in this book come from the Tattersall/McConnell Home Run Log, a database that is the property of the Society for American Baseball Research (SABR, www.sabr.org). John Tattersall, a Philadelphia shipbuilding executive, purchased baseball scrapbooks containing box scores for nearly every game in major league history from the *Boston Transcript* in 1941, when the newspaper was going out of business. During the 1950s, Tattersall started compiling lists of home runs from those historical box scores and for contemporary games from current newspapers. After his death in 1981, Bob McConnell, one of the original 16 members of SABR, assumed responsibility for maintaining the home run lists, by adding new years and expanding the data contained on the lists. This time-consuming, painstaking work was done by hand from newspaper box scores by both these gentlemen. In 1990, a committee of about 30 SABR volunteers started a project to convert the paper lists into an online format. Jim Johnston and Arnie Braunstein provided early leadership for the project and I later assumed the lead role. I verified and greatly expanded the information contained in the database and have maintained the data since the conversion, with the help of many other volunteers and data providers. Biographical information used in this volume comes from SABR's Biographical Committee, widely regarded as the standard for such information.

Other statistics used here come from Retrosheet (www.retrosheet.org). Modern baseball analysis has grown increasingly sophisticated and a number of new statistical categories have come into common usage among media and fans. All of these new methods require detailed play-by-play data for current games and several statistical organizations actively collect this information. Retrosheet, a group of some 100 volunteers, is collecting play-by-play of older games and making these game accounts publicly and freely available for all interested researchers on their website. This website is one of the most comprehensive baseball history sites on the Internet and, in addition to game accounts, it contains hundreds of thousands of pages of data, including complete game results for every team and complete daily standings of every league in history, plus many lists of historical interest.

All statistics in this book are valid through the 2005 season. Record changes that occurred in 2006 are covered in chapter 14.

David Vincent
May 2006

1
THE NINETEENTH CENTURY

Baseball in the nineteenth century was radically different than, and in many ways unrecognizable from, the twenty-first-century version. There are multiple reasons for the major differences in the game of 125 years ago and the one of today. Perhaps the primary reason is the many changes made to the playing rules through baseball's early days. The rulemakers of the time tried to maintain a balance in the game between the offense and defense as skills changed and grew and the delicate balance between the two tipped one way or the other. Since the rules changes themselves also altered the balance, players skills would change again in reaction to the new rules, thus changing the balance again—and on it went until the game matured and gradually settled into the form we know today.

It is a natural trend for the general level of playing skills to improve as a new sport is played by more people. As new techniques are tried and proven successful, others see the techniques or hear about them and use them to their advantage, thus raising the general skill level of all the players. Sometimes the new practice is employed by the offense and sometimes by the defense. This is part of the natural evolution of any sport, one that alters the balance between those trying to score points and those trying to prevent scoring. One commonly cited set of changes is in regard to the base on balls. When the National League began in 1876, a batter received a base on balls after nine pitches that were called balls. Rulemakers lowered this number in 1880, 1882, 1884, 1887, and finally in 1889 it became four balls for a walk, as is still the case in the twenty-first century. This set of changes was made to restore the balance between pitcher and batter.

The layout of the playing field also changed during this era. For example, the distance from the pitcher to the batter increased a number of times as did the size and shape of home plate and the size and shape of the pitcher's area. Equipment such as bats, balls, and gloves also changed through the early years of the sport. In the early days of the game, fielders did not wear gloves, and, as odd as it might seem, at one time it was legal for the bat to have one flat side, a practice not allowed in the modern game.

The evolutionary trend is not limited to the early days of a sport; indeed, it can be seen in baseball at various times in the twentieth century. Periods of high scoring are followed by periods of lower scoring and then followed by another high scoring era. Much of this pendulum-like swing between eras is because of changes in the playing rules, and these changes act to restore the balance of power between pitchers and batters.

The aforementioned changes in playing techniques also contribute to the general evolution of a sport. If the offensive side learns new ways to increase the chances to score, then the defensive side must design ways to counteract them. In the 1980s the rate of stealing bases increased as some players concentrated their game around that skill. Pitchers gradually learned new ways to prevent those runners from being as successful and a new balance between the sides evolved.

◆ ◆ ◆

In measuring how the four-bagger has become more prevalent in the game though the years, raw counting totals will not suffice. It is easy to state that 40 homers were hit in the initial year of the National League in 1876 and that 238 were clouted in 1883 in the major leagues by batters in the National League and the American Association, which started as a major league in 1882. At first glance, this looks as if homers were being hit at six times the rate in 1883 as in 1876. However, these numbers do not take into account the fact that more games were played in 1883 than in 1876, and adding some context to the raw counting totals better demonstrates the real difference between these two seasons (or between any two years).

The method employed here is a "home run production rate." It is calculated not by dividing homers by at bats (similar to batting average) but by calculating how many circuit drives were hit per 500 plate appearances. A straight calculation of homers divided by plate appearances would provide numbers not readily understandable by the reader. In 1876 the 40 homers were hit in more than 20,400 plate appearances. As a percentage (.196 percent), this number is hard to understand and hard to quantify as high or low. Similarly, the 238 home runs hit in 1883 were clouted in approximately 60,000 plate appearances. This result is 0.397 percent, which is also hard to quantify.

The 500 plate appearance standard was chosen because the official minimum performance standard for individual batting championships as listed in rule 10.23(a) is 3.1 plate appearances times the number of games scheduled for each team. Thus, in the 162-game schedule, 502 plate appearances is the minimum, but that was rounded here to 500 for simplicity. The home run production rate will generate numbers that can be compared to other numbers that have some context for the reader, such as a 30-homer season by a batter.

Look at the rates in the two previously discussed years as home runs per 500 plate appearances. In 1876, batters hit one homer for every 500 plate appearances, while in 1883, batters hit two four-baggers for every 500 plate appearances. Thus, 1883 batters were not hitting circuit drives six times more frequently than their 1876 brethren, as might be inferred by the raw totals, but rather only twice as often.

Figure 1.1 shows a graph of the home run production rate for all major league players each year since the start of the National League. It shows a gentle curve from 1876 through 1918 and then a gradual increase from 1919 to the present. The numbers in the charts do not represent the total homers hit in the major leagues for any one season but rather the home run production rate (homers per 500 plate appearances). Figure 1.1 will be used as a basis for dividing the game into eras from a

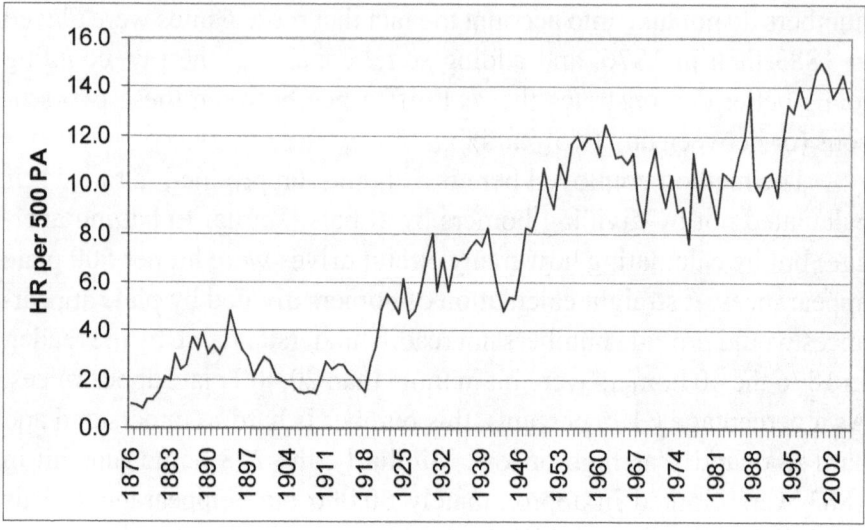

Figure 1.1 – Home Run Production Rate (1876–2005)

home run perspective. Each era will be discussed separately with a sub-chart of that time frame.

Ross Barnes of the Chicago White Stockings (now known as the Cubs) hit the first National League home run on May 2, 1876, off Cherokee Fisher of the Cincinnati Reds in the fifth inning of the fourth White Stockings game, which was played at the Avenue Grounds in Cincinnati. According to the *Chicago Tribune*, "Barnes, coming to the bat with two men out, made the finest hit of the game, straight down the left field to the carriages, for a clean home run." Two innings later, Cincinnati's Charley Jones hit another four-bagger in the same game. Also, in the seventh inning, Barnes hit a triple that was described as "very nearly repeating his former achievement" of a four-bagger.

The description of Barnes's homer is instructive about the playing fields of the day. The ball went "straight down the left field to the carriages." At that time many ballparks had no barrier fences in the outfield to show the farthest extent of the playing field. Spectators rode their horse-drawn carriages to the park and left them outside the normal playing area for the game beyond the outfield. They watched the game from various positions around the field, and batted balls occasionally traveled past the outfielders into the area where the carriages were parked with the ball

Brotherhood Park, Cleveland (1890). Note the horse-drawn carriages in the foreground, a common sight beyond the outfield in nineteenth century parks. *Transcendental Graphics*

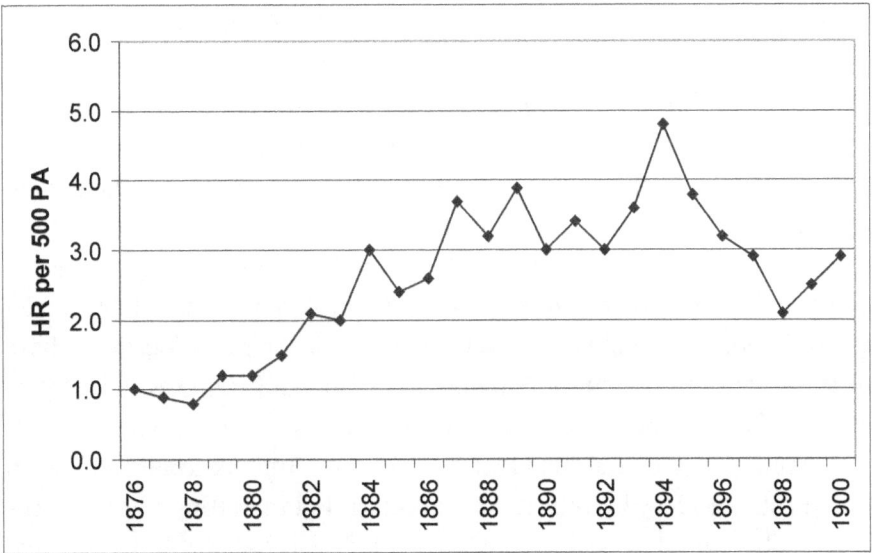

Figure 1.2 – Home Run Production Rate (1876–1900)

remaining in play. Gradually, ball fields were completely enclosed for business reasons, as the team owners wanted to increase their income by collecting admission fees from all spectators.

Nineteenth-century baseball did not feature the home run as a prominent part of the game. Figure 1.2 shows the home run production rate through 1900. In this 25-year period, the production rate never reached five in any season, topping out at 4.8 homers per 500 plate appearances in 1894. There is a lot of fluctuation from year to year in the rate as the game changed and matured, and as various factors influenced how the game was played.

The Boston Red Caps led the eight-team National League in its initial season with nine team homers. George Hall of the Philadelphia Athletics hit five circuit clouts to lead the league in the individual category, while Charley Jones of Cincinnati (and the second homer in league history) hit four. Jones was the only Cincinnati player to homer in 1876. Appendix D contains a list of the yearly home run leaders for each league. Ross Barnes, who clouted the first National League home run, only swatted one more four-bagger in his National League career, that coming in 1879. George Hall of the Athletics hit two homers in one game on June 17, 1876, off Amos Booth of the Cincinnati Reds at the Jefferson Street Grounds in Philadelphia, in the 24th game of the year, becoming the first player to hit more than one in a game. Twelve days later, catcher Pop Snyder of the Louisville Grays hit the first extra inning home run in National League history off Joe Borden of the Boston Red Caps. It came in the 10th inning of a game held at Louisville Baseball Park and won the game for the Grays.

In 1877, the league dropped to six teams, and only five of them hit at least one home run as Chicago failed to clout any during the season. This is another important factor in the game during the nineteenth century: teams went out of business and others replaced them, or sometimes clubs moved to a different city hoping to do a better business in their new location. These changes caused some turmoil in the early National League as did the creation of rival leagues three times in the century.

Paul Hines of the Providence Grays led the National League in home runs in 1878 by hitting four and also led in batting average. Before 1920, runs batted in were not an official statistic but historical research done in recent years has provided details of runs batted in for players before 1920. Hines has been credited with 50 RBI in 1878 to lead the league, thus giving him the title in homers, batting average, and runs batted in, the so-called Triple Crown. Hines became the first player to achieve this feat, although his is unofficial.

George Bradley, a pitcher for the Troy Trojans, became the first hurler to surrender at least 10 home runs in one season. In 1879, he watched 12 batters circle the bases, with six at home at Putnam Grounds and six on the road. This season's total included two games in which he surrendered three gopher balls, on July 19 and July 31, thus becoming the first pitcher in history to give up three circuit clouts in one game.

Charley Jones, a prominent 1876 home run hitter, provided more excitement in 1880. On June 10, Jones, now playing for the Boston Red Caps, hit for the circuit twice in the eighth inning against the Buffalo Bisons in Boston. Jones became the first to accomplish this, but four other batters smashed two homers in one inning during the nineteenth century: Lou Bierbauer of the Brooklyn Wonders in the Players League on July 12, 1890; Ed Cartwright of the St. Louis Browns of the American Association on September 23, 1890; Bobby Lowe of the National League's Boston Beaneaters (later Braves) in his four-homer game of May 30, 1894; and Jake Stenzel of the Pittsburgh Pirates at Boston on June 6, 1894. All players except Jones hit their two four-baggers in the third inning, and all except Stenzel did it in their home park.

> *The first known instance of two players hitting home runs back-to-back was performed by Dan Brouthers and Hardy Richardson in the eighth inning on June 21, 1881. They were teammates on the National League Buffalo Bisons playing the Trojans that day in Troy, New York. The consecutive solo homers came off Mickey Welch but the Trojans won the game in spite of these four-baggers, 8-7.*

In 1883, an American Association player, Harry Stovey, became the first batter to hit at least 10 homers in a season. Stovey, of the Philadelphia Athletics, hit his 10th four-bagger of the year on August 1 off Jack Neagle of the Pittsburgh Pirates and ended the season with 14 home runs. Both Charley Jones in the American Association and Buck Ewing in the

National League also hit 10 homers that season. Stovey led the Association in four-baggers that season having already led the National League in 1880. He was the first batter to lead two different leagues in home runs for a season and is the career home run leader for the American Association with 76 in that circuit.

Tip O'Neill, who spent most of his career as an outfielder, pitched in 19 games for the New York Gothams as a rookie in 1883. He surrendered five home runs in those 19 games, with four of them on July 5 at the Polo Grounds. O'Neill surrendered three homers in the first inning and then another in the second, thus becoming the first pitcher to give up four home runs in one game and three in one inning. The Providence Grays won the contest, 18-1.

The following year in Chicago, many cheap home runs were credited to batters. The White Stockings (Cubs) played at Lake Front Park, which is listed as having the shortest outfield fences ever in the major leagues. According to Phil Lowry in his wonderful book on ballparks, *Green Cathedrals*, the left field fence was only 180 feet down the line with the right field fence only slightly deeper at 196 feet. However, the right field fence cut across at a different angle than most fences so Lowry estimates the distance in right-center field at only 252 feet. In addition to the short distances, the wall itself was not very high, thus providing an inviting target for batters.

In 1883, batters were credited with a double on any ball hit over the fence at the newly opened park, but management changed the ground rule for the park before the 1884 season. The new ground rule stated that all balls hit over the fences would be home runs for the batter. This change had its intended effect in creating a livelier game in 1884 in Chicago, which is clearly evident by examining two sets of numbers for the club. In 1883, the White Stockings hit 277 doubles and only 13 homers, with 11 of those at home. The following year, with the new ground rule in effect, the White Stockings hit 162 doubles and 142 home runs and they took advantage of the new ground rule by hitting 131 four-baggers in their cozy little park. The White Stockings team hit 16.0 homers for every 500 plate appearances that season, a ridiculous rate for a team at this time, since the previous high had been set only the previous year by the Boston Beaneaters in the National League and the

Cincinnati Reds in the American Association at 4.5, and the next team to have a rate of 10.0 or higher was the 1921 New York Yankees with a rate of 11.1. The first team with a single-season production rate higher than the White Stockings was the 1947 New York Giants, at 18.7. The Buffalo Bisons had the second highest team home run total in the 1884 National League with 39 and the Columbus Colts led the American Association with 40 four-baggers and, even added together, these two teams did not match the home run output of the White Stockings playing at Lake Front Park.

Eleven players hit two homers in one game that season for the White Stockings while two players had three-homer games. Ned Williamson became the first batter in history to hit three circuit clouts in one game when he popped three balls over the fence on May 30 in Chicago. Player/manager Cap Anson hit home runs on three successive at bats on August 6 in Chicago, having hit two the previous day. Jack Manning of the Philadelphia Athletics, who hit 13 home runs in his career, hit three of his five 1884 homers in successive at bats at Lake Front Park on October 9 off John Clarkson of the White Stockings. Four White Stockings players hit at least 20 home runs that season. Ned Williamson led the majors with 27, while Fred Pfeffer (25), Abner Dalrymple (22), and Cap Anson (21) also contributed heavily to the overblown home run totals of the 1884 Chicago club. Pfeffer's four-baggers were all hit in Chicago, the most home runs hit in a season by a batter who hit all his four-baggers in his home ballpark.

Williamson became the new single-season standard bearer for home runs July 9 when he poked his 15th ball over the fence. He had hit one in Buffalo in June but set the new season record by knowing how to stroke the ball over the short fences in Chicago. In total, he hit 25 four-baggers at Lake Front Park and only two on the road for a single-season home run mark that stood for 35 years. Williamson's total, and indeed all the home run totals for the Chicago players in 1884, was obviously inflated by the change in the ground rule for Lake Front Park. Williamson hit no more than nine four-baggers in any other season and his anomalous 27 homers in 1884 represent nearly half his career total, in great part owing to the White Stockings' home games being moved to West Side Park in 1885.

Table 1.1 – Progression of the Season Record

Batter	Team (League)	Year	HR
George Hall	Philadelphia (NL)	1876	5
Charley Jones	Boston (NL)	1879	9
Harry Stovey	Philadelphia (AA)	1883	14
Ned Williamson	Chicago (NL)	1884	27
Babe Ruth	Boston (AL)	1919	29
Babe Ruth	New York (AL)	1920	54
Babe Ruth	New York (AL)	1921	59
Babe Ruth	New York (AL)	1927	60
Roger Maris	New York (AL)	1961	61
Mark McGwire	St. Louis (NL)	1998	70
Barry Bonds	San Francisco (NL)	2001	73

Table 1.1 shows the progression of the season home run record. Charley Jones, he of the second National League home run, held the record for a few years until Harry Stovey became the first to hit in double-figures in 1883.

Table 1.2 removes the unusual 1884 totals acquired by Chicago batters and shows how the record would have progressed otherwise. Buck Freeman's 1899 output will become newsworthy in 1919.

An 1884 change to the rules regarding pitching motion altered offensive production. Before then a pitcher's hand had to pass below

Table 1.2 – Progression of the Season Record without 1884

Batter	Team (League)	Year	HR
George Hall	Philadelphia (NL)	1876	5
Charley Jones	Boston (NL)	1879	9
Harry Stovey	Philadelphia (AA)	1883	14
Billy O'Brien	Washington (NL)	1887	19
Sam Thompson	Philadelphia (NL)	1889	20
Buck Freeman	Washington (NL)	1899	25
Babe Ruth	Boston (AL)	1919	29

the hip while delivering the ball but, starting in 1884, he could throw a pitch with his hand as high as his shoulder.

Figure 1.2 (page 5) shows a general spike in home run production in 1884, the first time that the rate reached three homers per 500 plate appearances, and much of this increase can be tied to the Lake Front Park situation. The Union Association played its only season in 1884, making this the first year with three major leagues (and thus more games played), but the production rate takes this into account by not using counting totals for comparison. The home run production rate was up in all three circuits in 1884, so the spike in home run production is not explained only by the ground rule changes at Lake Front Park, but that ground rule change appears to be the first time a major league team used a ballpark to gain an advantage over its competitors (although it certainly would not be the last).

The 1884 increase affected more than the hitters, however. In 1883, the White Stockings pitchers surrendered 21 home runs over the season with only six at home. In 1884, the White Stockings pitching staff surrendered 83 four-baggers with 66 of those at home. The increase from 21 to 83 is a large one but pales in comparison to the increase in output by the batters (13 to 142). Larry Corcoran of the White Stockings pitching staff surrendered 35 home runs in 1884 to establish a new record for gopher balls surrendered, breaking the old mark of 17 set by John Coleman of the Philadelphia Quakers in 1883. Corcoran surrendered 29 of the 35 at Lake Front Park in 1884 and those 35 homers for the season represent half of his career total of 68. He never surrendered more than 10 in any other season. The next pitcher to surrender 30 home runs in one season was Phil Collins of the 1934 Philadelphia Phillies, who led the National League that year with exactly 30 gopher balls. Murry Dickson of the St. Louis Cardinals broke Corcoran's record in 1948 by surrendering 39 home runs. See Table 1.3 for the complete progression of the gopher ball record.

Fred Dunlap, who had played in the National League since 1880, led the 1884 Union Association with 13 home runs. Dunlap, who played for the St. Louis Maroons, reached his career high in homers that season, and since the league only existed for the one season, Dunlap's total set the

Table 1.3 – Progression of the Season Surrendered Record

Pitcher	Team (League)	Year	HR
Bobby Mathews	New York (NL)	1876	8
George Bradley	Troy (NL)	1879	12
Jim McCormick	Cleveland (NL)	1882	14
John Coleman	Philadelphia (NL)	1883	17
Larry Corcoran	Chicago (NL)	1884	35
Murry Dickson	St. Louis (NL)	1948	39
Robin Roberts	Philadelphia (NL)	1955	41
Robin Roberts	Philadelphia (NL)	1956	46
Bert Blyleven	Minnesota (AL)	1986	50

single-season and career marks for the circuit. The American Association played from 1882 through 1891 as a major league. Rookie James "Bug" Holliday of the Cincinnati Reds and Harry Stovey of the Philadelphia Athletics set the single-season mark for the league by each hitting 19 homers in 1889. Stovey also set the career record by clouting 76 home runs during his seven years with the Athletics in his native Philadelphia. Stovey became the first full-season player/manager to lead his league in home runs by hitting 13 for the 1885 Athletics. Only Mel Ott of the New York Giants also performed this feat by leading the National League in 1942.

On August 15, 1886, pitcher Guy Hecker of the Louisville Colonels in the American Association beat the Baltimore Orioles, 22-5, in the second game of a double header. Hecker, who also played first base on days he was not pitching, hit three inside-the-park home runs in the victory at Louisville's Eclipse Park to become the first pitcher to stroke three homers in one contest. Only Jim Tobin of the 1942 Boston Braves also hit three round-trippers in one game.

There was one other far-reaching result because of the White Stockings 1884 ground rule change. The National League passed a new rule for the 1888 season that stated that a batter hitting a ball over a fence at a point less than 210 feet from home plate would receive credit for a double, not a home run, and the spot at which the fence crossed the 210 foot distance was to be marked distinctively. This distance was increased to 235 feet in 1892 and to 250 feet in 1926. A slightly different version of this rule would be passed before the 1959 season. It is obvious that this rule was put in place to counteract the type of ground rules instituted in Chicago in 1884 and help preserve the delicate balance between offense and defense.

Another rule change that affected the balance between pitcher and batter was enacted in 1887. Starting that season, a batter could no longer ask for a pitch in a particular location. Previous to this rule, a batter could call for a high pitch or a low pitch, thus getting a pitch to his preference. Now the pitcher was allowed to use his own preference in delivering the ball. While the change seemed advantageous to the pitchers, batters must have liked this new rule as the home run production rate unexpectedly increased in 1887.

Tip O'Neill played for the St. Louis Browns of the American Association during the 1887 season and he led the league in home runs that year with 14 circuit clouts, a fairly typical total for the era. He also led his league in batting average and runs batted in, thus becoming the second batter in history to win a Triple Crown.

In 1890, Harry Stovey became the first batter to hit 100 career home runs. Stovey, playing for the Boston Reds in the Players League, hit number 100 on September 3 at the Congress Street Grounds in Boston off Jersey Bakely of the Cleveland Infants. Stovey had started his career in the National League and then played for many years in the American Association before joining the Players League during its only season of operation in 1890. Stovey ended third in the Players League with 12 homers, two behind the leader, Roger Connor.

Like the Union Association, the Players League was an attempt by players to break the hold of the National League owners, who controlled the players with a reserve clause. The effect of this clause was that a player could only work for the team that "reserved" him. At the start, five players from each club could be reserved, which made it an honor of sorts, since only the best players would be reserved. Eventually, all players were reserved by a team, thus turning the honor into involuntary servitude. The two rival leagues both failed after one season and most players returned to the National League.

Table 1.4 shows the progression of the career record. The home run total is as of the end of the season listed. Harry Stovey had become the career leader on August 11, 1885 by hitting home run number 46 and passing Charley Jones. He hit the inside-the-park four-bagger off Hardie Henderson of the Baltimore Orioles at the Jefferson Street Grounds in Philadelphia. Stovey held the career mark until June 29, 1887 when Dan Brouthers of the Detroit Wolverines passed him with homer number 59, a two-run shot off Charlie Buffinton of the Philadelphia Phillies at Detroit's Recreation Park. Stovey regained the top spot two years later on August 13, 1889, when he hit two round-trippers off Lee Viau of the Reds at Cincinnati's League Park and Stovey held the mark the second time for almost five years. Stovey is the only player to hold the career record, be passed by another batter at the end of a season, and then regain the record. Stovey also hit more home runs from 1881 through 1890 than any other major league batter by stroking 95 four-baggers.

Roger Connor of the St. Louis Browns passed Stovey on the career list on June 23, 1895, when he hit two homers off Frank Dwyer of the Cincinnati Reds at Robison Field in St. Louis. The first one, an inside-the-

Table 1.4 – Progression of the Career Record

Batter	Year	HR
George Hall	1876	5
Charley Jones	1877	6
Charley Jones	1884	40
Harry Stovey	1885	50
Dan Brouthers	1887	65
Harry Stovey	1889	89
Harry Stovey	1893	122
Roger Connor	1895	126
Roger Connor	1897	138
Babe Ruth	1921	162
Babe Ruth	1935	714
Hank Aaron	1974	733
Hank Aaron	1976	755

park drive hit in the first inning of the contest, gave Connor 123 career home runs, making him the all-time leader. He held the record of 138 from his retirement in 1897 until 1921, when Babe Ruth passed him on the list. Stovey remained in the top five on the all-time home run list until 1924 when Rogers Hornsby passed him.

In 1891, a new rule allowed for substitute players in games. Prior to 1891, a person could be substituted only when a player in the game was injured or, in rare cases, the opposition could agree to a new player in the lineup without an injury, but the latter was an exceptional situation. With the new rule, a player could be substituted for a batter at the plate, pinch hitting for the original player. Tom Daly of the Brooklyn Bridegrooms hit the first pinch-hit home run in major league history on May 14, 1892, off John Clarkson of the Boston Beaneaters at the South End Grounds in Boston, when he substituted for left fielder Hub Collins. After his circuit drive, Daly remained in the game replacing Collins in left field. In 1889, Bug Holliday led the American Association in home runs by slugging 19 for the Cincinnati Reds. This was

Harry Stovey, 1886, the first important home run hitter. *Transcendental Graphics*

Holliday's only season in the Association, since the Reds moved to the National League in 1890. In 1892, Holliday led the National League in four-baggers with 13 and became the second player to lead two different major leagues for a season, after Harry Stovey.

Stovey led the National League for the second time in 1891 while a member of the Boston Beaneaters, thus leading a league for a season while playing for three different teams: the Worcester Ruby Legs of the National League in 1880; the Philadelphia Athletics of the American Association in 1883, 1885, and 1889; and the Beaneaters. Only Reggie Jackson in the second half of the twentieth century also led his league while playing for three different teams. Stovey, now mostly forgotten, became the

- first batter to hit 10 four-baggers in one season,
- first to reach 100 career home runs,
- first to lead two different major leagues in home runs for one season,
- first player to lead the league in home runs for three different teams,
- career leader for the American Association,
- single-season leader for the American Association,
- player to hit the most home runs from 1881 through 1890,
- only batter to hold the career major league mark in home runs at two different times, and,
- first player/manager to lead his league in homers.

In 1893, the distance between pitcher and batter increased to 60 feet 6 inches from the pitcher's plate to the back of home plate. The previously listed distance of 50 feet was measured from the front of the pitcher's box to the middle of home plate, but the pitcher had to start his delivery from the back of the box, another 5 feet 6 inches farther away from home plate. Thus, this new rule moved the pitching distance back only about 4 feet. More importantly, the pitcher now had to be in contact with a 12-inch-wide slab when releasing the ball, whereas before this time he could move laterally across a 4-foot-wide line and release the ball from anywhere on that line. Now the hurler had to be directly in front of the plate when pitching and this restriction proved more important to the hitters than the change in distance. The home run production rate increased slightly in 1893 back to the 1891 level, an increase that mirrored the general increase in offense that season. However, in 1894, the home run production rate jumped to its highest level in the nineteenth century, as batters stroked homers at a rate of 4.8 for every 500 plate appearances that season. The homer rate dropped off immediately the next season as pitchers adjusted to the new pitching restrictions and did not reach that level again until 1921.

On May 30, 1894, Boston second baseman Bobby Lowe performed a feat never before recorded in the major leagues. In the afternoon game of a Memorial Day doubleheader, Lowe led off the third inning and stroked a home run off Cincinnati Reds hurler Ice Box Chamberlain. The Beaneaters scored nine runs in the inning, and Lowe came to the plate a second time in that frame. He proceeded to smash another ball over the outfield barrier for his second home run of the inning. Lowe also hit circuit drives in the fifth and sixth innings to become the first major league batter to hit four home runs in one game. The *Boston Globe* on May 31 described Lowe's four homers, all off Chamberlain at Boston's Congress Street Grounds: "His home runs were on line drives far over the fence, and would be good for four bases on an open prairie." (Refer to Appendix C for details of all four home run games.)

> **On April 30, 1891,** Hardy Richardson of the Boston Reds of the American Association hit an inside-the-park home run in Philadelphia's Jefferson Street Grounds. As he slid into home plate, he broke a bone in his right leg, costing him half the season.

Bobby Lowe was not the only slugging star that day. The visitors featured two four-baggers by Bug Holliday, who hit for the circuit in the first and fifth frames. Boston won that afternoon contest, 20-11, in 2 hours and 10 minutes. They had already won the morning contest, 13-10.

Hugh Duffy, a teammate of Bobby Lowe on the Beaneaters who clouted 18 homers, led the National League in the Triple Crown statistics in 1894. By winning the title in home runs, batting average, and runs batted in, he became the third player to lead in all three for a season, following Paul Hines in 1878 and Tip O'Neill in 1887.

John Clarkson, who pitched from 1882 through 1894, surrendered 159 home runs in his career. He became the career gopher ball leader in 1890, a mark which he held until 1929. That season, Grover Cleveland "Pete" Alexander passed Clarkson with his 165 career total home runs surrendered.

Ed Delahanty repeated Lowe's four-homer feat in a game at Chicago's West Side Grounds, the successor to the infamous Lake Front Park, two years after Lowe performed the feat. On July 13, 1896, Delahanty of the

Philadelphia Phillies hit for a quartet of circuit drives off Colts' pitcher Adonis Terry. In the first and fifth innings, the right-handed hitting Delahanty drove the ball over the right field fence. The first four-bagger landed in the right field bleachers. The *Chicago Tribune* described the second homer as "over the scoreboard and out of the enclosure—the longest hit of the year on the local grounds." In the seventh inning, Delahanty hit the ball to deep center field and made the circuit before Colts' center fielder Bill Lange could get the ball back to the infield. Delahanty came to bat once more in the ninth inning and again stroked the ball to center field. This time after the ball got past Lange it was lost in the area of the clubhouse. Despite Delahanty's batting exploits, Chicago won the contest, 9-8. Delahanty, normally the Phillies left fielder, played first base that day because of the absence of the regular first-sacker, Dan Brouthers. As did Lowe in his game, Delahanty also hit a single in the game for 17 total bases, which was the record at the time for one game (Appendix C).

Bill Joyce started the 1896 season with the Washington Senators, but on August 1, the team traded Joyce to the New York Giants for two players and cash. After playing six games for the Giants, Joyce replaced Arthur Irwin as the team's manager, a position he held through the end of the 1898 season, except for 22 contests in the middle of 1898. Joyce led the National League in home runs in 1896, hitting eight for the Senators and five for the Giants, thus becoming the first single-season home run champ to be traded during the year in which he led the league.

In 1898, Sam Thompson ended his Hall of Fame National League career with 126 home runs, which set a new record for the league that stood until 1923. Thompson had passed the previous record holder, Roger Connor, on July 30, 1895, when he hit his 105th career home run and would be passed later by Cy Williams. Table 1.5 shows the complete progression of the National League career home run record.

In the 1890s, players regularly reached double figures in their seasonal home run totals. Batters such as Hugh Duffy, Mike Tiernan, Bobby Lowe, and Roger Connor performed the feat multiple times. Ed Delahanty reached 10 homers in three separate years, and Bill Joyce performed the feat four times. Buck Freeman had the highest single-season homer total in the 1890s when he hit 25 four-baggers in 1899, which would have been the record except for Ned Williamson's tainted mark from 1884.

Table 1.5 – Progression of the National League Career Record

Batter	Year	HR
George Hall	1876	5
Charley Jones	1877	6
Charley Jones	1880	23
Dan Brouthers (tie)	1884	35
Ned Williamson (tie)	—	—
Dan Brouthers	1885	42
Dan Brouthers	1889	81
Cap Anson	1891	84
Dan Brouthers	1892	86
Roger Connor	1893	96
Roger Connor	1894	104
Sam Thompson	1895	113
Sam Thompson	1898	126
Cy Williams	1923	149
Cy Williams	1928	246
Rogers Hornsby	1929	277
Rogers Hornsby	1933	298
Mel Ott	1937	306
Mel Ott	1946	511
Willie Mays	1966	542
Willie Mays	1971	646
Hank Aaron	1972	673
Hank Aaron	1974	733

As the nineteenth century came to an end, fours balls meant a walk, three strikes caused a strikeout, the pitching distance had settled at the modern 60 feet 6 inches, and home plate had changed from a 12-inch square in foul territory to a 17-inch wide five-sided figure completely in fair territory. The National League had survived the challenge of three other leagues—the American Association, the Union Association, and the Players League—and it was ready to move into the twentieth century. However, home runs were not a major part of the game of baseball as the century wound down, and the next era of play did nothing to change this.

2
THE DEADBALL ERA

"The Deadball Era" is the name historians have come to call the style of baseball played from 1901 through 1919. The name is derived from the concept that the ball changed in 1920 to a livelier version. This change in playing style will be discussed in chapter 5.

As in the nineteenth century, the Deadball Era game did not feature the home run; in general, the style of play was still the "get-him-on, get-him-over, get-him-in" of the previous century. This type of baseball uses base hits and walks to put runners on base and plays such as sacrifices and stolen bases to advance them. The concept of having a runner on for the big thumper to drive in came later.

As can be seen in Figure 2.1 (next page), the home run production rate for this period fluctuated between a high of 2.7 and a low of 1.4. It is interesting that the high marks came in the first and last years of the era with another peak close to the middle of the era in 1911. The first years started slightly higher than much of the rest of the period because of a slight surge in home run production at the end of the nineteenth century. The increase in production in 1919 is the precursor to a huge increase in the home run production rate that took place in the 1920s.

The low point in home run production rate during the Deadball Era is from 1906 through 1909, during which time it sat at 1.5, 1.4, 1.5, and 1.4. At the end of World War I in 1918, the 1.5 mark was repeated as part of a downward offensive trend in the mid-teens. The latter year represents a general low point in baseball as many players were away serving in the military or in other essential, defense-related jobs, and not appearing in the major league parks.

The general level of home run production rate during the Deadball Era is lower than that of most of the nineteenth century. A comparison of Figures 1.2 (page 5) and 2.1 shows this clearly. While the Deadball Era production rate never rose above 2.7 in any year, 13 of 25 seasons in the nineteenth century had a rate of 2.9 or above. The earliest years of the National League in the late 1870s and early 1880s are the exception with very low rates during that time. The production rate spiked slightly at the turn of the century but that increase quickly disappeared in the early years of the new era.

Although looking at raw counting totals generally is not instructive, Figure 2.2 shows the yearly total of home runs in the major leagues broken out by type. Before 1931, if a ball bounced in fair territory and then into the stands or over, through, or under a barrier, it was considered a home run. Rulemakers changed that statute for the 1931 season to the modern rule which states that those bounce hits are doubles. The modern hits are usually referred to as "ground-rule doubles" but this is not correct. A ground rule is a special ruling for one ballpark that deals with a particular physical element. For example, the centerfield wall in

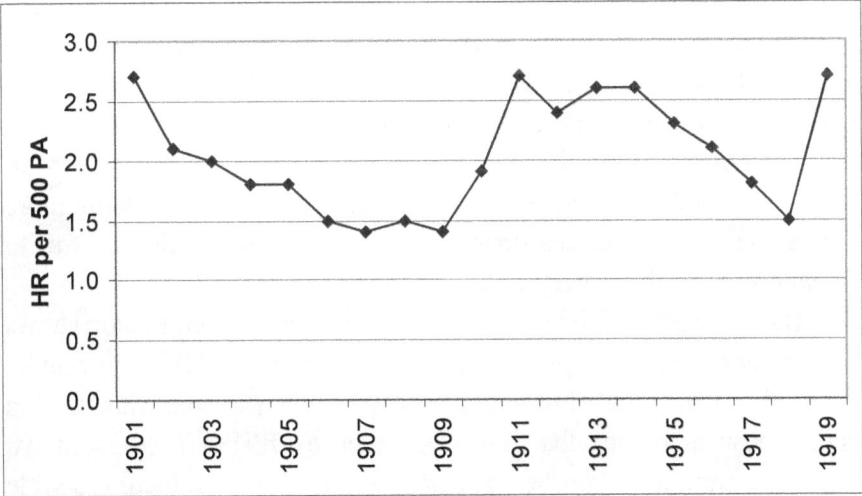

Figure 2.1 – Home Run Production Rate (1901–19)

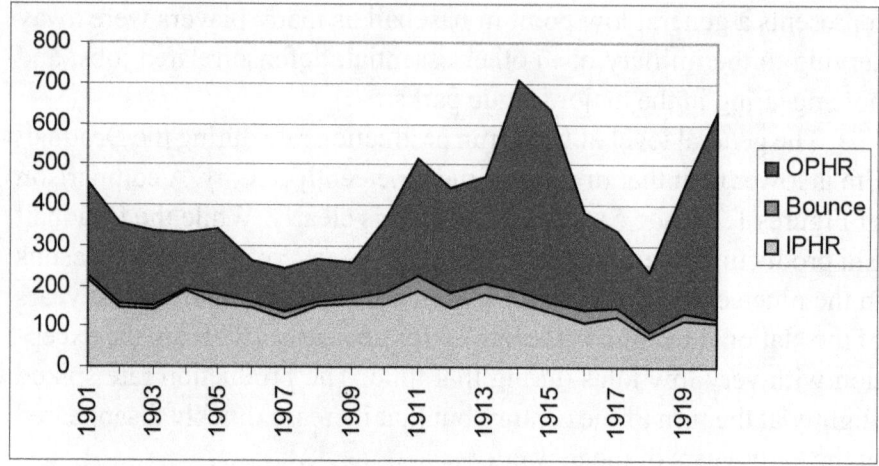

Figure 2.2 – Breakdown of Home Runs by Type (1901–19)

Fenway Park has a vertical line painted on it to show the spot where a ball is either in play or out of play. In this case, if the ball strikes the wall to the right of the line (toward the seating area), it is a home run. If it strikes the wall on or to the left of the stripe, it is in play. This is an example of a ground rule: tailored for one ballpark. The statute concerning a bounce hit as a double is in the official rule book as section 6.09(e) and applies to every game in every park in every league. Thus, it is not a "ground rule." It is more proper to call this a "rule-book double."

Figure 2.2 shows a stacked set of numbers indicating home run totals for each season. The total home run output is shown by reading across the top of the shaded area. Thus the most homers were hit in 1914 when batters smashed 710 four-baggers. The increase in total number of homers is owed partly to the formation of a new league, the Federal League, which increased the number of games played and thus the opportunity to hit more four-baggers. This is one reason that counting totals are not the best way to compare statistics between years.

There are three divisions within the chart. The bottom section shows the number of inside-the-park homers in each season (IPHR). The middle section shows the number of bounce homers in each season, while the top section shows all homers that flew over the fence (OPHR). The bottom two sections remain fairly constant through the era. However, there is a wide difference in the number of over-the-fence home runs in the 19 years of the

Deadball Era. The four seasons from 1906 through 1909, which have already been identified as the lowest home run production rate of the era, also show up as the lowest totals of over-the-fence home runs. In each of these four years, there are more inside-the-park homers than the over-the-fence variety.

As the home run production rate climbed in the early teens, so did the number of over-the-fence homers and both numbers dropped again during World War I. The number of inside-the-park home runs remained fairly constant. This latter type of home run is often the result of the ball being misjudged by a fielder, thus allowing it to get past him. Then the batter has time to circle the bases before the fielder can retrieve the ball and relay it into the catcher. Also, outfielders commonly allowed a ball to get between them in left- or right-center field with the same result for the batter. In both cases, the very large outfield area in many of the older ballparks assisted the batter as the ball had more space in which to roll.

Thus, in the Deadball Era we find a constant stream of inside-the-park and bounce home runs with the variance coming in the number of balls hit over the fence in the first two decades of the twentieth century. There is a strong correlation between the number of balls hit out of the park and the home run production rate for a season during this era even though there were many four-base hits that never left the playing field. This correlation is seen by comparing Figures 2.1 and 2.2. The general slope and height of the line in Figure 2.1 is closely matched by the top line in Figure 2.2, which shows the total home runs hit in each season, and, since the number of inside-the-park home runs do not vary much through the era, the over-the-fence totals are reflected by the top line of Figure 2.2.

◆   ◆   ◆

The first significant event in the Deadball Era was the formation of the American League. It started play as a major league in 1901 and became the first and only successful challenger to the National League's monopoly as a major league. Erve Beck of the Cleveland Blues (now Indians) hit the first home run in the history of the American League off

John Skopec of the Chicago White Sox on April 25, 1901, the second day that the league played. Beck hit a line drive over the right field fence in the second inning of the contest. The two teams met at Chicago's South Side Park, having played the first game in the history of the league there on the previous day.

Except for the first few years of the century, the National League generally hit home runs at a higher rate than its younger sibling. In fact the Senior Circuit batters hit homers at a significantly higher pace from 1911 through 1916, when they nearly doubled the rate of the American League hitters.

Nap Lajoie of the Philadelphia Athletics led the American League in homers in 1901 with 14 and Cincinnati's Sam Crawford led the National League by hitting 16. Lajoie also topped the league in batting average and runs batted in to become the first player to win the Triple Crown in the American League, in its first season. The following year, Ralph "Socks" Seybold, also of the Athletics, clouted 16 to set the top single-season total in the new league until 1919, when Babe Ruth hit 29. An Athletics batter would lead the American League in home runs in 11 of the first 19 years the league existed. Babe Ruth's single-season major league marks were all set in the American League, thus each higher total hit by Ruth also became the new record in the Junior Circuit. Table 2.1 shows the complete progression of the single-season home run record in the American League.

> *There was an unusual play* that occurred on August 14, 1901 at New York's Polo Grounds. The Boston Beaneaters were playing a double header against the Giants and, in the second game, player/manager George Davis of the Giants hit a ball down the left field line. There were two New York policemen standing in the corner of the field talking and before they could get out of the way, the ball struck one of them on the shoulder and bounced into the bleachers. Umpire Bob Emslie ruled it a home run over the protests of the Boston squad.

One prominent home run hitter in the early American League was Buck Freeman, who had whacked 25 circuit drives for the National League's Washington Senators in 1899 to lead the league in homers. He played for that league's Boston Beaneaters (later Braves) in 1900 and then jumped to

Table 2.1 – Progression of the American League Season Record

Batter	Team	Year	HR
Nap Lajoie	Philadelphia	1901	14
Socks Seybold	Philadelphia	1902	16
Babe Ruth	Boston	1919	29
Babe Ruth	New York	1920	54
Babe Ruth	New York	1921	59
Babe Ruth	New York	1927	60
Roger Maris	New York	1961	61

the new league's Boston club in 1901. Freeman placed in the top two in American League home runs from 1901 through 1904 and led the league in 1903 with 13 dingers, all while a member of the Boston Americans (now Red Sox). He became the third player to lead two different leagues in home runs for a season, following in the footsteps of Harry Stovey and Bug Holliday, who both performed the feat in the nineteenth century. Freeman held the career home run record for the American League from 1903 through 1905.

One of Freeman's 1899 teammates, Harry Davis, jumped to his hometown Philadelphia Athletics for the first year of the American League and enjoyed a long career in the City of Brotherly Love playing for Connie Mack. Davis led the Junior Circuit in four-baggers every year from 1904 through 1907 while playing his home games at Columbia Park. In June 1906, Davis hit his 47th American League home run to pass Freeman and set a new career mark for the fledgling league. Davis moved the mark up slightly in the next few years, finally setting his American League record at 69 after the 1911 season. Table 2.2 shows the complete progression of the American League career home run record.

In 1905, no player hit at least 10 home runs for the season, which, at first glance, does not seem unusual. However, it had been 23 years since the high total for a season did not reach double figures, when, in 1882, no batter hit more than seven four-baggers. In 1905, Fred Odwell of the Cincinnati Reds led the majors with nine round-trippers. This lack of individual production was repeated in 1909, the last year of the extremely

Table 2.2 – Progression of the American League Career Record

Batter	Year	HR
Nap Lajoie	1901	14
Socks Seybold	1902	24
Buck Freeman	1903	36
Buck Freeman	1905	46
Harry Davis	1906	50
Harry Davis	1911	69
Sam Crawford	1917	70
Home Run Baker	1919	80
Babe Ruth	1920	103
Babe Ruth	1934	708

low home run production rate in the first decade of the century, as discussed previously. In 1909, Ty Cobb of the Detroit Tigers carried the standard with nine homers. Since then, there has not been another season when fewer than two players hit 10 or more home runs for the year. Cobb won the American League Triple Crown in 1909, the second American Leaguer, the fifth player overall, and the first left-hander to do so. The Georgia Peach hit 117 home runs in his career with at least one in 24 consecutive seasons. Cobb's streak of years, which encompassed his entire career, was the longest in history until Rickey Henderson topped it in 2003. In 1908, Cobb's teammate, Sam Crawford, led the American League by hitting seven home runs—having already led the National League in 1901 with 16 homers—and became the fourth player to lead two different leagues in home runs for a season.

The advent of the American League brought with it eight new ballparks as each team needed a home in which to do business. None of these initial parks lasted more than 11 seasons as the teams moved into better accommodations after their first years. In fact, starting in 1909, a surge in building new parks occurred in the major leagues. Between then and 1915, 13 new parks were built to house major league clubs. This building period corresponded with the time frame in which the home run production rate increased.

The 13 new parks were home to 14 different teams, including all eight in the American League. The fifth and last structure known as the Polo

Grounds in New York became the new home of the National League Giants in 1911 and of the American League Yankees two years later. Only the Philadelphia Phillies and St. Louis Cardinals remained in the same park during this period of intensive ballpark construction.

However, there is no clear evidence that the new fields were more conducive to hitting the ball out of the yard. Remember that the number of in-the-park four-baggers remained fairly constant at this time and the surge was in balls hit over the wall. Some of these new fields were larger than their predecessors while some were smaller and, in many cases, extra seating was added in the outfield later, thus causing the distance to the fence to be shorter than before. In general, batters might find it easier to hit the ball out of a smaller park while the opposite is generally true of larger fields. In addition, the dimensions of some parks have been lost to history, therefore it is hard to draw a conclusion that the parks were a major factor in the overall increase in home run production rate in the early teens, but they probably were influential in many cities.

In September 1908, a 22-year-old man from the Eastern Shore of Maryland made his big-league debut with Connie Mack's Athletics. John Franklin Baker, who went by the name of Frank, would figure prominently in baseball's home run lore. Baker hit 96 regular-season home runs in his career, which lasted through 1922, with two years out of baseball in 1915 and 1920. He hit the fourth most home runs from 1911 through 1920 and led the American League in four-baggers each year from 1911 through 1914. From 1916 through 1919, Baker placed among the top four in American League home run hitters. As fit the era, Baker never hit more than 12 homers in a season, although he placed in the league leaders eight of those years.

In 1911, Baker hit 11 homers in his third full season in the major leagues and his first leading the league. During the four years that he led the American League, the National League standard-bearer always hit more home runs than Baker, reflecting the higher home run production rate of the Senior Circuit. However, leading the league is not why he is remembered as a home run slugger.

Baker and his Athletics teammates won the American League pennant in 1911 and with it the right to play the National League champion New York Giants in the World Series, a post-season event still in its

Frank "Home Run" Baker, who acquired his nickname from two World Series homers.
National Baseball Hall of Fame Library, Cooperstown, New York

infancy, having only been held seven times previously.

New York's Polo Grounds hosted the first game with the home team winning by a narrow 2-1 margin. Baker had two hits in four trips to the plate and scored the only run of the day for Philadelphia off the Giants' ace Christy Mathewson. The scene then shifted to Philadelphia's Shibe Park for game two. In the middle of the sixth inning, the visitor's Rube Marquard and home town hurler Eddie Plank were locked in a 1-1 pitching duel. In the bottom of the frame with two outs, Eddie Collins doubled down the left field line and then the left-handed-hitting Baker stepped to the plate. He hit a Marquard pitch over the right field wall for a two-run home run that provided the margin of victory for the Athletics. This win tied the seven-game series at one victory each as the teams headed back to New York for game three.

In that game, John McGraw's Giants held a slim 1-0 lead after eight innings. With one out in the top of the ninth, Baker hit a solo homer off Mathewson to tie the contest. In the top of the eleventh inning, Eddie Collins and Baker hit back-to-back singles and eventually both runners scored to give game three to Philadelphia.

Mack's squad went on to win the World Series and Baker continued to perform well through the six games of the series. When Baker retired after the 1922 season, his 96 career round-trippers placed him 17th on the all-time list of home run hitters. However, it is the two circuit drives in consecutive World Series games, both coming in critical situations off two of the greatest pitchers in history, which earned him the nickname "Home Run" Baker. This nickname first appeared in the *New York Times* on October 18, the day after Baker's second homer of the series, and spread quickly. It is a fair assumption that his performance in the 1911 World Series also helped propel him to the Hall of Fame after his career.

It is certainly a sign of that time that a batter who hit only 96 career home runs acquired a nickname related to homers because of two well-timed four-baggers. However, this effect is no different in the twenty-first century. Most lists of the "greatest" home runs of all time are drawn primarily from post-season and pennant-clinching contests. Few people remember any events from a Thursday afternoon contest in June 1963 in Boston between two teams going nowhere. It is almost always the struggle between two good teams late in the season that draws the attention of the average fan and is remembered years later.

The major leagues introduced a new ball in 1910 that had a cork center wrapped by a rubber core. Although not used regularly until 1911, the effects of this ball can be seen in the home run production rate. In 1910, the home runs per 500 plate appearances increased one-half point to 1.9 but in 1911 it jumped to 2.7. This new ball is the primary reason for the increased home run production in the early teens and perhaps the deterioration of ball quality, because sub-standard manufacturing materials were used during World War I, is the reason for the decrease in home run production rate during the mid-teens. This latter subject will be discussed in depth in chapter 3.

For 35 years, from the start of the National League in 1876 through 1910, only six batters slugged at least 20 homers in a season. The first four were the Chicago White Stockings hitters who benefited from the new ground rule at Lake Front Park in 1884: Ned Williamson (27), Fred Pfeffer (25), Abner Dalrymple (22), and Cap Anson (21). The next batter to perform this feat was Sam Thompson of the Philadelphia Phillies, who hit exactly 20 homers in 1889. Buck Freeman had the last 20-plus homer season in the nineteenth century when he led the National League with 25 in 1899 playing in the nation's capital for the Senators.

In 1911, Frank Schulte of the Chicago Cubs led the majors with 21 long-balls, with one inside-the-park and no bounce home runs. Schulte's home games were played at West Side Park, a spacious field up the middle with the center field wall 560 feet from home plate. However, with a right field fence only 316 feet down the line, the left-handed-hitting Schulte whacked 11 of his 21 four-baggers at home that season, with five at Boston's South End Grounds and the others split between St. Louis and Philadelphia. Thus Schulte hit no circuit drives on the road in New York, Brooklyn, Cincinnati, or Pittsburgh! Schulte had hit 10 homers in 1910 and would stroke 12 in both 1912 and 1915.

Two years after Schulte's 21 home runs, Clifford Carlton "Gavvy" Cravath swatted 19 for the 1913 Philadelphia Phillies to lead the National League and the majors. Cravath repeated the feat the next season as he again hit 19 homers to the lead the majors. In both seasons, another Philadelphia slugger, Home Run Baker, led the American League.

> **On May 30, 1913,** *Harry Hooper of the Boston Red Sox, who hit only four homers in 1913, led off both games of a doubleheader with a home run. Playing in Washington, Hooper connected off Bob Groom in the first game and Walter Johnson in the second. The latter was a game winner, as the Red Sox won, 1-0. Rickey Henderson repeated the feat with Oakland on July 5, 1993 and Baltimore's Brady Anderson also led off both games of a twin-bill with home runs on August 21, 1999.*

At that time, the Phillies played at Baker Bowl, and the right-handed Cravath aimed at a 40-foot right field fence that was only 279 feet down the line. In 1913, 14 of Cravath's 19 dingers were hit at home but the next season he really took aim at the Baker Bowl fences, as all 19 of his home runs were hit there. This is the second-highest single-season total of homers for a batter with all of them slugged at home, with only Fred Pfeffer's 1884 total of 25 being higher. Amazingly, even though Cravath hit 19 homers at Baker Bowl, all opposing National League players only hit a total of 16 home runs in Philadelphia for the entire 1914 season.

Cravath led the National League for the third consecutive year in 1915, when he smacked 24 circuit drives. As with the previous two years, he took great advantage of his home field, because 19 of his 24 clouts came at Baker Bowl. He again out-homered the combined total of all opposition batters for the season at the Bowl as opponents hit only 18 four-baggers there. Thus, over the three years he hit 52 of 62 home runs (84 percent) in Philadelphia. Robert "Braggo" Roth led the American League with seven homers in 1915. On August 21, the Chicago White Sox traded Roth, who had hit three homers to that point of the season, to the Cleveland Indians with two other players and cash for Shoeless Joe Jackson. Roth thus became the second and most recent player in history to lead a league in home runs while being traded during the season, repeating the feat of Bill Joyce in 1896. Mark McGwire took this feat one step further in 1997 when he led the major leagues in home runs while playing for two teams. Since those teams were in different leagues, he led neither the American nor the National League that year.

Gavvy Cravath continued to be among the National League leaders through the end of the decade. He led the league again for three consecutive years from 1917 through 1919 after finishing third in 1916. Gavvy hit more than any other major league batter from 1911 through 1920 with 117, and he led his league in six out of seven consecutive years. The decade total of 117 set a new high for a 10-year period, breaking the mark of 95 set by Harry Stovey from 1881 through 1890.

The Federal League, a third major league that formed in 1914, existed for two seasons and, as had happened in the nineteenth century, the new circuit drew many star players from the established leagues. For both of its years, Federal Leaguers out-homered their colleagues in the other two leagues. In 1914, the Feds batters hit 3.2 home runs for every 500 plate appearances, which dropped to 2.7 in 1915. The National League placed second among the three leagues in each of these seasons, with a rate of 2.9 and 2.5 those two years. The American League came in a distant third with rates of 1.6 and 1.7.

Dutch Zwilling, who had played briefly for the 1910 Chicago White Sox with no home runs, played two full seasons with the Chicago Whales in the Federal League, and in 1914 he led the league in homers with 16. Zwilling, whose name is last alphabetically in major league history, led another slugger with a great name, Duke Kenworthy, by one homer.

In 1915, Hal Chase led the Federal League with 17 and Zwilling finished second with 13 home runs. Chase had been in the American League since 1905 with New York and Chicago, but, in the middle of the 1914 season, he jumped to the Federal League. In its June 17 issue, the *Chicago Tribune* reported that Chase had told White Sox president Charles Comiskey that he was quitting the Sox and going into business with friends in Philadelphia. Chase denied having any dealings with the new league but soon after became a member of the Buffalo Blues squad.

Chase's story is typical of that time. Many players in the National and American Leagues were courted by the Federal League with offers of large increases in salary and some of them moved to the new league. The *Tribune* put it: "the ball players are determined to make hay while the haying lasts." After two seasons, the Federal League folded and many of the players returned to the two established leagues to continue their careers.

> *On May 6, 1916, Brooklyn's George Cutshaw hit a trick home run at Ebbets Field in the 11th inning. The hit fell into right field near the wall and looked to be a double for the batter. However, the ball slowly rolled up the fence and over the top into the street, thus becoming a game-ending homer. According to the* New York Times *story, "Instead of receiving the plaudits from 20,000 spectators, which ordinarily would follow a winning home run in the eleventh inning of a hard-fought battle, the Dodger second baseman crossed the plate amid a storm of laughter, which eventually turned into meek applause."*

Dutch Zwilling is the career home run leader for the Federal League with 29. He also hit one for the Chicago Cubs in 1916 to complete his career output. Hal Chase and Benny Kauff each hit 20 during the two-year lifetime of the Federal League but each player hit many more home runs in other leagues during his career.

In 1916, the New York Yankees had a slugging first baseman who led the circuit in home runs. Wally Pipp had played 12 games for the 1913 Detroit Tigers but in February 1915 that organization sold him to the Yankees. In 1916, Pipp hit 12 four-baggers to top runner-up Home Run Baker by two and become the first Yankee to lead the American League in homers. Baker had not played in 1915 owing to a contract dispute with Connie Mack and, when he returned in 1916, he played for the Yankees but was never the same home run hitter that he had been prior to his year hiatus. Pipp led the league again in 1917 when he slugged nine home runs. His homer production in comparison to his peers fell off after that season but Pipp continued as the regular first baseman for the Yankees into the first half of the 1920s as they started their impressive run of American League championships.

Sam Crawford, a star in the American League with the Detroit Tigers who had started his career in the National League, broke Harry Davis's American League career homer record in 1917 by hitting homer number 70 in the Junior Circuit. However, Crawford did not hold the mark very long as Home Run Baker set a new standard of 80 American League homers in 1919 that Babe Ruth broke in 1920. Ruth's final total of 708 four-baggers in the American League is still the record for that circuit, as shown in Table 2.2.

The increase in home run production in the majors in the early teens reversed itself in the latter half of the decade as the home run production rate dropped steadily from 1914 through 1918. The effects of World War I on the field started to be felt in 1917 but became much more prominent during the 1918 campaign, because many players had been drafted

---

Two remarkably similar freak home runs were hit at Boston's Braves Field at the end of the Deadball Era. At the time there was a ground-level scoreboard in left center field, which had a three-column lineup area with each player listed by a number. The number for the player currently at bat would be slid into the center column leaving a 12 x 6 inch hole in the board at his lineup spot. In the first game of two on July 11, 1919, Cincinnati Reds catcher Bill Rariden, a former Brave, hit a ball that bounced a couple of times and headed for the scoreboard. Rariden's hit hopped into the hole at his slot in the lineup. The young man running the scoreboard was looking through the hole at the game and the ball nearly struck him before he could move out of the way. This tied the score at two each and the Reds eventually won in extra innings, 4-2. Johnny Rawlings repeated the feat on August 14, 1920. Playing for the Philadelphia Phillies (to whom the Braves sold him that June), Rawlings's hit came in the seventh inning of the second game that day. This time the ball went through a spot in the lineup board where the hole was half open, the number being party in two different columns. The solo shot put the visitors ahead, 3-2, but the Braves won the game in 10 innings, 4-3.

into the military or had left baseball to take essential, war-related jobs in other industries to avoid being drafted. The 1918 season ended early because of the war and with many players gone, the 1919 season was considered to be in jeopardy. However, the war ended in November 1918 and the players returned to the field the next year.

> **Baldy Louden hit 12** homers in his career and none were more unusual than his last four-bagger, hit on June 1, 1916, at Forbes Field in Pittsburgh. In the seventh inning, the Cincinnati second baseman hit a pitch down the left field line for an apparent double. However, base umpire Bob Emslie briefly lost sight of the baseball as it caromed around behind a section of the grandstand that jutted out into the field and awarded Louden a home run.

The home run production rate rose sharply in 1919 to 2.7 home runs per 500 plate appearances from 1.5 the previous year, partly owing to the return of some of the game's best players, thus marking the start of a steady, dramatic rise in homer production that would span the next 10 years. One man from Baltimore led this sudden predominance of the home run hitter.

3

RULES CHANGES IN 1920

Before the start of the 1920 season, changes were made to the game that had a great effect on the balance between offense and defense. New playing rules were put into place that affected home runs and, in addition, the ball itself changed.

The first of three rules changes stated that fly balls hit over the fence along the left and right field lines would be judged fair or foul according to where the ball passed the fence rather than where it landed. The previous version of the rule had seemed reasonable and helpful to the umpires: they would call a fly ball fair or foul after watching it land since judging the flight of the ball without a pole at the intersection of the line and the wall could be difficult, and there were no poles on the lines at this time.

This rule changed a few times during the 1920s. On June 25, 1920, with fewer than 60 games played by most teams under the new statute, the rule reverted to the 1919 version which stated "the umpire shall judge it fair or foul according to where it disappears from view." Before the 1928 season, the rule again became "where the ball crosses the fence." National League president John Heydler stated that trying to determine where the ball actually landed was often very difficult. However, this applied only to balls crossing the barrier that indicated the edge of the playing field and that landed in the seating area. If a ball flew completely out of the park it was to be judged not where it flew over the inner barrier but where it crossed the outer barrier. Therefore there were two different interpretations of the rule, which depended on how far the ball traveled before deciding the proper interpretation to use.

National League president Heydler held a meeting with all league umpires in his New York office on August 5, 1928. Part of the discussion regarded the double interpretation of judging a fly to be fair or foul. The umpires favored one rule for both situations, to call the ball fair if it crossed the inner barrier in fair territory regardless of the flight of the ball after that. Since most of the poles recently constructed to help umpires judge fly balls were not tall enough to allow a single interpretation of the rule as requested by the arbiters, Heydler decided not to

Table 3.1 – Game-Ending Hits before 1920

Date	Batter	Team (League)/ Opponent	Credited Hit
06/17/1884	Roger Connor	New York (NL)/ Boston	single
09/06/1884	Hardy Richardson	Buffalo (NL)/ Boston	triple
04/21/1885	Fred Mann	Pittsburgh (AA)/ Louisville	double
07/30/1885	Tommy McCarthy	Boston (NL)/ Detroit	double
08/20/1885	Paul Hines	Providence (NL)/ Boston	single
07/10/1888	Bob Caruthers	Brooklyn (AA)/ St. Louis	double
06/05/1890	Sam Thompson	Philadelphia (NL)/ Brooklyn	single
07/30/1890	Al McCauley	Philadelphia (NL)/ Chicago	triple
06/17/1890	Mike Griffin	Philadelphia (PL)/ New York	double
08/16/1890	Bill Joyce	Brooklyn (PL)/ Philadelphia	single
05/07/1891	King Kelly	Cincinnati (AA)/ Boston	single
09/13/1891	George Wood	Philadelphia (AA)/ Milwaukee	double
07/07/1892	Buck Ewing	New York (NL)/ St. Louis	single
05/13/1893	Lou Bierbauer	Pittsburgh (NL)/ Louisville	single
08/09/1893	George Van Haltren	Pittsburgh (NL)/ Chicago	double
06/24/1894	Hugh Duffy	Boston (NL)/ Baltimore	triple
08/27/1895	Bill Lange	Chicago (NL)/ Washington	single
09/02/1895	Mike Tieman	New York (NL)/ Cleveland	triple
09/27/1895	Duke Farrell	New York (NL)/ Baltimore	triple
07/27/1896	Charlie Irwin	Cincinnati (NL)/ Cleveland	triple
06/04/1897	Parke Wilson	New York (NL)/ Louisville	double
07/15/1899	Jimmy Collins	Boston (NL)/ Pittsburgh	single

change the rule interpretation during the 1928 season.

However, the league adopted a new rule for the 1929 season regarding those poles. It stated that a pole must be constructed at least 25 feet above the outer barrier to aid the umpires in calling balls fair or foul. The taller poles were constructed on either the top of the grandstand roof or the outer fence of the park and the umpires got their wish for a single interpretation of the rule concerning calling flies fair or foul in 1929 to the "where the ball leaves the playing field" version. The American League continued to use the double interpretation of the rule through 1930.

Table 3.1 – continued

Date	Batter	Team (League)/ Opponent	Credited Hit
07/24/1899	Ginger Beaumont	Pittsburgh (NL)/ Philadelphia	triple
07/24/1900	Jimmy Collins	Boston (NL)/ St. Louis	single
07/27/1900	Chick Stahl	Boston (NL)/ Pittsburgh	single
05/17/1901	Bill Coughlin	Washington (AL)/ Philadelphia	single
09/01/1902	Ed Gremminger	Boston (NL)/ Cincinnati	double
06/26/1903	Pat Moran	Boston (NL)/ Chicago	triple
08/31/1903	Barry McCormick	Washington (AL)/ Boston	triple
09/10/1904	Roger Bresnahan	New York (NL)/ Philadelphia	double
05/05/1906	Sherry Magee	Philadelphia (NL)/ Brooklyn	triple
06/02/1906	Tim Jordan	Brooklyn (NL)/ Boston	double
04/30/1908	Frank Bowerman	Boston (NL)/ New York	double
05/25/1908	Joe Tinker	Chicago (NL)/ New York	double
09/28/1908	Cy Seymour	New York (NL)/ Philadelphia	single
04/23/1910	Doc Crandall	New York (NL)/ Brooklyn	single
08/24/1911	Tex Erwin	Brooklyn (NL)/ Chicago	triple
05/06/1913	Jay Kirke	Boston (NL)/ Pittsburgh	double
06/17/1914	Sherry Magee	Philadelphia (NL)/ St. Louis	double
04/19/1917	Ping Bodie	Philadelphia (AL)/ Boston	triple
07/08/1918	Babe Ruth	Boston (AL)/ Cleveland	triple
07/18/1918	Home Run Baker	New York (AL)/ Detroit	single
04/19/1918	Irish Meusel	Philadelphia (NL)/ Boston	triple

National League president John Heydler had experience regarding calling plays on the field since he had been a National League umpire for four years in the 1890s. He served as league president on an interim basis in 1909 and then was elected the chief executive from 1918 through 1934. One other arbiter later became league president. Tom Lynch, who umpired from 1888 to 1902 in the National League, served as league president from 1910 through 1913.

The second change in the playing rules for 1920 concerned game-ending hits. Previously, if a batter hit a ball over the fence to end a game, he received credit only for enough bases on that hit to allow the winning run to score. In other words, if the game was tied and a runner was on second base, a ball hit out of the park became a double since, when the runner on second scored, the game ended. The new rule allowed the batter and all runners to score on such game-ending hits and the batter received credit for a home run.

Table 3.1 shows the game ending hits before 1920 and how they were recorded. Since the rules of the day were clear about these hits not being home runs, it is not correct to state that the players listed in Table 3.1 "lost" a homer. They were never home runs under the playing rules. Jimmy Collins of the Boston Beaneaters (later Braves) hit two of these game-ending blows, one in 1899 and one in 1900 and Sherry Magee of the Philadelphia Phillies hit two, in 1906 and 1914. They are the only batters who had two of these game-ending hits. The Boston Braves had the most as a team with nine and the New York Giants hit eight of them.

Major League Baseball formed a special rules committee in 1968 to make decisions regarding record keeping in the early days of professional baseball. The committee attempted to make the old statistics consistent with modern scoring rules and one of its rulings changed the 39 known pre-1920 game-ending hits to home runs. Note that on July 8, 1918, Babe Ruth hit one of these game-enders and received credit for a triple at the time. Thus, the committee's ill-advised ruling changed the record for most career home runs from 714 to 715. To make it worse, as part of this ruling the committee had to change the final score of the affected ballgames and the pitching records of the hurlers surrendering the hits.

When the committee announced this decision, many sports reporters wrote stories regarding the change in Ruth's record. Leonard Koppett, writing in the *New York Times* on April 27, 1969, stated: "For several years now, Willie Mays has been gradually closing in on Babe Ruth's career total of 714 home runs, one of the most hallowed statistics of all sports lore. Well, here's a shock for Willie and all his fans: the Babe just gained ground on him." Koppett discussed the entire computerization project that produced the first comprehensive baseball record book, published in 1969. He was generally complimentary about the project and the records committee, however, he ended his story with: "But it just lends support to those who believe that Ruth was the supreme slugger, the giant among giants. Here he is, after all, adding to his total 34 years after he played his last game."

Koppett's remarks helped focus attention on the ruling concerning game-ending hits. If the Babe had not been on the list, the ruling might have remained in place. However, changing the most recognizable statistic in all of sports generated a lot of negative feedback. Therefore, in May 1969 the special committee reversed themselves on this one ruling, thus leaving the Babe's home run record intact at 714. It should be stated again that these batters did not lose home runs at this time because those hits were never homers according to the playing rules. The initial decision by the special committee granted something to the batters in conflict with the playing rules at the time of the event and the reversal of this decision, although made for the wrong reason, achieved the correct status for these hits.

Since the committee published its list of 39 game-ending hits, four more have been discovered by baseball historians. They are Hugh Duffy in 1894, Barry McCormick in 1903, Frank Bowerman in 1908, and Jay Kirke in 1913. All known instances of this event are listed in Table 3.1.

On July 11, 1920, the Boston Braves were tied with the Reds, 3-3, after eight innings in Cincinnati. In the bottom of the ninth, the Reds had Hod Eller running at second base and Morrie Rath at first when Jake Daubert came to the plate with two out. Daubert hit Hugh McQuillan's 1-1 pitch to center field, where it bounced once and hopped into the bleachers. Under the new rule on game-ending hits passed before this season, Daubert got credit for a three-run home run to win the game, 6-3, thus becoming the first batter to receive credit for a homer because of the rule change. Four days later, the St. Louis Browns and the New York Yankees were tied, 10-10, after 10 innings at the Polo Grounds in New York. In the bottom of the 11th inning, with Aaron Ward the runner at second base and Wally Pipp running at first base, Babe Ruth came to bat with no one out. Ruth hit the ball onto the right field roof for a three-run, game-ending home run. This was the Babe's 29th of the season, tying his record set the previous year, and the first American League home run under the new rule. These were the only two game-ending home runs under the new rule in 1920. There were two more of these home runs in 1921, by Jack Tobin of the St. Louis Browns and Roger Peckinpaugh of the Yankees. Four batters smashed game-enders under the new rules in 1922, Wally Pipp of the Yankees, Tilly Walker of the Philadelphia Athletics, Babe Ruth (again!), and Andy High of the Brooklyn Robins. Ruth is the only batter on the list of game-ending hits under the old rules who hit a game-ending homer under the new rules.

The third playing rule that changed for the 1920 season had a huge effect on hitting. It stated that the spitball and other unorthodox deliveries were outlawed. In other words, hurlers were no longer allowed to apply substances to the ball or scar its surface before pitching it, which included using rosin. Here is the wording agreed on at the meeting in February 1920:

> At no time during the progress of the game shall the pitcher be allowed to (1) apply a foreign substance of any kind to the ball; (2) expectorate either on the ball or his glove; (3) to rub the ball on his glove, person or clothing; or (4) to deface the ball in any manner or to deliver what is called the "shine" ball, "spit ball," mud ball or emery ball. For a violation of any provision of this rule the pitcher shall be ordered from the game and be barred from participation in any championship contest for a period of ten days.

This change led to an increase in offense in 1920 and the following seasons because hurlers were no longer allowed to throw a "trick" or "freak" pitch to fool the batter. However, teams registered a group of pitchers already in the majors with the league presidents and those hurlers could continue throwing the spitball (but not any other banned pitch) through the 1920 season only. After that year, all use of the spitball would be abolished.

However, at a meeting the following December, the leagues extended the rule concerning these registered spit ballers to allow them to continue throwing that pitch until they retired. Burleigh Grimes, who pitched until 1934, became the last of these grandfathered hurlers still in the major leagues.

These outlawed pitches were common during the Deadball Era. Applying a substance to the ball or scuffing it would cause it to curve, sometimes in an unusual way. Pitchers who did not have a good curve ball liked these freak pitches because throwing one gave them a kind of breaking ball to use as a part of their arsenal. However, the unusual flight of these pitches meant that the hurler often had no control over where the pitch went and sometimes that meant directly at the batter.

Because of the fear of a scuffed ball veering in toward a batter's head and causing serious injury, starting in 1920 umpires threw out any scuffed or discolored ball and placed a new ball into play immediately. Previous to this time, one baseball might be used for the entire contest regardless of its condition. With the elimination of the "freak" pitches and cleaner, easier-to-see balls in use, the batters had less fear of being injured by a baseball striking them. Therefore, they could stand in the batter's box with more confidence and have a better chance of hitting the ball long and hard.

The fact that balls hit into the stands were usually kept by the fans and not returned to the field became another consideration in ball replacement during a game. As the number of homers hit out of the park increased, so did the need to use a new baseball during the game as each home run ball would be unavailable to the players, thus providing another situation in which a new, clean baseball replaced a used ball.

◆ ◆ ◆

The last change in 1920 involved the baseball itself. At the time, each league used a ball from a different manufacturer. The A. G. Spalding Company manufactured the National League baseball while Reach and Company made the sphere for the Junior Circuit. They were all made to the same specifications, the only difference being that the stitching on the cover of the National League ball had two colors, red and blue, while the American League ball had red yarn holding the outer cover on the ball.

The league presidents and representatives of the manufacturers all agreed during the 1921 season that no changes had been made to the specifications of the baseball. The primary theory discussed at the time as the cause of the "rabbit" ball was the fact that during World War I the government took the best quality wool for its own use and commercial enterprises, such as Reach and Spalding, had to use wool of lower quality than they had previously used. With the end of the war, importers brought better quality wool from Australia into the United States. The yarn made from this wool was of better quality and was able to be wound tighter around the core of the baseball by the machines that completed that part of the process. The tighter winding was as a result of the better-quality yarn, not a change to the machines, and created a slightly harder, more elastic ball – one that batters could hit farther than the old baseball.

The war had also depleted the ranks of workers in baseball factories, just as it had on the ball field. With new, inexperienced workers in the factories, the quality of the product was sure to deteriorate until the veteran laborers returned after the end of the war. Although machines performed the first part of the manufacturing process, workers hand-stitched the cover on the ball, and the post-war covers were probably more uniform in their quality than those used at the end of the Deadball Era.

4

BABE RUTH

On July 11, 1914, a highly-touted young pitcher made his big league debut with the Boston Red Sox, George Herman Ruth Jr., a 19-year-old Baltimore native. George was born to a saloon-keeper and his wife in 1895 and by the age of seven, his parents decided that they could not control the young man so they sent him to St. Mary's Industrial School for Boys, an institution for orphans and delinquent boys run by the Catholic order of the Xaverian Brothers. One of the teachers at the school, Brother Matthias, became Ruth's mentor and later Ruth referred to Brother Matthias as one of the most important people in his life.

Young George played baseball at the school and soon professional scouts came to watch him. In February 1914, Ruth signed a contract to play with the Baltimore Orioles of the International League whose owner and manager, Jack Dunn, played in the majors from 1897 through 1904. Ruth's first professional contract listed a salary of $100 per month, which meant $600 for the season. Shortly after the team started its spring training practice, his teammates sarcastically called the 19-year-old one of "Dunn's babes." This name, picked up by writers covering the team, appeared in the newspapers and George Ruth soon turned into "Babe" Ruth.

The Babe made his professional debut on April 22, 1914, with the Orioles and in the first few weeks of the season, he quickly became popular with the fans. He pitched so well that by May, Dunn doubled Ruth's salary and by the end of June, Dunn increased Ruth's salary again to an $1,800 yearly figure. However, Dunn started experiencing financial troubles because of the competition from the Federal League team in Baltimore, so he sold off some of his players to raise money.

On July 9, 1914, Dunn sold Ruth's contract along with two other players to the Red Sox for an unconfirmed sum of more than $25,000. In August, after only two games with Boston, management sent Ruth to its minor league team in Providence for more work. On September 5, he pitched the first game of a double header in Toronto, winning 9-0. His pitching feats while with Baltimore were the reason the Red Sox were interested in Ruth, and he showed that skill while pitching for Providence.

Perhaps more importantly that day, the Babe hit his first professional home run and the only minor league four-bagger of his career. The Toronto team played their games at Hanlan's Point, located on an island in the Don River, and it became the site for an event that many people would want to see in the 1920s: Babe Ruth smashing a ball over the fence.

In early October, the Red Sox recalled Ruth to Boston, thus ending his minor league career. Over the next three seasons, Ruth pitched impressively for the Sox including in the 1916 (and later the 1918) World Series. He also hit nine home runs during those three years, which included one as a pinch hitter in June 1916 in addition to eight as a pitcher. He hit four as a hurler in 1915, the most home runs in one season for any pitcher in the years 1915 through 1917. He hit those nine as a part-time player, but nine homers in three years was not impressive for a home run hitter, even during the Deadball Era—Ruth's slugging ability had not surfaced yet in the American League.

In 1917, the Babe had shown great improvement in his batting, so in 1918 while he continued to pitch, Red Sox manager Ed Barrow also had the Babe play in the outfield on some non-pitching days. Ruth hit 11 circuit drives that season, seven of them as an outfielder. Now the Sultan of Swat was starting to appear.

Those 11 homers in 1918 tied Ruth with Tilly Walker of the Philadelphia Athletics for the lead in the American League and the majors since the National League standard bearer, Gavvy Cravath, hit only eight home runs. From 1918 through 1931, Ruth led the American League outright or shared the lead in home runs 12 of those 14 years. In 1922, his 35 dingers placed third in the league and, in 1925, Ruth hit 25 long balls, good for second in the league in a season in which he only played two-thirds of his team's games. He also finished second in the home run race in 1932 and 1933; thus, in the 16 years from 1918 through 1933, Ruth led the league 12 times, finished second three times, and finished third once. During that same period, the Babe also led the American League in walks 11 times and placed second twice. Obviously, that many walks made it harder to hit the ball out of the park, thus making Ruth's home run achievements much more impressive.

His 1918 blasts came in five of the eight league parks but he hit none at home. At the end of the 1918 season, Ruth had hit 20 major league home runs but only two of them were hit in Boston. The home field for the Red Sox, Fenway Park, has always been more friendly to right-handed hitters than to left-handed hitters and when Ruth played, there were no bullpens in right field, thus making the distance to the fence longer. Those bullpens were added to the park in 1940 by owner Tom Yawkey to help another left-handed slugger by the name of Ted Williams.

In general, home run production was down in the majors for the fourth consecutive year in 1918. The Babe showed some promise of what the future held for him and other sluggers in the 1920s, but he had not changed the game yet. That started in 1919.

In the last year of the Deadball Era, Gavvy Cravath continued his home run hitting in the National League as he again led the circuit with 12 four-baggers, the sixth time in seven years that the Phillies star led the National League in home runs. His 12 blasts were a fairly typical total for the league leader at that time as four major league players swatted 10

A young Babe Ruth as a member of the Boston Red Sox; the Babe held the single-season homer record from 1919 through September 1961. *National Baseball Hall of Fame Library, Cooperstown, New York*

homers that season, including three in the American League.

However, all those batters finished a great distance behind Babe Ruth that year, as the man who would eventually accumulate many nicknames based on his batting heroics slugged 29 home runs in 1919. He hit his first homer of the season at the Polo Grounds in New York in the first inning on Opening Day. (It was the first of 10 inside-the-park four-baggers that Ruth would hit in his career. It should be noted that the Babe never hit a home run that bounced over the fence.)

On September 5, Ruth hit his 25th homer of the season, thus tying Buck Freeman's 1899 total. The blast came off Win Noyes of the Athletics in Philadelphia in the third inning of the contest. Newspaper stories the next day proclaimed that the Babe had tied the major league record set by Freeman. On September 8, Ruth hit his next homer, off Hank Thormahlen of the Yankees in New York, thus becoming the new record holder—at least in some circles. That morning, before the Red Sox played their double header in New York, National League president John Heydler sent a telegram to the *Boston Globe*. The newspaper quoted the telegram in the next day's edition:

> The National League has no official record of [N]ed Williamson's 27 home runs in 1883 [sic]. Granting that he made this record, it could hardly be fair to compare it with the modern records. Freeman's record of 25 home runs was made under the same rules as are followed today. In 1883 the pitching distance was different. The batsman could call for a high or low ball and he could have the benefit of seven unfair fouls. In my opinion 26 homers will establish a new record, and my congratulations to the big lad when he does it.

Note that Heydler referred to the wrong year for Williamson's record in his telegram and made no mention of the real reason all those four-baggers were hit: the changed ground rules at Lake Front Park in Chicago. Thus, the baseball writers declared Babe Ruth the new home run king upon his hitting number 26 that day. Ruth actually did set a record for left-handed batters, however, as Freeman had hit the most of any port-sider in one season. Table 4.1 shows the progression of the

Table 4.1 – Progression of the Left-Handed Season Record

Batter	Team (League)	Year	HR
George Hall	Philadelphia (NL)	1876	5
John O'Rourke	Boston (NL)	1879	6
Dan Brouthers	Buffalo (NL)	1881	8
Abner Dalrymple	Chicago (NL)	1884	22
Buck Freeman	Washington (NL)	1899	25
Babe Ruth	Boston (AL)	1919	29
Babe Ruth	New York (AL)	1920	54
Babe Ruth	New York (AL)	1921	59
Babe Ruth	New York (AL)	1927	60
Roger Maris	New York (AL)	1961	61
Barry Bonds	San Francisco (NL)	2001	73

single-season record for left-handed batters.

When Ruth struck his 27th homer, which tied the actual record set by Ned Williamson in 1884, the writers made no mention of it in the newspapers. The Babe hit this blast on September 20 off Lefty Williams of the Chicago White Sox over the left field wall at Fenway Park, as perhaps this was an easier target than the spacious right field area. Ruth finally did break the real record with a fly ball over the right field grandstand at the Polo Grounds in New York on September 24 off Bob Shawkey of the New York Yankees and the news stories reported that fact. Newspapers listed Williamson's 1884 record (with the correct year cited) and for the second time that season, Ruth was given credit for "breaking" the single-season mark. He left no doubt about being the Sultan of Swat.

His last 1919 homer came in the first game of a double header on September 27 in Washington. Until this point, Ruth had not hit a long-distance smash at Griffith Stadium even though he had at least two in each of the other seven American League venues. He had finally started hitting four-baggers at Fenway Park, with nine that season, and he hit five circuit drives at Detroit's Navin Field (later known as Tiger Stadium), thus making that park his favorite road stadium. Ruth was the first twentieth-century batter to homer in all eight league parks in one season, a feat he performed 11 times.

Ruth's 29 home runs in 1919 not only set a new season record but trumpeted to the baseball world that he was a special hitter, a type of hitter that had not been seen before in baseball. To illustrate just how much better the Babe was at hitting homers, consider that his Boston teammates only hit four home runs that season. Four of the other seven American League clubs and six of the eight National League squads belted fewer home runs than Ruth in 1919 and his homers represented 12 percent of the American League total for the 1919 season.

The Bambino garnered a lot of attention as his exploits made headlines in newspapers across the continent and he was the single biggest drawing card in either the American or National League that season. He was so popular that he was signed to star in a movie which was released in 1920 titled, *Heading Home*. He later appeared in other movies as well.

On January 5, 1920, Red Sox owner Harry Frazee announced that he had sold Babe Ruth's contract to the New York Yankees. He would not announce the amount of money involved but later reports put that figure at $125,000 with a loan by Yankees owner Jacob Ruppert of $350,000 to Frazee, with Fenway Park used as collateral for the loan. In announcing the contract sale, Frazee stated that the 1919 Red Sox were a one-man team that finished in sixth place (out of eight teams in the American League) and that the fans of Boston wanted a winning team, not a one-man team. The actual memorandum of agreement on the sale of Ruth to the Yankees is at the National Baseball Hall of Fame Library. It contains a sale price of $100,000 and no mention of a loan to Frazee, which would probably have been contained in a separate agreement.

Frazee was a theatrical producer and if his shows were successful he had money to spend on the Red Sox. In 1919, his shows were not doing well so he needed cash. He seemed more interested in raising money for Broadway than for Lansdowne Street (the location of Fenway Park), thus he turned his biggest baseball asset into cash for his other enterprises. Frazee's time as owner in Boston is not regarded as a good period for the Red Sox. They were one of the best teams in baseball when Frazee bought the club in 1917, having won the World Series in 1912, 1915, 1916, and then again in 1918, but the club did not finish higher than fifth place again until 1934 when they placed fourth. In fact, Boston finished last in the American League in 1922, 1923, and 1925 through 1930. Frazee sold the team in 1923, having converted it from a first-place championship team into a last-place club.

The *Boston Globe* carried the story of Ruth's move to New York on the front page, as might be expected. Many people viewed this as a disaster for the Red Sox but it was part of a pattern by Frazee in his time as owner. Ruth might have been the biggest star to be sold off by the owner but he was not the only star to be sent away for cash and this type of behavior is certainly not unique in baseball history among owners, carrying even into the twenty-first century.

Through his slugging exploits and friendly persona, the Babe pulled baseball into a new era, although aided some by the rulemakers as discussed in the previous chapter. The Babe had gained a lot of attention in 1919 for his slugging when he hit 29 homers, but in 1920 he set the world on fire with his batting. He started slowly for his new team, not hitting his first four-bagger as a Yankee until the 12th game on May 1. And, of course, the fates laughed at Frazee and the Boston fans as this blast came against Ruth's former teammates, the Red Sox.

As the month of May progressed, however, Ruth picked up his homer-hitting pace. By the end of the month, he had whacked 12 circuit drives. He hit nine at home in the Polo Grounds and three at Fenway Park, because the Yankees spent most of the month of May at home. Ruth swatted another dozen homers in June and the writers covering the team could not come up with enough adjectives to describe him or new nicknames to call him as they glowingly wrote stories extolling his feats. The Babe became the toast of Broadway and most of the rest of the country as he closed in on the record he had set the previous September.

On July 15, the Yankees played the St. Louis Browns at the Polo Grounds in the rain. In the bottom of the 11th inning with two runners on base, Ruth hit a Bill Burwell pitch off the roof of the right field grandstand to win the game and tie his record 29 homers with a fly ball that ended the contest and would not have been a home run the previous season. Four days later, the Babe hit two homers off Dickie Kerr of the Chicago White Sox to break his own record and become the first batter to reach the 30 home run mark for a season. Ruth is the only batter to break his own single-season home run record. In July, Ruth hit 13 four-baggers to reach 37 for the year with 53 games left on the Yankee schedule. On August 6, Ruth reached the 40 milestone when he hit a Hooks Dauss pitch out at Detroit's Navin Field (later Tiger Stadium).

On September 24, the Babe hit home run number 50 for the season, the first batter to achieve this milestone. The blast came off Jose Acosta of the Washington Senators in the first game of a double header at the Polo Grounds in New York. In game two, Ruth hit another four-bagger, this coming off Jim Shaw in the first inning, and this blast made Ruth the 11th batter in history to hit 100 career home runs. By the end of the season, Ruth had hit 54 home runs to smash his single-season record. This represented an 86 percent increase over the previous mark and only four homers from doubling it. He became the first batter to hit 30, 40, and 50 home runs in one campaign—and he did this all in one season! (Refer to Appendix B for details of each home run number 50 in history.) He ended the year ninth on the all-time list after only three seasons playing primarily as a hitter and not a pitcher. The Babe out-homered all seven other American League teams and seven of eight in the National League in 1920. George Sisler of the St. Louis Browns had the second-highest individual total for the year with 19. Clearly, Ruth was in a league of his own as a slugger.

Ruth hit 15 percent of the American League home runs in 1920, an even higher percentage than the 12 percent in 1919. To show the difference between eras, Roger Maris, when he set his major league record by hitting 61 circuit drives in 1961, hit 4 percent of the American League homers. Mark McGwire hit 3 percent of the 1998 National League homers with his 70 and Barry Bonds only 2.5 percent of the National League four-baggers in 2001 when he slugged 73. The increased number of teams in a league and the longer schedule of games played are not enough to explain the great difference in percentages between Ruth in the 1920s and later sluggers. The Babe was simply that much better than his contemporaries.

As with the single-season record in 1919, baseball writers reported that Ruth broke the career record a little early in 1921. On June 10, when he hit his 120th homer, which came off a pitch by Jim Bagby of the Cleveland Indians at the Polo Grounds, the *New York Times* stated that he had become the "undisputed champion of major league sluggers of all time" by beating the mark set by Gavvy Cravath. Unfortunately, three nineteenth-century players had hit more four-baggers than Cravath, whose career ended in

1920. On July 18, Ruth hit career homer 139 off Bert Cole of the Tigers in Detroit, which set the new record for the major leagues, topping Roger Connor. Ruth really became the all-time champ that day but the newspapers made no mention of it. (Table 1.4 shows the progression of the career record.)

◆ ◆ ◆

In 1921, for the second consecutive year, Ruth topped his newly-minted single-season record when he slammed 59 homers. He reached the 50 milestone on September 3 with a blast off Harry Courtney of the Washington Senators in New York, and hit number 55 to set the new mark on September 15 with a drive off Bill Bayne of the St. Louis Browns at the Polo Grounds. (Refer to Appendix B for details of each home run number 50 in history.) From 1919 through 1921, Babe hit 142 total homers, thus, in just three seasons, he had hit more homers than any other player in history. In comparison, Roger Connor, whose career mark Ruth had broken, took 18 years to accumulate his 138 dingers. As great as his home run hitting was, Ruth's slugging was not limited to just homers. In 1920, his slugging average was .847 and almost identical at .846 in 1921. These were the top two single-season slugging averages in the major leagues until 2001, when Barry Bonds slugged .863 for the year. Before Bonds, Ruth had four of the top five major league marks for slugging average, with only Lou Gehrig's 1927 slugging average of .765 appearing in fourth place. Ruth held the record for highest slugging average for a very impressive 81 years.

Ruth's slugging exploits continued through the 1920s and his every move was documented to a greater extent by the news reporters than any other celebrity of his time, with hyperbole a great part of that coverage. For example, Ruth often would hit a home run that was called the longest ever seen at the local field. This kind of statement was impossible to verify but easy to write. Any performance by Ruth garnered him top billing in the next day's newspapers regardless of the feats of his teammates.

As early as 1920, the *New York Times* ran tables comparing Ruth's home run output for the season to the previous record. For example, on June 3, a table titled "Ruth's Home Run Speed Five Times as Great as in 1919" ran on the baseball page. The table contained a listing of the Babe's

15 1920 homers to date with a similar listing of the three 1919 homers to the same date. For each blast, the table listed the date, pitcher, pitcher's team, and city in which the homer was hit. This kind of special listing about Ruth was not limited to the New York newspapers as regular items appeared in many big league cities. Later in the twentieth century, similar tables would be created comparing other sluggers to Ruth.

Ruth was suspended (for arguing with an umpire) by Commissioner Kennesaw Mountain Landis at the start of the 1922 season and played only 110 games. However, in that time he hit 35 home runs to finish third in the American League. Ruth had an off year in 1925 in many ways. He only played in 98 games that season, having been sick during spring training, and he also showed more and more signs of a lack of discipline until he was fined $5000 by the Yankee manager, Miller Huggins, in mid-season. After losing an appeal to the club's owner, Ruth's attitude improved, but he only hit 25 homers that season to finish behind teammate Bob Meusel, who hit 33, in the American League race. On September 8, 1925, the Babe hit his 300th career round-tripper, a blast off Buster Ross of the Red Sox into the right field bleachers at Fenway Park, and the environment seemed to have stabilized for the Yankees, as everyone seemed happy again.

Although he had been a pitching star for the Red Sox in two World Series, Ruth starred as a hitter for the Yankees in the Fall Classic. In game four of the 1926 Series, Ruth hit three home runs against the St. Louis Cardinals. He repeated that feat in game four of the 1928 Series, also against the Cardinals. Ruth had never hit three or more home runs in one regular season game to that point, and no other batter would hit three in a World Series game until 1977, when Reggie Jackson performed the feat. See chapter 9 on post-season home runs for more details.

On September 2, 1927, Ruth hit his 400th career homer, off Rube Walberg of the Athletics in Philadelphia. The four-bagger cleared the right center field fence at Shibe Park in the first inning. Lou Gehrig followed with a back-to-back homer on the first pitch he saw that left the park and landed on the roof of a house across the street.

In 1927, Ruth upped the season record again when he stroked 60 home runs. At the end of August, Ruth had hit 43 circuit drives. In September, he hit an incredible total of 17 four-baggers, more long balls in one month that any batter had ever hit, topping the previous record of 15 by Cy Williams of the Philadelphia Phillies in May 1923. Ruth's previous best one-month total had been the 14 home runs he hit in July 1924. Only two batters have hit more homers in one month than Ruth: Rudy York of the Detroit Tigers with 18 in August 1937 and Sammy Sosa of the Chicago Cubs with 20 in June 1998. Later in the century as batters seemed likely to approach Ruth's single-season record, comparisons would be made to Ruth's total at a particular point in the season. The proclamations of a hitter being "ahead of Ruth's pace" were misinformed and even silly since the Babe had hit nearly one-third of his 60 in the last month of the season. No one would reach the 60 milestone for 34 years and Ruth would hold the single-season home run record for a total of 42 years, starting in 1919.

Ruth's 60th swat came on September 30, 1927 at Yankee Stadium. The two-run blast into the right field seats off southpaw Tom Zachary of the Washington Senators broke a 2-2 tie to win the penultimate game of the season for the pennant-winning team from the Bronx. The Babe hit Zachary's 1-1 pitch, a fastball on the inside corner, down the right field line and the sphere curved around the pole and landed just fair about half way up the seating area. Thus, Ruth broke his six-year-old record and became the first slugger to reach the 60 milestone in a season. (Refer to Appendix B for details of each home run number 60 in history.)

The Babe had hit at least 50 home runs in consecutive seasons in 1920 and 1921. In 1928, he clouted 54 homers, thus hitting over 50 in consecutive seasons for the second time in his career. Ruth hit 50 or more home runs in one season four times in his career and they came in two pairs of consecutive years: 1920–21 and 1927–28. No other player would match this feat of consecutive 50 homer seasons until the late 1990s, when it became fairly common.

On August 11, 1929, Ruth hit his 500th career home run at Cleveland's League Park off Willis Hudlin of the Indians. The ball sailed over the screen near the right field line onto the adjoining street. The man who retrieved the sphere was brought into the dugout and exchanged it with the Babe for two autographed balls and $20. The price of historic baseballs on the memorabilia market would change radically in 70 years when comic book writer Todd McFarlane paid $3 million at auction in February 1999 for the baseball that Mark McGwire hit in 1998 for his 70th home run. (Refer to Appendix A for details of each home run number 500.)

On May 21, 1930, Ruth hit three homers in one regular season game for the first time. This occurred in the first game of a double header in Philadelphia. The next afternoon, also in the first of two games, Ruth swatted two home runs and then followed with another in the second game. Thus, the Babe hit six circuit drives in four games in two days to tie the record for four consecutive games held by many players, including the Babe himself in 1921.

On August 21, 1931, the Babe reached another unprecedented milestone when he hit his 600th career home run off George Blaeholder in St. Louis. Ruth was 36 years old at the time, making him younger than any of the three players to follow him into this exclusive club. The Bambino also took fewer trips to the plate to reach the milestone than the other three batters. (Refer to Appendix A for details of each home run number 600.)

During the 1933 season, the first All-Star game was played at Chicago's Comiskey Park and, naturally, one of the American League starters was Babe Ruth. In the third inning with one man on base, the Babe slugged the first homer in the history of the Midsummer Classic to help the American League win the game, 4-2. See chapter 11 on the All-Star Game for more details of this event.

In 1933, Ruth, now 38 years old, had slowed down. After seven consecutive years of hitting more than 40 home runs, he hit "only" 34. The following year he hit 22 and his general level of play was down dramatically. On July 13, 1934, the Babe connected for the 700th time of his career, accompanied by the usual flowery news accounts in the New York papers. He hit the milestone home run on a 3-2 pitch by Tommy Bridges at Detroit's Navin Field (later called Tigers Stadium) in the third inning of a game won by the Yankees, 4-2. As he was at number 600, Ruth was younger when he reached 700 home runs than either of the sluggers who later achieved that milestone. (Refer to Appendix A for details of each home run number 700.)

On February 26, 1935, the New York Yankees released Babe Ruth, and he signed the same day with the Boston Braves. After 659 home runs in 15 seasons with the Yankees and 708 home runs in more than 20 years playing in the American League, Ruth returned to the city where he started his major league career but now in the National League.

At age 40, Ruth's skills were greatly diminished. He appeared in 28 games for the Braves and hit very poorly. However, there were a few flashes of the Sultan of Swat, such as on Opening Day, when he clouted a homer off the New York Giants ace Carl Hubbell in his third National League at bat. Then, on May 25, with the Braves playing in Pittsburgh, the Babe hit three homers, the 72nd time Ruth had hit at least two homers in one game, still the record at the end of the 2005 season. The last one flew completely out of Forbes Field, bounced on an adjacent street, and rolled into a city park down the street. These were the last three home runs of Ruth's career and they came 20 years and 19 days after he stroked his first circuit drive in the majors.

Having already had a three-homer game in the American League, Ruth became the first player to hit three in an American League game and in a National League game. In the next 48 years, only one other player would perform this feat: Johnny Mize. Ruth became the first 40-year-old batter to hit three homers in one game, a feat not repeated until 1962 when Stan Musial smacked three at age 41.

Ruth played his last game five days after hitting his last home run and retired with 714 home runs with his former teammate, Lou Gehrig, second on the career list that day; Gehrig had hit 353 circuit clouts at that time – fewer than half the Babe's total. The Baltimore native was clearly the Home Run King.

The Babe made his major league debut at the age of 19 and played until after his 40th birthday. Most of the members of the 500 Home Run Club came to the big leagues young and played a long time with little time out for injuries or other events. Ruth hit 198 home runs after his 35th birthday, which stood as the record until Hank Aaron topped it with 245.

Babe Ruth became the first batter to hit 30, 40, 50, and 60 home runs in one season, with the first three all occurring in one year (1920). He became the first batter to hit 200, 300, 400, 500, 600, and 700 career home runs. From 1920 through 1933, the only season in which he did not hit at least 34 homers was 1925, when he stroked 25, and for seven consecutive years from 1926 through 1932, Ruth hit at least 40 homers, which is still the record. The Babe led or tied for the lead in homers in the American League for 12 seasons, the most years any batter has led any league.

For the decade 1911 through 1920, Babe hit the second-most home runs in the majors (103) behind Gavvy Cravath's 117, even though he played three fewer years in that decade than Cravath and was primarily a pitcher for two of the years he did play. Ruth led the majors in four-baggers from 1921 through 1930 with 462 and also hit the most homers in American League history. Ruth has the second-best career home run production rate of all time, having hit 33.6 homers for every 500 plate appearances. Only Mark McGwire's production is higher at 38.1. In his career, Ruth split playing time almost evenly between left and right field, usually playing the easier position in every park. In his career, he swatted 313 home runs while playing left field and 354 while playing right field. When Ruth retired, he was the career leader at both those positions by more than 100 but now places fourth in left field and fifth in right field. Only Ernie Banks has hit at least 200 home runs at each of two positions in his career with 277 at shortstop and 210 at first base through the end of the 2005 season. (See chapter 14 for an addendum to this note.)

The list of superlatives goes on and on. Ruth's fame even made it to the entertainment industry when legend has it that his career home run figure became the badge number for Sgt. Joe Friday on the 1950s television show, *Dragnet*. There is no wonder, then, that Ruth, the Sultan of Swat, is still the premiere legend of the game.

5

THE ROARING TWENTIES

As the 1920s started, Americans were flush from victory in the Great War, and the economy was growing. As the decade progressed, personal excess became a way of life for many people. At the same time there was a great loosening of social and moral restraints. The next era of baseball was played on this stage.

The style of baseball in the 1920s reflected the social milieu of the era: brash and loud. The term the "Roaring Twenties" correctly describes the baseball era as well as the decade. Owners, managers, and players all learned the lessons of Babe Ruth, that a high octane offense put more fans in the seats (owners), won more ballgames (managers), and increased salaries (players). A new philosophy encouraged batters to "hit one out," and the general level of home run production in the major leagues increased dramatically as did the individual totals of the yearly leaders in each league.

The home run production rate for the era, as shown in Figure 5.1, increased dramatically over the previous periods. The lowest point in the decade, the 3.3 production rate in 1920 is higher than almost all previous years and the production rate had never before topped 5.0 in any single year but six of the eleven years in this graph are above that level. The era began with a small increase from 1919 to 1920 but then a larger increase occurred from 1920 to 1921. This higher level held through much of the decade and then surged at the end of the period to 8.0 in 1930, a year truly

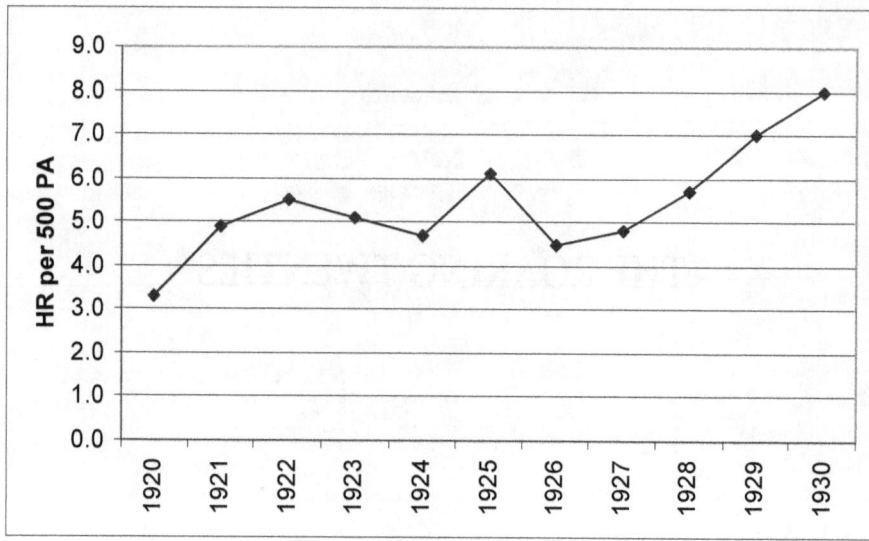

Figure 5.1 – Home Run Production Rate (1920–30)

dominated by the hitters. The largest American League increase in home run production at the start of the era occurred in 1920, as that circuit's production rate jumped from 2.8 in 1919 to 3.9. In the National League, the largest increase occurred one year later from 1920 (2.8) to 1921 (4.9), a much bigger increase than that of its rival league.

Early in the decade, players such as Tilly Walker of the Philadelphia Athletics, Ken Williams of the St. Louis Browns, and Bob Meusel of the New York Yankees joined Babe Ruth at the top of the American League home run charts. In the Senior Circuit, Rogers Hornsby of the St. Louis Cardinals, George "High Pockets" Kelly of the New York Giants, and Cy Williams of the Philadelphia Phillies led the charge. Bob Meusel's brother, Irish, made it a family affair as he slugged many homers in the National League. From 1921 through 1930, Ruth hit 462 home runs, a previously unheard-of total for any 10-year span. In fact, Gavvy Cravath had hit 117 homers from 1911 through 1920 to become the first player to hit at least 100 for a decade, with Ruth also topping the century mark at 103 in that period. Rogers Hornsby slugged 243 in the National League from 1921 through 1930, higher than any previous total but not close to matching the Babe's output.

The reason for this increase in home run totals is the sudden dramatic increase in the number of baseballs being hit over the fence rather than any increase in the number of inside-the-park home runs. Batters were taking mighty swings at the pitchers' offerings and hitting the ball farther in the air than in past eras. Many of these extended flights landed in the grandstand or out on the street producing instant runs for the batter's team, thus decreasing the need to play hit-and-run to score since one swing of the bat could produce multiple runs in a blink of the eye. However, old habits are hard to break and the managers and veteran players—highly schooled in the Deadball Era style of play—continued to play that style of baseball for a few more years. During the decade, teams frequently used first inning bunts and what might be considered crazy base running by twenty-first century observers, such as trying to go from second to third on a grounder to shortstop and attempting many unsuccessful double steals of second and home.

Many people around baseball began speaking out about the dramatic rise in home run production and their perception of the negative effect this had on the sport. To counteract this growing trend, on June 5, 1920, Thomas Shibe, an employee of the Reach Company, which manufactured the baseball for the American League (and Vice President of the Philadelphia Athletics at the same time), stated that the increase in home runs in the first part of the 1920 season could not be tied to a change in the ball. The next day's *New York Times* quoted him as saying: "The specifications this year called for the same yarn, the same cork centre, the same size and weight of rubber and the same horsehide. It has not changed one iota and no effort has been made to turn out a livelier ball." He credited the abolishment of the spit ball and other "freak" pitches for the increase in offense, a reasoning cited by many people in the next few years.

The National League leader in 1920, Cy Williams of the Philadelphia Phillies, hit 15 home runs, fewer than any of the top three sluggers in the American League: Ruth with 54, George Sisler of the St. Louis Browns with 19, and Tilly Walker of the Philadelphia Athletics with 17. At the end of the 1920 season, the top five players on the all-time home run list were Roger Connor (138), Sam Thompson (126), Harry Stovey (122), Gavvy Cravath (119), and Jimmy Ryan (118). Babe Ruth passed all five players before the end of July 1921 to take over the top spot on the all-time list. The career totals of the 1920 Top Five add up to 623 home runs, but at the end of the 2005 season four players had hit more than that combined total.

In 1921, there was a large jump in home run production in the major leagues, and homer totals for individual batters increased along with that as six sluggers hit at least 20 for the season. Babe Ruth hit more than double the four-baggers of his nearest competitor, as both Ruth's teammate Bob Meusel and Ken Williams of the St. Louis Browns hit 24 blasts compared to the Babe's 59. In the National League, High Pockets Kelly of the New York Giants led the circuit with 23 homers.

Partway into the 1921 season, umpires in both leagues were instructed to rub baseballs before their use in a game. The intent was two-fold: to take some of the gloss off the surface and to allow the pitchers to grip the ball better. In the American League, the umpires were told to use a white powder created by a Philadelphia chemist, which created the same effect as when rosin had been permitted on the baseball before 1920. The Senior Circuit arbiters were instructed to use moist dirt on the balls.

Table 5.1 – Progression of the American League Season Surrendered Record

Pitcher	Team	Year	HR
Watty Lee (tie)	Washington	1901	14
Ted Lewis (tie)	Boston	—	—
Bill Reidy (tie)	Milwaukee	—	—
Al Orth	Washington	1902	18
Eddie Rommel (tie)	Philadelphia	1921	21
Urban Shocker (tie)	St. Louis	—	—
Urban Shocker	St. Louis	1922	22
George Blaeholder (tie)	St. Louis	1928	23
Jack Ogden (tie)	St. Louis	—	—
George Earnshaw	Philadelphia	1932	28
Bobo Newsom	St. Louis	1938	30
Fred Hutchinson	Detroit	1948	32
Camilo Pascual	Washington	1956	33
Pedro Ramos	Washington	1957	43
Bert Blyleven	Minnesota	1986	50

In 1921, both Eddie Rommel of the Philadelphia Athletics and Urban Shocker of the St. Louis Browns surrendered 21 home runs during the season, establishing a new American League record for gopher balls. Al Orth of the 1902 Washington Senators had held the mark by surrendering 18 home runs. Table 5.1 shows the progression of the American League home runs surrendered record. None of the listed pitchers set a major league mark until Bert Blyleven in 1986, who is the only hurler to surrender 50 homers in one season.

As the decade progressed, new players entered the majors with the concept of swinging for the fences as a primary offensive strategy rather than the small-ball style of play common in the Deadball Era. This trend was unpopular with people who had been around the game for years and many spoke out against the new style of play.

The *New York Times* published a story on May 24, 1921, titled "Home Run Epidemic Hits Major Leagues." The story cited the fact that players who had not hit many homers in the past were now sluggers and stated that the change in pitching rules was not a satisfactory reason for this increase. The ball manufacturer claimed that it was following the same procedures in the process but that they were getting a better quality of Australian wool than before. Four days later, Johnny Evers, manager of the Chicago Cubs, stated that there was a danger of a pitcher or infielder getting hurt by a batted ball and that he was hesitant to pull the infielders in on the edge of the grass to prevent a run from scoring as he thought it too dangerous for the fielder.

In 1922, the grand total of four-baggers hit in the major leagues crossed the 1,000 line for the first time. Also that year, a National League batter hit 40 homers for the first time as Rogers Hornsby of the St. Louis Cardinals clouted 42 to lead the majors. This set a new single-season mark for the National League, beating Ned Williamson's 1884 record of twenty-seven but less than Ruth's American League (and major league) record 59. Table 5.2 shows the progression of the single-season home run record in the National League. Hornsby won the National League Triple Crown in 1922, a feat he would repeat in 1925. In 1922, Ken Williams of the St. Louis Browns led the American League with 39 home runs and stole 37 bases (second only to teammate George Sisler's 51) for a unique combination of power

Table 5.2 – Progression of the National League Season Record

Batter	Team	Year	HR
George Hall	Philadelphia	1876	5
Charley Jones	Boston	1879	9
Buck Ewing	New York	1883	10
Ned Williamson	Chicago	1884	27
Rogers Hornsby	St. Louis	1922	42
Chuck Klein	Philadelphia	1929	43
Hack Wilson	Chicago	1930	56
Mark McGwire	St. Louis	1998	70
Barry Bonds	San Francisco	2001	73

and speed. Williams was the first player to top the 30 mark in both homers and steals in the same season, a feat that would not be duplicated until 1956 when Willie Mays had two consecutive 30/30 seasons. The long drought in this achievement of power and speed occurred because stolen bases became less of a factor in the offensive arsenal of teams by the end of the 1920s as the power half of the pair became more dominant in the game. In 1922, Ken Williams hit 32 of his 39 round-trippers at home in Sportsman's Park, the largest percentage of four-baggers hit at home for a player with at least 30 in a season.

As part of his league-leading 39 homers, Ken Williams set a record in 1922 by hitting a home run in each of six consecutive games to break the old mark of five set by Babe Ruth in 1921. The St. Louis slugger homered in contests from July 28 through August 2 all played at Sportsman's Park. High Pockets Kelly of the New York Giants matched the record by hitting seven home runs in six consecutive games in July 1924.

On September 24, 1922, Rogers Hornsby of the St. Louis Cardinals hit a pair of home runs in a game at New York's Polo Grounds. He victimized Virgil Barnes of the Giants in the fourth inning and then Virgil's brother, Jesse, in the sixth. This was the first time that brothers each had surrendered a home run to the same batter in the same game, a feat that has been duplicated twice. In 1927, Jesse Barnes pitched for the Brooklyn Dodgers and, on May 3, the brothers each surrendered a homer as opponents in the contest, the first time that opposing brothers had surrendered home runs in the same game.

The dramatic increase in the major league home run production rate can be seen also in the rise in the number of players who hit multiple homers in one game. In the 1880s and 1890s, this type of event had occurred frequently and in the early teens some players were proficient at it. However, the highest previous total for any one season was in 1884 with 35 single-player, multi-homer games. In the 1920s, homers came in bunches for batters with 59 multi-homer games in 1922, 62 in 1925, and 98 in 1930. It would be 1950 before the latter level was achieved again.

In 1923, Cy Williams of the Philadelphia Phillies stroked 41 circuit drives to lead the National League and tie Ruth for the major league-leading total for the year. Table 1.5 shows the progression of the career home run record for the National League. Sam Thompson had held the National League mark since 1895, a record that stood until June 2, 1923, when Cy Williams

> *The first time a father/son pair* had each hit a home run in the major leagues occurred in 1924. James Joseph "Jimmy" Cooney hit all four of his major league homers in 1890 for the Chicago Colts (now Cubs) in the first year of a brief big league career. His son, James Edward "Jimmy" Cooney hit the first of his two major league home runs on June 17, 1924 while playing for the St. Louis Cardinals. The younger son, Johnny, also played in the majors and hit both his career homers on consecutive days in 1939 for the Boston Bees.

hit career homer number 127 at Philadelphia's Baker Bowl. By the end of the decade, Rogers Hornsby would surpass Williams's total in the league, finishing with 298 National League home runs and Hornsby's mark in turn would be broken in the late 1930s by Mel Ott.

In 1924, Babe Ruth led the American League with 46 swats, while Jack Fournier of the Brooklyn Dodgers hit 27. Joe Hauser of the Philadelphia Athletics finished second to Ruth with 27, while Rogers Hornsby was runner-up to Fournier with 25 clouts. Bob Meusel of the Yankees led the American League in 1925 with 33 homers, and Ruth hit 25, although he started the year sick and later was fined and suspended by the Yankees.

That year was the first that the top five home run sluggers in each league hit at least 20 circuit drives, with Rogers Hornsby, who was appointed the manager of the St. Louis Cardinals on May 31, leading the majors with 39. Hornsby won the National League Triple Crown for the second time in 1925, the first player to perform this feat multiple times. The only other hitter to lead in all three categories in one season multiple times is Ted Williams, who won the American League Triple Crown in 1942 and 1947. In 1926, only two batters hit at least 20 home runs, as Ruth once again led the American League with 47 and Hack Wilson, in his first year with the Chicago Cubs, led the National League with 21.

In 1925, the Yankees replaced Wally Pipp, one of the home run stars of the late teens, with another left-handed-hitting slugger. New York City native Lou Gehrig, who attended Columbia University on a football scholarship, became the every day first baseman for the Yankees, as evidenced by his 2,130 consecutive games played from June 1925 through May 1939. In 10 of those seasons, the "Iron Horse" hit at least 30 home runs, and he led the league three times in the 1930s.

As great as Gehrig was as a player and person, he was overshadowed by his larger-than-life teammate, Babe Ruth, and then, shortly after Ruth retired, by a new teammate, Joe DiMaggio. Each year from 1925 through 1930, no matter how many home runs Gehrig hit, the Babe hit more. Finally in 1931, Lou tied the Babe with 46 circuit drives for the season. This tie must have been bittersweet for him, however, as on April 26, Gehrig hit a home run into the center field bleachers at Griffith Stadium in Washington. The ball caromed back to the center fielder and the base runner, Lyn Lary, thought the ball had been caught to end the inning. He left the field without completing the circuit of the bases and when Gehrig passed the spot Lary had stopped running, the umpires called Gehrig out for passing the preceding runner, thus losing credit for the four-bagger. That one homer would have given the undisputed home run crown for the season solely to Lou for the first time in his career.

In 1927, when Ruth raised the single-season record to 60, Gehrig actually led the Babe as late as August 19 and was still even with him on September 5. Figure 5.2 shows how the race between the sluggers progressed. On September 6, both batters hit number 45 although Gehrig would

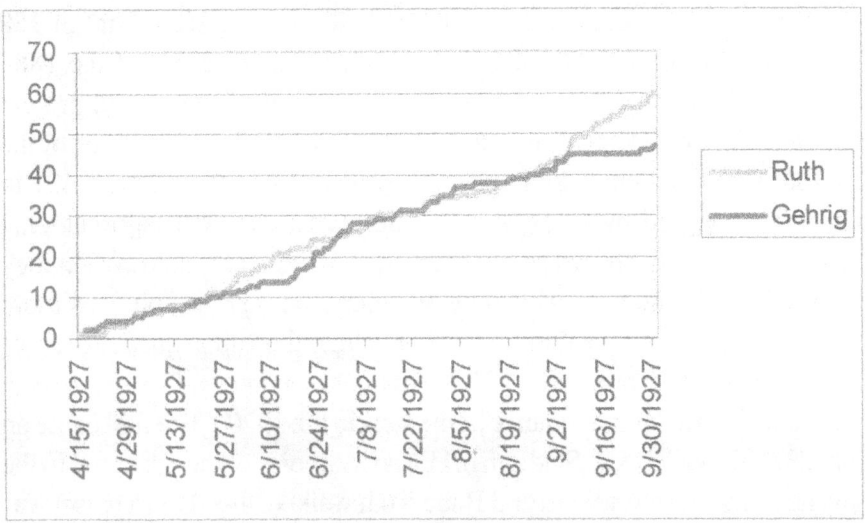

Figure 5.2 – The 1927 Home Run Race

not slug another circuit drive for three weeks while the Babe went on his September run of 17 homers to beat the record and win the home run championship for that year. The 107 combined home runs for the two batsmen were more than every other major league team for the season except the New York Giants, who clouted 109. During his dash to 47 homers in 1927, Gehrig hit three in one game on June 23 at Fenway Park in Boston. He also hit three in one contest in 1929 and 1930. His four-homer game will be discussed in chapter 6. While Ruth and Gehrig dominated the American League, Cy Williams of the Philadelphia Phillies and Hack Wilson of the Chicago Cubs tied for the National League lead in 1927 by hitting 30 homers each. Rogers Hornsby placed third with 26.

Before the 1927 season, only Ruth had hit at least 45 home runs in one year, having performed the feat in 1920 (54), 1921 (59), 1924 (46), and 1926 (47). Indeed, only two other batters had hit even 40 circuit drives in one season, Rogers Hornsby with 42 in 1922 and Cy Williams with 41 in 1923, both in the National League. Thus the fact that two batters each hit more than 45 in 1927 was an unprecedented feat but in retrospect simply one more indication that this *was* baseball's "Roaring Twenties."

The 1927 Yankees, led by Ruth and Gehrig, swatted a total of 158 home runs for the year, beating the previous tainted record of the 1884 Chicago White Stockings, who hit 142 as a result of the altered ground rules at Lake Front Park. With the 1927 total, the Yankees had three of the top four single-season team totals as they had hit 134 in 1921 and 121 in 1926. In 1930, led by Hack Wilson's 56 homers, the Chicago National League team, now known as the Cubs, reclaimed their record when they smashed 171 home runs. This time, the club's home/road split was more evenly divided than it had been in 1884. While the 1884 squad hit 131 of 142 four-baggers at home, the 1930 team hit 96 at home and 75 on the road.

Lou Gehrig hit two bounce home runs in the 1920s. The first came on July 23, 1925, at Yankee Stadium off Firpo Marberry of the Senators. In the seventh inning, Aaron Ward and Babe Ruth walked, then Bob Meusel was hit on the hand by a pitch to load the bases. Gehrig hit a pop fly down the left field line that landed a few feet inside the line and bounced into the grandstand for a homer. This was the first grand slam of Gehrig's career, a feat he would perform 23 times, which is still the major league mark. Lou hit his second bounce home run in the first of two games on July 30, 1927, at Yankee Stadium. In addition to the pair of bounce homers, Gehrig raced around the bases 10 times in his career on inside-the-park homers. These came at the beginning and the end of his career with none from 1930 through 1933. As stated in the previous chapter, Babe Ruth had no bounce homers but he hit 10 inside-the-park four-baggers during his time in the big leagues.

◆ ◆ ◆

On September 4, 1927, brothers Paul and Lloyd Waner, teammates on the Pittsburgh Pirate squad, both hit home runs off Dolf Luque in the fifth inning of a game at Cincinnati's Redland (later Crosley) Field. They became the first brothers to homer in the same game as each Waner hit a bounce home run down the left field line with no runners on base. They repeated the feat in 1929 and 1938, with the latter instance occurring back to back. Many other teammate brothers have homered in the same game since then, with some of those being in the same inning. Table 5.3 lists all occurrences of the event. Hank and Tommie Aaron homered in the same game three times in one season (in 1962), more than any other pair for a year. The Guerreros and the Giambis have each performed the feat four times in their careers, more than any other pair of brothers. There also have been many occasions when brothers on opposing teams have clouted circuit drives in the same game. The first opponents to do so were the Ferrells. In the top of the fourth inning on July 19, 1933, at Boston's Fenway Park, Cleveland pitcher Wes Ferrell homered off Red Sox hurler Hank Johnson. Johnson's catcher, Wes's brother Rick, returned the favor in the bottom half of that inning when he hit a four-bagger off his brother.

Table 5.3 – Brothers Homering in the Same Game

Teammate Brothers

Date	Players	Team (League)	Notes
09/04/1927	Lloyd & Paul Waner	Pittsburgh (NL)	1, 2
06/09/1929	Lloyd & Paul Waner	Pittsburgh (NL)	2
09/15/1938	Lloyd & Paul Waner	Pittsburgh (NL)	2, 3
05/15/1961	Felipe & Matty Alou	San Francisco (NL)	
06/12/1962	Hank & Tommie Aaron	Milwaukee (NL)	
07/12/1962	Hank & Tommie Aaron	Milwaukee (NL)	1
08/14/1962	Hank & Tommie Aaron	Milwaukee (NL)	
08/12/1965	Matty & Jesus Alou	San Francisco (NL)	
07/04/1970	Billy & Tony Conigliaro	Boston (AL)	
09/19/1970	Billy & Tony Conigliaro	Boston (AL)	
09/15/1990	Billy & Cal Ripken	Baltimore (AL)	1, 2
05/28/1996	Billy & Cal Ripken	Baltimore (AL)	1, 2
08/15/1998	Vlad & Wilton Guerrero	Montreal (NL)	
10/02/1999	Vlad & Wilton Guerrero	Montreal (NL)	2
05/08/2000	Jason & Jeremy Giambi	Oakland (AL)	2
05/18/2000	Vlad & Wilton Guerrero	Montreal (NL)	2
09/15/2000	Jason & Jeremy Giambi	Oakland (AL)	
09/18/2000	Vlad & Wilton Guerrero	Montreal (NL)	2
06/21/2001	Jason & Jeremy Giambi	Oakland (AL)	2
08/11/2001	Jason & Jeremy Giambi	Oakland (AL)	2
07/31/2005	Benji & Jose Molina	Anaheim (AL)	2

Key to Notes: 1 – Same Inning   2 – Same Pitcher   3 – Back to back

Table 5.3 – Brothers Homering in the Same Game (continued)

Opponent Brothers

Date	Players	Teams (League)	Notes
07/19/1933	Rick & Wes Ferrell	Boston & Cleveland (AL)	1
07/05/1935	Al & Tony Cuccinello	New York & Brooklyn (NL)	
06/30/1950	Dom & Joe DiMaggio	Boston & New York (AL)	
10/15/1964	Clete & Ken Boyer	New York AL & St. Louis (NL)	4
06/11/1972	Graig & Jim Nettles	Cleveland & Minnesota (AL)	
09/14/1974	Graig & Jim Nettles	New York & Detroit (AL)	
05/04/1981	Hector & Jose Cruz	Chicago & Houston (NL)	
09/01/1999	Aaron & Bret Boone	Cincinnati & Atlanta (NL)	
05/11/2000	Aaron & Bret Boone	Cincinnati & San Diego (NL)	
06/07/2001	Cesar & Felipe Crespo	San Diego & San Francisco (NL)	

Key to Notes: 1 – Same Inning   4 – World Series

The Nettles brothers homered as opponents in 1972 and 1974 and each brother changed teams between instances! In game seven of the 1964 World Series, St. Louis Cardinals third baseman Ken Boyer homered in the seventh inning. In the top of the ninth inning, brother Clete, the third baseman for the New York Yankees, hit a solo shot. Other brothers, such as the Meusels in the 1920s, had the opportunity to homer in the same World Series game, but the Boyers were the first to accomplish this feat.

There were no surprises on the home run leader board in 1928. Ruth (54) and Gehrig (27) finished first and second in the American League, and Hack Wilson tied for the National League lead with 31, this time with Jim Bottomley of the St. Louis Cardinals. From 1927 through 1930, the home run production rate in the major leagues increased rapidly from 4.8 to 8.0. In 1929, the production rate reached a new high, topping the previous record level from 1925 (6.1) at 7.0. The following year, another new mark was set, which was a whole point higher. Individual totals also climbed during this time. For the first time in 1929, three batters hit more than 40 circuit clouts in the same season: Babe Ruth (46), National League leader Chuck Klein (43) of the Philadelphia

Phillies, and the New York Giants' Mel Ott (42). Rogers Hornsby and Hack Wilson, both with the Chicago Cubs, each missed the mark by one long ball. Klein's total in his first full major-league season increased the National League season record for most home runs by one from Hornsby's 1922 mark. (See Table 5.2 for the progression of the National League single-season record.)

On May 8, 1929, there were eight homers hit in the major leagues and one of those was home run number 25,000 in big league history. It took 53 years for the first 25,000 homers to be hit, but the amount of time to hit each succeeding 25,000 circuit drives has decreased dramatically. Table 5.4 shows the progression of dates for each 25,000 home runs in big league history.

On July 14, 1929, the results of a survey concerning the home run epidemic were published in the *New York Times*. Fifteen of sixteen major league managers answered the survey conducted by the *St. Louis Post-Dispatch* with the general response being that the epidemic of home runs was ruining the game. Several solutions were proposed by the skippers, such as altering the ball, discoloring it, and keeping it in play longer during the game. Some managers said that the pitching was weak owing, in part, to rules restrictions such as the outlawing of the spitter. However, four of the team leaders said that they were in favor of the

Table 5.4 – Dates of Each 25,000 Home Runs

Date	HR Number	Years to Accomplish
05/02/1876	1	—
05/08/1929	25,000	53
06/30/1948	50,000	19
08/14/1960	75,000	12
04/29/1970	100,000	10
08/19/1978	125,000	8
08/03/1986	150,000	8
08/24/1993	175,000	7
06/12/1999	200,000	6
04/09/2004	225,000	5

increased homers, among them Yankees manager Miller Huggins, which should be no surprise, since his club had been the leading group of sluggers through the 1920s. Wilbert Robinson of Brooklyn termed the home run a "joke." This kind of response to a large increase in home run production has been repeated by the game's observers as recently as in the first years of the twenty-first century.

Grover Cleveland "Pete" Alexander surrendered his 160th home run on August 17, 1929, to become the new career leader in that category as he passed John Clarkson. Clarkson had held the record since 1890 but Alexander's tenure would be a lot shorter, as George Blaeholder, Earl Whitehill, and Red Ruffing would each set a new record before the end of the 1930s.

◆　　　◆　　　◆

In 1930, the first challenge came to Babe Ruth's single-season mark set in 1927. Cubs outfielder Hack Wilson, who had led the National League in home runs in 1926 and tied for the lead in 1927 and 1928, had hit 16 four-baggers by the end of May 1930. This put him two ahead of Ruth's 1927 total at the end of May. Wilson remained ahead at the end of July at 34-33 but lost ground in August when he hit 11 long balls. Starting September three behind Ruth's pace, Wilson was not likely to break the record, especially since the Babe had swatted 17 in September 1927. Wilson hit number 50 on September 15 off Phil Collins of the Phillies in Philadelphia to become the first National League slugger to reach the 50 milestone. (Refer to Appendix B for details of each home run number 50 in history.) Wilson ended the campaign with 56 home runs but set a new major league mark by collecting 191 RBI. His home run total increased the National League record for a season for the second consecutive year, a mark that would not change again until 1998. (Refer to Table 5.2 for the progression of the National League single-season record.)

Wilson hit at least 30 home runs in four consecutive years from 1927 through 1930. He led the National League in four of five consecutive years from 1926 through 1930 and hit the third-most homers from 1921 through 1930 with 193, coming in behind Babe Ruth with 462 and Rogers Hornsby with 243. This ranking for the decade came despite the fact that Wilson played only three games before 1924 and 172 before 1926. As part of his 56 clouts to lead the National League in 1930, Wilson hit three in one game on July 26 at Philadelphia's Baker Bowl.

Three other sluggers hit at least 40 home runs in 1930: Ruth (49), Gehrig (41), and Chuck Klein (40). For the first time in history, four batters hit at least 40 home runs in the same season; 10 sluggers clouted 35 or more homers, which was also a first. Rookie Wally Berger of the Boston Braves placed in the latter category as he smashed 38 circuit drives that season to establish a rookie record that would stand until 1987 when Mark McGwire hit 49 home runs.

In the latter half of the 1920s, a new group of sluggers had emerged who carried the game into the next decade. Names such as Ott, Foxx, and Klein would be joined soon by Greenberg, DiMaggio, and Mize in the 1930s.

6
THE GOLDEN AGE OF BASEBALL

In the 1930s, a worldwide economic depression left many people out of work, but in baseball, batters continued beating up on pitchers with their high-octane offensive style inherited from the previous decade. The Roaring Twenties style of baseball continued even though the social environment had changed dramatically from the style in the 1920s. Many historians refer to this decade as the "Golden Age of Baseball."

The home run production rate reached a record high of 8.0 in 1930 and the 1929 average of 7.0 homers per 500 plate appearances became the norm during the 1930s, as shown in Figure 6.1. With the exception of 1931 and 1933, all years in the 1930s had a home run production rate of at least 6.9, while the aberrant years both had averages of 5.6. Not until the United States entered World War II did the home run production drop back to the 1933 level. The large drop in home run average from 1930 (8.0) to 1931 (5.6) can be attributed to three changes made during the winter of 1930–31.

Before the 1931 season, two rules changes were enacted that affected home runs slightly. The American League finally dropped the rule that stated a ball was fair or foul depending on where it landed and adopted the National League version of the rule. Now both leagues would judge a fly ball based on where it flew over the fence (the modern rule). The second rule change eliminated the bounce home run, turning a hit that bounced in fair territory and then out of play into a two-base hit rather than the four-base variety, which is the modern rule. There had been 14 of those bounce homers in 1930 with the last hit by Brooklyn outfielder Eddie Moore on September 27, one day before the end of the 1930 season. Only two seasons are known to have had more than 40 bounce home runs, 1922 (56) and 1923 (52), but since those 108 are part of the 2,035 hit those two seasons, the rule had a very small effect on home run totals. This change removed one of the last vestiges of old-style baseball.

In addition to rules changes, both leagues made changes to the specifications of the baseball before the 1931 season that caused most of that year's drop in the home run production rate. The American League required heavier, raised stitching on the cover with longer stitches while in addition the National League also adopted a heavier cover. The stitching had been counter-sunk in previous years and the raised stitches gave a pitcher a better grip to spin the curve ball. Also, the wind resistance created by those raised stitches improves the aerodynamics that allow the ball to curve when thrown by a pitcher. In the mid-1920s, the threading used on the cover of the ball broke frequently, thus making the ball unusable. Manufacturers began using a finer thread with greater strength and the stitching was sewn flush with the cover. The intent of the 1931 change was to deaden the "rabbit" ball slightly so as to curb the home run barrage that had peaked in 1930 with more than 1,500 home runs in the major leagues for the first time. No changes were made to the interior of the baseball at this time.

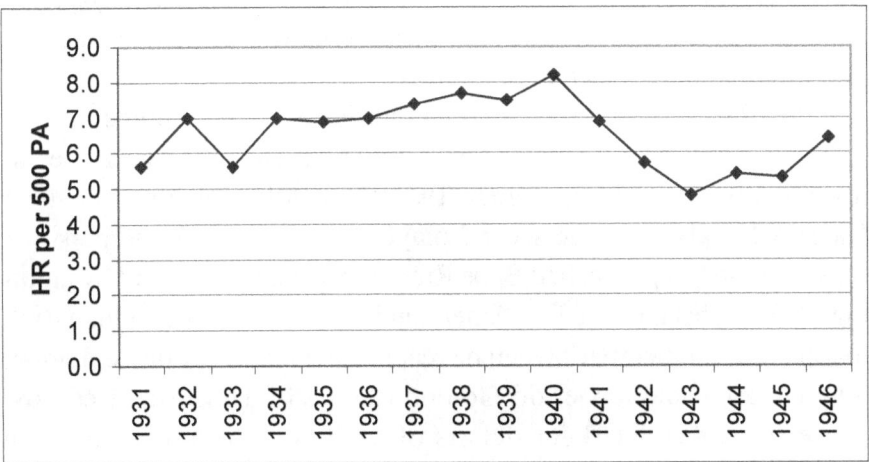

Figure 6.1 – Home Run Production Rate (1931–46)

A drop in individual totals in 1931 reflected the general decrease in home runs produced by the rules and ball changes as only two batters, Yankees teammates Babe Ruth and Lou Gehrig, who tied for the American League lead with 46 homers, hit more than 32 blasts. Chuck Klein of the Phillies led the National League for the second of four times in his career with 31 home runs. Giant's outfielder Mel Ott, who had hit his career-high 42 four-baggers in 1929, placed second to Klein in 1931 with 29 home runs. In the American League, Earl Averill of the Cleveland Indians hit 32 and Jimmie Foxx clouted 30 for the Philadelphia Athletics. As part of Gehrig's 46 home runs in 1931, he hit one in each of six consecutive games from August 28 through September 1. This streak tied the mark for homering in the most consecutive games held by Ken Williams and High Pockets Kelly set in the early 1920s. On July 12, 1931, Mel Ott of the New York Giants hit his 100th career homer at age 22 off rookie Frank Watt of the Philadelphia Phillies in the second game of the day at the Polo Grounds. He is the youngest to reach the 100 homer level and only Tony Conigliaro and Eddie Mathews also hit 100 home runs before age 23.

> *The visiting Washington Senators beat the Philadelphia Athletics on April 18, 1932, 15-7, at Shibe Park. In the ninth inning, Washington first baseman Joe Judge hit his first homer of the season, which crashed through a window of a house overlooking right field and a woman came out of the house to see what had caused the crash to the amusement of those in the park.*

In 1932, Jimmie Foxx, who had hit 33, 37, and 30 homers in the previous three campaigns, led the majors with 58 home runs as he enjoyed the best year of his career. Two years earlier, National Leaguer Hack Wilson became the second player to hit at least 50 homers in a season when he approached Babe Ruth's single-season record by clouting 56. Foxx became the first American League slugger other than Ruth to top the 50 homer mark when he reached the milestone on September 3 by hitting a solo homer off Gordon Rhodes of the Boston Red Sox. (Refer to Appendix B for details of each home run number 50 in history.) Foxx set a new single-season record for home runs by a

Table 6.1 – Progression of the Right-Handed Season Record

Batter	Team (League)	Year	HR
Charley Jones	Cincinnati (NL)	1876	4
Charley Jones	Boston (NL)	1879	9
Harry Stovey	Philadelphia (AA)	1883	14
Ned Williamson	Chicago (NL)	1884	27
Rogers Hornsby	St. Louis (NL)	1922	42
Hack Wilson	Chicago (NL)	1930	56
Jimmie Foxx	Philadelphia (AL)	1932	58
Mark McGwire	St. Louis (NL)	1998	70

right-handed batter with his 58, breaking Wilson's 1930 mark. Foxx held the single-season record for right-handed batters until Mark McGwire broke it in 1998 by hitting 70 home runs, but Foxx still holds the American League mark for right-handed batters. (See Table 6.1 for the progression of the season record for right-handed batters.) Foxx was from the Eastern Shore of Maryland and had been recommended to Athletics manager Connie Mack by a former Athletic slugger also from the Eastern Shore, Home Run Baker. Foxx made his major league debut at age 17 in 1925 and was a part-time player for the first three years of his career. However, once he became a regular member of Mack's lineup, Foxx quickly became one of the most feared sluggers in the league.

From 1929 through 1940, Foxx never hit fewer than 30 home runs in a season and led the league four times in that period. For the 10-year period 1931 through 1940, Foxx slugged 414 homers to become only the second batter to hit over 400 in a decade. His output for the decade places him second to Babe Ruth's 462 in the 1920s. In 1932, Foxx had smashed 41 circuit drives by the end of July and was seven ahead of Ruth's 1927 pace. In August, he only hit seven homers after consecutive months with 13, 12, and 12 four-baggers but was still five ahead of Ruth. However, as discussed in chapter 4, Ruth's last lap in September proved the death of many a pursuit. Foxx hit 10 homers in September, which is an admirable total, but fell behind the Babe at the end because of the latter's 17 homer month in September 1927. Ruth himself was still swatting the ball out of American League parks as he hit 41 home runs in 1932. Chuck Klein and Mel Ott, both of whom played in ballparks well-suited to left-handed pull hitters, tied for the National League lead with 38 circuit drives.

◆ ◆ ◆

On June 3, 1932, the Yankees beat the Athletics at Philadelphia's Shibe Park, 20-13. Jimmie Foxx collected a triple and his major-league-leading 19th home run in the game, while Babe Ruth hit a double and his 15th homer of the season in the contest. However, Lou Gehrig was the star of the day as he hit home runs in each of his first four trips to the plate to become the first American Leaguer and first twentieth-century player to hit four in one game. It had been nearly 36 years since Ed Delahanty had hit four homers in one game and this was only the third time in history that the feat was accomplished. In the first and fifth innings, Gehrig whacked the ball over the left center field fence while, in the fourth and seventh innings, he homered over the right field wall. Before the game, Gehrig was the only player to have hit three or more home runs in one game on three occasions, having socked three in 1927, 1929, and 1930. On this day he became the first to hit at least three in a game four different times. Gehrig had two chances to hit another homer in the game, but he grounded out in the eighth inning in his first attempt and in the ninth hit a long fly ball to the deepest part of the park in center field, which was caught only a few feet from the fence. (Refer to Appendix C for details of all four home run games.)

Gehrig had been part of the late-1920s group of sluggers who dominated the pitchers of the era but also qualifies as one of the elite home run hitters in the 1930s. He led the American League three times in the decade, hitting his career-high 49 four-baggers in both 1934 and 1936, and hit 306 round-trippers from 1931 through the end of his career in 1939, the second-highest total for the decade behind Jimmie Foxx. On July 10, 1936, Gehrig hit his 400th career homer to join the retired Babe Ruth as the only two batters with that many circuit clouts. On that day, Jimmie Foxx was third on the all-time list with 324 homers and Rogers Hornsby had exactly 300. Gehrig also continued his assault on pitchers with the bases loaded through the decade, compiling 23 grand slams by the end of his career. For Gehrig to hit that many homers with the bases full is quite an achievement when one considers that for almost all of his career, Gehrig had either Babe Ruth or Joe DiMaggio hitting before him in the lineup, both of whom had a knack for driving in runs. Of course, through that entire period the Yankees had a lot of base runners for all of them to knock in as the New York squads led the American League in runs scored in 11 of 14 years from 1926 through 1939. When Gehrig retired, he had hit 493 homers to place second on the career list, a spot he had held since April 1934. Jimmie Foxx passed him on August 16, 1940.

Foxx (48) and Klein (28) led the way in the two leagues again in 1933, although each of them hit exactly 10 fewer homers than the previous year, reflecting the general downturn in home run production for the season. For the only time in history, the home run champ in each league also won the Triple Crown. In the American League, Babe Ruth, in his last big year, finished second in homers with 34 and Lou Gehrig finished third right behind the Babe with 32 blasts. In the National League, Wally Berger of the Boston Braves placed second with 27. Chuck Klein, having led the National League as a member of the Philadelphia Phillies squad, was traded to the Cubs before the 1934 season. This had happened before in 1920 when Babe Ruth was sent to New York by the Red Sox during the off-season after leading the league in home runs.

In 1934, the New York Giants' Mel Ott and James "Ripper" Collins of the St. Louis Cardinals, who should not be confused with the 1920s pitcher Harry "Rip" Collins, led the National League tied with 35 home runs with Wally Berger of the Boston Braves close behind with 34 clouts. In the American League, Lou Gehrig carried the banner with his 49 homers, winning the Triple Crown as well, and Jimmie Foxx continued his assault on the pitchers around the circuit with 44 drives. Rookie Hal Trosky Sr. of the Cleveland Indians hammered 35 homers.

Ripper Collins set a new mark for single-season home runs for switch hitters in 1934 with his 35. He had raised the record to 21 in 1932 by breaking Buzz Arlett's previous record of 18 set in 1931 (in the only year of Arlett's major league career). Collins would hold the record until Mickey Mantle broke it in 1955 by hitting 37 home runs.

Hank Greenberg of the Detroit Tigers and Jimmie Foxx of the

Athletics tied for the American League lead in 1935 with 36 dingers each, while Wally Berger of the Boston Braves led the Senior Circuit with 34. Outfielder Babe Herman of the Cincinnati Reds hit the first home run in a night game off Brooklyn Dodgers' hurler Dutch Leonard on July 10, 1935, at Cincinnati's Crosley Field as Brooklyn lost in its first-ever night game, 15-2. Philadelphia's Connie Mack traded his star slugger, Jimmie Foxx, to the Boston Red Sox after the season, the second time in three years that an American League home run leader had been traded before the next season. Foxx was part of a deal that included other players and $150,000, which was part of Mack's general trend of selling off his best (and most expensive) players to raise money for his cash-strapped organization.

Three American League sluggers hit 40 homers in 1936, as Lou Gehrig of the Yankees led with 49, Hal Trosky of the Cleveland Indians hit 42, and Jimmie Foxx hit 41 in his first season with the Red Sox. This season marked the third time that three batters each hit 40 home runs in one year, with Babe Ruth, Mel Ott, and Chuck Klein performing the feat in 1929 and Ruth, Hack Wilson, Gehrig, and Klein reaching 40 in 1930. Ott led the National League with 33 homers in 1936, the only batter to top the 30 home run level in that league. Highly touted rookie Joe DiMaggio of the Yankees hit 29 to place fourth in the American League. A slow climb in major league home run production started in 1936 that culminated with the 1940 rate of 8.2 home runs per 500 plate appearances, which set a new single-season high for the major leagues. The 1936 Yankees squad hit 182 home run to set a new mark for most homers by a team in one season, topping the previous mark of 172 set by the 1932 Philadelphia Athletics. The 1936 Bronx squad hit 14.2 home runs for every 500 plate appearances, the best mark since the tainted 16.0 rate set by the 1884 Chicago White Stockings. The 1936 Yankees, when the 1884 mark is ignored, set the single-season production rate for a team, which would stand until 1947.

Tony Lazzeri of the New York Yankees hit two grand slam home runs in one game in Philadelphia on May 24, 1936. No other batter had ever socked two home runs with the bases full in a game before Lazzeri, who hit another homer to lead off the seventh inning. He almost hit a fourth home run in the eighth inning but settled for a two-run triple as the ball stayed in the park. Lazzeri drove in 11 runs to set a new American League record in that category, topping the record set by Jimmie Foxx in 1933. Lazzeri led the Yankees as they beat the Athletics, 25-2.

On July 10, 1936, Chuck Klein of the Phillies hit four home runs in one game at Forbes Field off three Pittsburgh Pirate hurlers and became the first National Leaguer to perform the feat in the twentieth century. Bobby Lowe and Ed Delahanty had hit four homers in one National League game in the 1890s and Lou Gehrig hit a quartet in the American League in 1932. Klein's fourth clout came in the 10th inning and provided the winning margin for the visiting team. All four drives were over the right field fence, and in the second inning, Klein almost got a fifth as he hit a fly ball that Paul Waner caught against the fence. Previous to Klein's big day, only Rogers Hornsby in 1931 and Babe Ruth in 1935 had hit three homers in one game at spacious Forbes Field, and no Pirate player accomplished the feat there until Ralph Kiner in 1947. Klein's 10th inning blast made him the first batter to use extra innings to complete a four-homer game. Later, Pat Seerey and Mike Schmidt both hit the last of a four-homer game in extra innings. Klein is the oldest player to hit four homers in one game at 31 years 276 days. (Refer to Appendix C for details of all four home run games.)

> *The visiting Cincinnati Reds beat the Brooklyn Dodgers, 7-2, on June 22, 1936 at Ebbets Field. In the fifth inning, Ival Goodman hit a fly ball to right field that landed on top of the scoreboard and remained there. The ball was still in play but it did not come down to the field so that the outfielders could retrieve it but rather sat on the ledge at the top of the scoreboard. Meanwhile, Goodman raced around the bases for a very unusual inside-the-park home run.*

Joe DiMaggio led the American League with 46 four-baggers in 1937, while Hank Greenberg hit 40 to place second. DiMaggio led the league in homers twice in his career (11 years apart, which is the longest time between leading a league for any batter) and had hit 361 career home runs when he retired. One indication of DiMaggio's hitting ability is shown by comparing his career strike out total (369) to his home run total. No other player with 300 career homers stuck out fewer than 400 times. Ted Kluszewski with 279 home runs and 365 strikeouts is the only other player with more than 250 homers to strike out fewer than 400 times.

When Rogers Hornsby ended his National League career on July 26, 1933, to begin his position as player/manager of the American League St. Louis Browns, he had hit 298 home runs in the Senior Circuit, setting the career record for the league. Hornsby also placed second on the all-time list that day behind Babe Ruth, who had hit 676 of his 714 career home runs at that point. Mel Ott, who would become player/manager of the New York Giants in 1942, passed Hornsby's National League mark on August 12, 1937. At the Polo Grounds, Ott swatted career homer number 299 off Guy Bush of the Boston Bees (a team nickname used by the Braves from 1936 through 1940). In 1937, Ott tied for the National League lead in home runs with Joe Medwick of the St. Louis Cardinals as both sluggers clouted 31 four-baggers. Medwick won the Triple Crown that year, the most recent National Leaguer to do so.

In August 1937, Rudy York of the Detroit Tigers hit 18 home runs to set a new record for one month. Babe Ruth had set the previous mark of 17 in September 1927 on the way to his then record 60 for the season. A handful of players have since hit 17 in a month but Sammy Sosa of the Chicago Cubs topped York's record in June 1998 when he smacked 20 home runs as part of his 66 that year.

Jimmie Foxx, in his third year with the Boston Red Sox, hit 50 home runs in 1938. Foxx, who had hit 58 for the 1932 Athletics, became the first batter to slug 50 or more home runs for two different teams, and only Babe Ruth, with four years of at least 50 had hit that many homers multiple times before this season. Foxx hit number 50 on October 1, a grand slam off Johnny Murphy of the New York Yankees at Fenway Park. Foxx also is the only batter to be the single-season home run leader for two franchises, although Albert Belle held the top spot for both the Cleveland Indians and Chicago White Sox for a few years before Jim Thome topped Belle's Cleveland total. (See chapter 14 for an update to Foxx' marks.) Foxx hit 35 of his 50 in 1938 at Fenway Park, the most by any batter in one season at that ballpark. He hit his 400th career homer on June 27, 1938, off Indians fireballer Bob Feller to become the third player with that many home runs. Even with 50 circuit clouts in 1938, Foxx only placed second in the American

League as Hank Greenberg hit 58 home runs for the Tigers. Greenberg hit 15 homers in July to end the month with 37, three more than Ruth's 1927 total to that point. Greenberg remained three ahead after August but Ruth's 17 homers in September proved too much for Greenberg to overcome, as they had for Hack Wilson in 1930 and Jimmie Foxx in 1932. Greenberg hit number 50 on September 12 off Jack Knott of the Chicago White Sox in Detroit, and hit 39 of his 58 clouts at home at Briggs (later Tiger) Stadium, the record for any one ballpark in one season, topping the previous record of 33 hit by Hack Wilson at Chicago's Wrigley Field in 1930. Greenberg and Foxx became the first pair of sluggers to each hit 50 homers in the same season and Foxx thus became the first batter to drive at least 50 home runs in a season without leading his league. Mel Ott led the National League in 1938 with 36 home runs. (Refer to Appendix B for details of each home run number 50 in history.) Johnny Mize of the St. Louis Cardinals hit three home runs in one game on July 13 (off Jim Turner of the Boston Braves in consecutive at bats) and then again one week later on July 20 (off two New York Giants hurlers), becoming the first player to have two three-homer games in one season. Bobo Newsom of the St. Louis Browns became the first American League pitcher to surrender 30 homers in 1938 with exactly 30 gopher balls. Table 5.1 (page 60) shows the progression of the American League gopher ball record.

Another future member of the 500 Home Run Club, Ted Williams, made his major league debut in 1939. The Splendid Splinter hit 31 homers for the Boston Red Sox, good for third place in the American League behind teammate Jimmie Foxx (35) and Detroit's Hank Greenberg (33) and led the league in runs batted in with 145. Williams would hit at least 30 homers in five of his first six seasons. Johnny Mize of the St. Louis Cardinals, who had been among the top five home run sluggers in the National League since his 1936 debut, led the way in that league with 28 homers in 1939.

The New York Giants clouted six home runs in one game at home in the Polo Grounds against the Cincinnati Reds on June 6, 1939. Jo-Jo Moore hit one in the second inning and Mel Ott in the third before the fireworks started in the fourth inning. With two outs in the fourth, Harry

Danning homered, and after two more batters reached base, Frank Demaree hit the second of the frame. After a change of pitchers, Burgess Whitehead hit a two-run shot, then pitcher Manny Salvo hit an inside-the-park homer to right field and Jo-Jo Moore hit the third consecutive round-tripper and his second of the contest. Thus, the Giants hit five homers in the inning to break the record of four in one frame held by the 1894 Pittsburgh Pirates and the 1930 Cincinnati Reds.

On June 28, 1939, the New York Yankees beat the Philadelphia Athletics twice at Shibe Park by scores of 23-2 and 10-0. In the first game, the club set a new record for homers in one game with eight. Joe DiMaggio and Babe Dahlgren each hit two, while Bill Dickey, George Selkirk, Joe Gordon, and Tommy Henrich each hit one in the contest. The previous record had been seven, which had been done by six teams, including the Giants just three weeks before on June 6, 1939, when they hit five in one inning. The Giants would hit another seven in one game in August 1939 to become the first club to hit at least seven in a game twice in one season. The Yankees hit five more homers in the second game on June 28 with Gordon hitting two, and Frank Crosetti, DiMaggio, and Dahlgren hitting one apiece. Not until 1953 would another team hit eight homers in one game when the Milwaukee Braves did so. The record for most home runs in two consecutive games had been eleven, which had been set by the Yankees in May 1936. The thirteen clouted on this day in 1939 is still the record for consecutive games, having been tied since by the San Francisco Giants in 1961. Three of the 1939 sluggers, Dickey, Crosetti, and DiMaggio, were involved in the 1936 fireworks for the Yankees, which also came at the expense of the Athletics pitching staff.

Lou Gehrig, who had played his last game on April 30, 1939, but was still with the team in his role as captain, received a standing ovation from the Philadelphia fans while presenting the lineup to the umpires for game two on June 28. Athletics skipper Connie Mack, who seldom left the bench, walked to home plate to shake Gehrig's hand.

Jim Tabor of the Boston Red Sox hit four home runs in a holiday doubleheader at Philadelphia on July 4, 1939, with two of the three in the nightcap coming with the bases loaded. This was the second time a batter had smashed two grand slams in one contest and both came at the expense of the hapless Athletics at Shibe Park. Tony Lazzeri had first performed the feat in 1936. The Sox swept the twin bill, 17-7 and 18-12, by hitting seven homers in the two games.

Red Ruffing of the New York Yankees became the career leader for home runs surrendered on May 30, 1939, when he surrendered three long balls to pass George Blaeholder. Ruffing would hold the gopher ball mark until 1956 when Murry Dickson passed him. Table 6.2 shows the complete progression of the career gopher ball record.

Table 6.2 – Progression of the Career-Surrendered Record

Pitcher	Year	HR
Bobby Mathews	1876	8
Tommy Bond	1878	12
Tommy Bond (tie)	1880	21
George Bradley (tie)	—	—
Tommy Bond	1881	24
George Bradley	1882	28
Will White	1883	39
Larry Corcoran	1884	63
Larry Corcoran	1885	66
Jim McCormick	1886	70
Jim McCormick	1887	82
Pud Galvin (tie)	1888	86
John Clarkson (tie)	—	—
Pud Galvin	1889	105
John Clarkson	1890	116
John Clarkson	1894	159
Pete Alexander	1929	160
Pete Alexander	1930	165
George Blaeholder	1936	173
Earl Whitehill	1938	184
Red Ruffing	1939	196
Red Ruffing	1947	254
Murry Dickson	1956	269
Robin Roberts	1957	288
Robin Roberts	1966	505

The year 1940 saw a new all-time high in home run production in the major leagues as the sluggers of the two loops hit 8.2 homers per 500 plate appearances. For the second time in history, major league batters hit at least 1,500 home runs in a season, with the 1,571 hit in 1940 skimming above the previous high count of 1,565 in 1930. The home run average was slightly better than the 1930 record of 8.0 as well. For the second consecutive year, Johnny Mize of the St. Louis Cardinals led the National League, hitting 43 circuit drives, while Hank Greenberg of the Detroit Tigers led the American League for the third time with his 41 four-baggers. Jimmie Foxx of the Boston Red Sox hit 36 home runs to place second in the Junior Circuit, the seventh time since 1932 that Foxx had been in the top two in homers in the American League. Johnny Mize once again had two three-homer games during the 1940 season, a feat he first accomplished in 1938. Mize became the first and only slugger to have multiple three-homer games in a season twice in his career.

◆ ◆ ◆

On September 24, 1940, the Red Sox were in Philadelphia for a double header. In the first game Ted Williams homered in the fourth inning and then again in the sixth, both off George Caster. In the latter inning, the Red Sox hit four home runs as Jimmie Foxx and Joe Cronin followed Williams with consecutive blasts. Bobby Doerr then hit a triple and when the third base coach stopped him at the hot corner, many observers thought Doerr could have scored on an inside-the-park homer. Jim Tabor then hit the fourth ball of the inning out of the park for Boston scoring Doerr in front of him as the Sox beat the Athletics 16-8. This was the fourth time in history that a team hit four long balls in one inning, with the most recent occurrence by the 1939 New York Giants. The home run by Foxx in the midst of the Red Sox barrage was his 500th career blast, making him the second slugger in history with that many home runs, 11 years after Babe Ruth initiated the club, and the only player in history to hit his 500th against a team for whom he formerly played. Foxx, a month shy of his 33rd birthday on that day, is still the youngest player to hit home run number 500 and he retired second on the all-time list with 534 home runs in 1945. Over the course of his career, Foxx hit 27.6 home runs for each 500 plate appearances, placing him second on the all-time batter list for home run production at the time he retired. Foxx, who had slugged 302 homers for the Philadelphia Athletics, hit 222 for the Red Sox, thus becoming the first batter to clout at least 200 for two different teams, an accomplishment achieved by only two other players, Mark McGwire and Rafael Palmeiro. Like Ruth before him, and Hank Aaron in the 1970s, Foxx ended his career in the same city in which it began but in the other league. Ruth started his career with Boston in the American League and finished with the National League Braves. Aaron began in Milwaukee with the Braves and returned to Wisconsin to play for the American League Brewers. Foxx started with the Athletics and finished with the National League Phillies. (Refer to Appendix A for details of each home run number 500.)

The 1941 baseball season is chiefly remembered for two outstanding hitting performances: Red Sox left fielder Ted Williams hitting .406 for the season (including a six-for-eight day to end the year), and Yankee center fielder Joe DiMaggio hitting safely in 56 consecutive games. As part of Williams's supreme hitting that year, he clouted 37 home runs to lead the majors, while Dolph Camilli of the Brooklyn Dodgers led the National League with 34 homers.

On April 17, 1941, Wes Ferrell of the Boston Braves hit his 37th home run as a pitcher, the record for hurlers, off Si Johnson of the Philadelphia Phillies. Ferrell also smacked one as a pinch hitter in 1935, and in his career he out-homered his catcher brother, Rick, by 38-28 in 4,800 fewer at bats.

Ted Williams led the majors for the second consecutive year in 1942 with 36 home runs and won the American League Triple Crown that season before leaving to join the Marine Corps. Mel Ott hit 30 homers in 1942 to lead the National League for the sixth and last time. This was the first year of Ott's managerial career with the Giants, and he became the only full-year player/manager of the twentieth century to lead his league in home runs. Both Gavvy Cravath in 1919 with the Phillies and Rogers Hornsby in 1925 with the Cardinals had taken over the managerial responsibilities in mid-season when they led the league in four-baggers. Only Harry Stovey managed this feat in the nineteenth century when he skippered the 1885 Philadelphia Athletics of the American Association and topped the circuit with 13 homers.

Jim Tobin, a pitcher for the Boston Braves, pinch hit a home run on May 12, 1942, in a 9-8 defeat by the Chicago Cubs at Braves Field. The next day he pitched against the Cubs, winning 6-5 and hitting three home runs in consecutive at bats to drive in four of the six Braves runs that day. He is one of two pitchers to hit three homers in one game, following Guy Hecker in 1886, and the only one to hit them over the fence as all of Hecker's trio for the Louisville Colonels were inside-the-park.

The home run production rate slipped from 1943 through 1945 because of World War II, as some of the best players were away in the military or working other war-related jobs. As was the case during World War I, inferior materials used to create baseballs probably contributed to the lower level of offense across the board. After the all-time high home run percentage of 8.2 in 1940, the production in the next few years dropped to a 1943 low of 4.8; the home run rate had not been this low since 1927 and had not been below 6.0 since 1933.

On June 17, 1943, manager Joe Cronin of the Boston Red Sox inserted himself as a pinch hitter for pitcher Lou Lucier with the visiting Philadelphia Athletics leading 4-1, in the seventh inning. Cronin smacked a three-run homer into Fenway Park's left field screen to tie the score and his team later won the game 5-4. In the second game of the Bunker Hill Day twin bill, Cronin again pinch hit for his pitcher, this time Mike Ryba, and again hit a three-run homer. This time it was not enough, as the Athletics won the contest 8-7. Only one other batter has pinch hit home runs in both halves of a double header, Hal Breeden of the Montreal Expos on July 13, 1973.

Later in the 1943 season, Vern Stephens of the St. Louis Browns hammered two home runs in extra innings in the same game, a first for any batter. Stephens performed the feat in game one of two on September 29, 1943, in Boston. The first of the pair came in the 11th inning to put the Browns ahead 3-2. After the Red Sox tied the score and the two teams played a scoreless 12th inning, Stephens blasted another in the 13th inning to win the game 4-3. Both solo homers came off Tex Hughson and went into the left field screen. It would be 20 years before another batter hit two extra-inning homers in one game.

In 1943, with the home run production rate dropping to levels not seen in years, no batter hit at least 35 homers, which had not happened since Babe Ruth led the majors with 29 in 1919, a period of 24 seasons. Detroit Tigers first baseman Rudy York led the majors with 34 home runs while Bill Nicholson, another slugger from the Eastern Shore of Maryland originally signed by the Philadelphia Athletics but now a Chicago Cub, led the National League with 29. Nicholson led his league in homers and runs batted in for two consecutive seasons during the war, having placed in the top five three times earlier in his career. As the war progressed and star players left the big leagues, the names at the top of the home run charts became less recognizable. In 1944, Nick Etten of the Yankees led the American League with 22 home runs; this was the only season he clouted at least 20 home runs in a career in which he hit only 89 home runs. No batter hit 30 homers in 1945, with Boston Braves outfielder Tommy Holmes leading the majors with 28 circuit drives. Holmes never hit more than 13 home runs in any other season and finished his 11-year career with 88, the all-time lowest career total for a season leader since 1920. Etten and Holmes are the only two league leaders since the end of the Deadball Era with fewer than 100 career home runs. Vern Stephens of the St. Louis Browns led the American League in 1945 with 24 homers. No other batter in the Junior Circuit hit 20 home runs that season.

Two teams showed great futility in the home run department in 1945. The Chicago White Sox hit only 22 homers that season, led by Guy Curtright and Johnny Dickshot with four home runs each. The club's 22 was the lowest team total for a season since 1931 when the Cincinnati Reds hit 21 circuit drives. The Washington Senators hit 27 homers in 1945 but only one of those was hit at spacious Griffith Stadium. That four-bagger was an inside-the-park homer hit by Joe Kuhel on September 7 and was the last home run of the season hit by the Senators.

◆ ◆ ◆

Mel "Master Melvin" Ott joined the 500 Home Run Club on August 1, 1945, when he hit a ball, appropriately enough, into the right field seats at the Polo Grounds. Ott became the first National Leaguer to join the club and the third member overall, joining Babe Ruth and Jimmie Foxx, and he was the first to hit number 500 in a night game. Ott's home run ball bounced off a fan's hands back onto the field and was presented to the Giants' skipper as a souvenir on the field where he hit so many of his career blasts. It would be another 15 years before the fourth batter would join the club. Ott, the Giants' right fielder, also played well in right field that night. In the sixth inning, Carden Gillenwater of the Braves singled to right, rounded the first base bag too far and was put out when Ott threw behind him to first base. Ott slugged 323 (63 percent) of his total output at home, taking advantage of the 258-foot distance down the line to the right field wall at the Polo Grounds. This is the highest percentage hit at home for any batter with at least 350 career four-baggers, which contrasts greatly with Joe DiMaggio's percentage at home. "Joltin' Joe," who played his home games at Yankee Stadium, hit only 41 percent of his career output in New York. Ott held the National League career record for homers until 1966 when Willie Mays passed him on the list while Babe Ruth's 708 is still the American League record. Ott placed among the top three home run sluggers in the National League in 1929, 1931 through 1939, and 1941 through 1944, in other words, 14 times in 16 years. Ott led the Senior Circuit six times to tie Gavvy Cravath in that category, a mark that would be broken by Ralph Kiner. For the 10-year period from 1931 through 1940, Ott hit 302 home runs, good for third place in the majors behind Jimmie Foxx (414) and Lou Gehrig (306). (Refer to Appendix A for details of each home run number 500.)

Tommy Brown, a part-time shortstop for the 1945 Brooklyn Dodgers had made his big league debut in August 1944 at age 16. On August 20, 1945, he hit his first major league home run, which landed in the upper left field seats at Ebbets Field. Brown, born December 6, 1927, in Brooklyn, homered again five days later and is the only 17-year-old to hit a home run in the major leagues. After the game on August 20, Brown was presented with a carton of cigarettes by the radio broadcast sponsor but they were taken from him by the Dodgers manager, Leo Durocher, who explained that Brown was too young to smoke.

In 1946, with players back from war duty, the game rebounded and offense picked up, although not yet to the 1941 level. Hank Greenberg and Ted Williams, who both returned to their teams and played as if they had never left, topped the American League with 44 and 38 homers respectively, and a Pirate rookie named Ralph Kiner led the National League with 23, the first time that a Bucco led the National League since Tommy Leach in 1902. Kiner would lead the National League in homers in each of his first seven seasons—an unprecedented feat as Babe Ruth is the only other batter to lead a league for six consecutive years, having led the American League from 1926 through 1931. Kiner tied for the lead in three of those seasons, while Ruth tied for the American League lead once in his span of years. The next highest total of consecutive years leading a league in home runs is four, which has been performed three times, all in the American League: Harry Davis (1904 through 1907), Home Run Baker (1911 through 1914), and Ruth (1918 through 1921). Kiner beat the record of three consecutive years leading the National League, set by Gavvy Cravath (1913 through 1915 and 1917 through 1919), Hack Wilson (1926 through 1928), Chuck Klein (1931 through 1933), and Mel Ott (1936 through 1938). The Detroit Tigers sent Hank Greenberg to the Pittsburgh Pirates after the 1946 season, where he played his final year. Greenberg's 44 homers to lead the league in 1946 were the most hit in a season by a league leader immediately before being traded to another team. Ken Griffey Jr. topped this mark after his 48-homer 1999 season when the Seattle Mariners traded him to the Cincinnati Reds. Griffey's mark would be tied by Adrian Beltre, who left the Los Angeles Dodgers after the 2004 season as a free agent to go to those same Mariners. Greenberg hit 27.1 home runs for every 500 plate appearances in his career, a mark that placed him third on the all-time list for home run production when he retired behind Babe Ruth (33.6) and Jimmie Foxx (27.6), and Greenberg retired fifth on the all-time list with 331 round-trippers.

For the third time in history, a player slugged two grand slams in the same game. On July 27, 1946, Rudy York, now with the Boston Red Sox performed the feat in St. Louis. Both shots came off Tex Shirley as the Sox beat the Browns 13-6 on the way to the American League championship.

On October 23, 1945, the Brooklyn Dodgers signed an undrafted player who, although he did not hit many home runs, helped change the face of the game and open doors for many sluggers in the 1950s.

7
INTEGRATION

Many players who are important in the history of the home run have been discussed in previous chapters. However, there is one significant fact about that list of names: a large segment of the population was not allowed to join it. On April 15, 1947, Jackie Robinson made his National League debut for Branch Rickey's Brooklyn Dodgers at Ebbets Field. He has been referred to as the first African American in major league baseball by many people, but this is not correct. In 1884, two brothers, Fleetwood and Welday Walker, played for the Toledo Blue Stockings of the American Association. They were the first African Americans to play major league baseball but neither hit a home run during his short big league career. Thus, Jackie Robinson was not the first African American to play in the majors but the first after a long period of discrimination by the leagues and the first in the modern history of the game. Robinson's career, life, and legacy helped break down barriers and made it possible for many people to play in the major leagues who had no chance before 1947. Although Robinson hit only 137 homers, his pioneering efforts paved the way for sluggers who collectively have hit thousands of four-baggers since 1947, including four of the top five on the all-time list.

In the years immediately after the end of World War II, there was a sharp rise in the home run production rate, which had held around 5.0 during the war years. After a small increase in 1946 from 5.3 to 6.4, 1947 had the largest single-season increase to that point as production jumped to

8.2, an increase of 1.8 home runs per 500 plate appearances. The rate matched the 1940 mark for the highest production rate to date, and this increased production became the new standard for home runs in the majors. Only one year since (1976 at 7.6) has had a home run rate lower than 8.0. Figure 7.1 shows the production trend for 1947 through 1960 with two important factors: a minimum of 10.0 as the base level for the period and a production rate with no year less than 11.0 after 1954.

In 1947, two players hit 50 home runs for the season as Pittsburgh's Ralph Kiner and Johnny Mize of the New York Giants tied for the National League lead with 51 clouts each. It had been nine years since any batter had hit 50 home runs, when Jimmie Foxx and Hank Greenberg each performed the feat. Kiner and Mize became the second pair of sluggers to reach the 50 level in the same year, following that Foxx/Greenberg pairing in 1938. (Refer to Appendix B for details of each home run number 50 in history.) Kiner hit three homers in one game twice during the 1947 season, joining Johnny Mize as the only two batters to have accomplished this. Also that year, Ted Williams of the Red Sox led the American League for the third time in his career with 32 circuit clouts and won the league's Triple Crown for the second time. Williams is the only American Leaguer to win the Triple Crown twice in his career, joining Rogers Hornsby of the National League, who won the Triple Crown twice in the 1920s. The New York

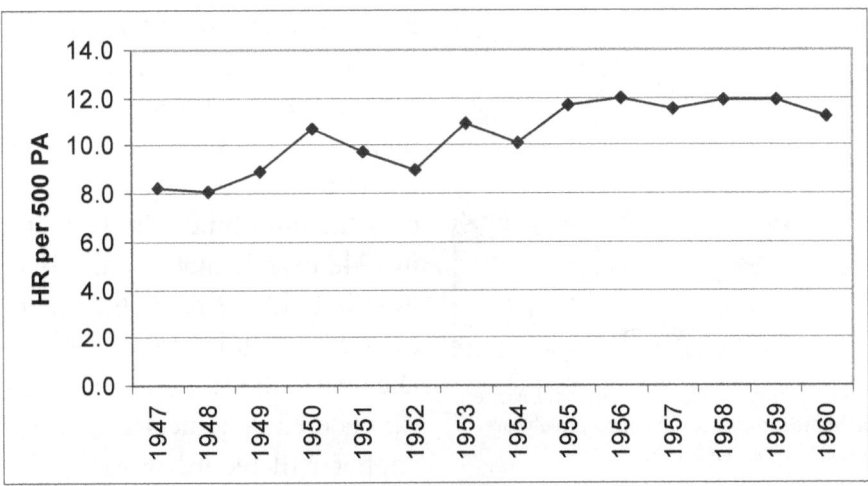

Figure 7.1 – Home Run Production Rate (1947–60)

Giants, led by Mize, hit 221 homers for the season, thus becoming the first squad to hit 200 for a year. They broke the single-season team mark set by their crosstown rivals, the 1936 New York Yankees, who had slugged 182 four-baggers. The Giants had a team home run production rate of 18.7 in 1947, breaking the single-season team record set by the 1884 Chicago White Stockings of 16.0. Discounting that tainted 1884 mark, the team record had been set by the 1936 New York Yankees, who had a production rate of 14.2.

From June 22 through June 28, 1947, Walker Cooper of the New York Giants hit at least one home run in six consecutive games to tie a record held by three other sluggers: Ken Williams, High Pockets Kelly, and Lou Gehrig. Cooper clouted 35 home runs that season, his career high, but never hit more than 20 in any other campaign.

Kiner and Mize tied for the National League lead for the second consecutive year in 1948, although with a much lower total. After hitting 51 the previous year, the sluggers topped the circuit with 40 home runs apiece with Stan Musial of the St. Louis Cardinals one behind at 39. The American League leader, Joe DiMaggio of the Yankees, matched Musial's total for the year. Del Ennis of the Philadelphia Phillies hit only eight of his 30 home runs at Shibe Park in Philadelphia, the lowest percentage at the time for any batter with at least 30 home runs. Although no team hit 200 homers in 1948, the total for all teams topped the 1,500 mark for only the third time. The 1,565 hit in 1948 exactly matched the 1930 total but did not reach the record of 1,571 set in 1940. Murry Dickson of the St. Louis Cardinals surrendered 39 homers to set a new gopher ball record in the major leagues, breaking the mark set in

Ralph Kiner, who led the National League in home runs for seven consecutive years from 1946 through 1952. *National Baseball Hall of Fame Library, Cooperstown, New York*

1884 by Larry Corcoran. See Table 1.3 for the complete progression of the single-season gopher ball record.

For the fifth time in history, a batter hit four home runs in one game during the 1948 season. Pat Seerey of the Chicago White Sox hit his quartet off three Athletics pitchers on July 18 at Shibe Park, the site of the only other American League four-homer game, by Lou Gehrig in 1932. Of the five instances to this point of a batter slugging four home runs in one game, four had involved a Philadelphia team. The first batter to accomplish the feat, Bobby Lowe in 1894, was the exception because he had no Philadelphia connection on his big day. Seerey had been traded by the Cleveland Indians to the White Sox on June 2 and may be the most unlikely name on the list of four-homer batters with his 86 career blasts. Seerey's first home run cleared the roof of the left field stands and the next two landed on that same roof. Seerey is the youngest player to accomplish the feat and, like Chuck Klein before him, needed extra innings to finish off the quartet of long balls with his last blast winning the game in the 11th inning for the White Sox, 12-11. (Refer to Appendix C for details of all four home run games.)

The Philadelphia Phillies smacked six home runs, including five in one inning, on June 2, 1949, to beat the Cincinnati Reds, 12-3, in Philadelphia. Andy Seminick hit a solo shot in the second inning for the first run of the game. In the eighth inning, Del Ennis and Seminick hit back-to-back home runs, and two batters later, Willie Jones clouted one. Pitcher "Schoolboy" Rowe homered for the 18th and last time of his career as part of the 10-run inning. Later in the inning, Andy Seminick came to the plate for the second time in the frame and hit his second home run of the inning and third of the game. The Phillies were the second team to smash five homers in one inning, repeating the feat first performed by the 1939 New York Giants, also against the Reds.

Ralph Kiner of the Pittsburgh Pirates led the National League for the fourth consecutive season in 1949 by hitting 54 home runs. Kiner thus set a new record for consecutive years leading the Senior Circuit, breaking the old mark of three set by Gavvy Cravath (twice), Hack Wilson, Chuck Klein, and Mel Ott. (See Appendix D for the season leaders for all leagues.) Kiner also became the first National League hitter to smack 50 homers in multiple seasons, since only two other players had performed the feat in the league—Hack Wilson in 1930 and Johnny Mize in 1947. (Refer to Appendix B for details of each home run number 50 in history.) Ted Williams led the American League for the fourth and final time of his career in 1949 with 43 home runs. For the decade 1941 through 1950, Williams hit more home runs than any other player with 239 in his war-shortened time in the American League. As part of the general homer production rate increase in the late-1940s, a new high mark was set in 1949 with 8.9 homers for every 500 plate appearances, but that level would be short-lived, topped in each of the next 18 years.

In fact, during the next season, 1950, the production rate climbed above 10.0 for the first time in history, at 10.7 for the campaign, as batters hit over 2,000 total homers in the majors for the first time. Ralph Kiner paced the National League and the majors with his 47 home runs while rookie Al Rosen of the Cleveland Indians, a team which had never had a league leader before, led the American League with 37. Before the season began, the strike zone had been redefined slightly for the first time since the nineteenth century. Previously, the definition stated that the zone was not higher than the batter's shoulders and not lower than his knees, but in 1950 this was shrunk by the new definition: between the batter's armpits and the top of the knee.

Joe DiMaggio moved into fifth place on the all-time home run list on June 25, 1950, by hitting his 332nd homer and passing Hank Greenberg. Greenberg had held that spot since April 20, 1947, when he knocked Al Simmons out of the top five. At this point in 1950, Lou Gehrig held fourth place with 493 clouts and there was no batter between Gehrig and DiMaggio's 332—a large gap between the top four and DiMaggio.

On August 31, 1950, Brooklyn first baseman Gil Hodges hit four home runs in one game off four different Boston Braves hurlers at Ebbets Field in Brooklyn. The progression of how many pitchers surrendered homers in each instance of a batter slugging four reflects the growing trend of managers to use relief pitchers rather than relying primarily on starters to throw complete games. Both Bobby Lowe and Ed Delahanty in the nineteenth century hit all four of their blasts off one pitcher, while Lou Gehrig in 1932 homered on offerings from two pitchers. Chuck Klein in 1936 and Pat Seerey in 1948 each hit their homers off three different hurlers. (Refer to Appendix C for details of all four home run games.)

Johnny Mize had played in the National League for the St. Louis Cardinals and the New York Giants from 1936 into the 1949 season with three years out during World War II. During that time, Mize hit three homers in one game four times, including twice both in 1938 and 1940. He was the first slugger to have two three-homer games in one season and he did it twice in his career. In fact, Mize is the only player to do this in two separate years. On August 22, 1949, the Giants sold Mize's contract to the Yankees where he played until the Yankees released him after the 1953 season. On September 15, 1950, the Big Cat walloped three home runs at Detroit's Briggs Stadium (later called Tiger Stadium) to become the second player to have a three-homer game in both the National and American Leagues, joining Babe Ruth who had completed the two-league feat in 1935. Mize hit three home runs in one game six different times in his career, a record that Sammy Sosa tied in August 2002.

For the sixth consecutive year, Pittsburgh's Ralph Kiner led the National League in home runs in 1951 when he hit 42 for the season. This streak of six years tied him with Babe Ruth, who led the American League from 1926 through 1931, for the most consecutive years leading a league. Gil Hodges hit 40 homers to take the runner-up spot in the National League in 1951 while a pair of American League left fielders hit at least 30 homers, with Gus Zernial on top with 33 and Ted Williams of Boston close behind with 30. Zernial started the season with the Chicago White Sox but was one of six players involved in a three-team trade on April 30, at which point Zernial had hit no homers in four games for the Pale Hose. Thus, he became the third player to be traded during a year in which he led the league in four-baggers, following Bill Joyce in 1896 and Braggo Roth in 1915.

On October 3, 1951, the Brooklyn Dodgers and New York Giants played the third of a three-game series to determine the National League champion after the two squads had finished the season tied for first place. The Giants had won a close contest in the first game of the series at Ebbets Field 3-1, and the Dodgers had won the second game 10-0 at the Polo Grounds. In the middle of the ninth inning of the third game, also at the Polo Grounds, the Dodgers were leading 4-1 with their starting pitcher, Don Newcombe, still on the mound. After three hits, the Giants had scored once and had runners on second and third with one out. Ralph Branca came out of the bullpen to pitch to Bobby Thomson, who had homered off Branca in the first game of the series. Thomson lined Branca's 0-1 pitch into the left field seats for a three-run, game-ending, pennant-clinching home run, thus sending the Giants to the 1951 World Series. This blast off Thomson's bat has become one of the most celebrated homers of all time, mostly owing to the game situation in which it was

Bobby Thomson is greeted at home plate by his teammates after hitting "The Shot Heard 'Round the World" on October 3, 1951. In the foreground is Jackie Robinson (#42) and to the right is Ralph Branca, who surrendered the home run. *National Baseball Hall of Fame Library, Cooperstown, New York*

hit but also because it is one of the earliest homers of its type to have been recorded on film. (One other note from that day: Hall of Famer Dave Winfield, who slugged 465 home runs in his career, was born in St. Paul, Minnesota, on October 3.)

In 1952, five years after Jackie Robinson made his major league debut, Larry Doby of the Cleveland Indians, the first African American to play in the American League, led that circuit in home runs with 32. His teammate, Luke Easter, hit 31, and Yogi Berra of the Yankees hit 30. In the National League, Ralph Kiner led the league for the seventh and final time, tied with Hank Sauer of the Chicago Cubs with 37 homers each. In three of the seven years Kiner led the National League, he tied for that lead with another batter. Kiner holds the record for most consecutive years at the top of a league list with his seven years from 1946 through 1952.

◆   ◆   ◆

For the second time in history, a team hit more than 200 homers for a season in 1953, as the Brooklyn Dodgers smacked 208 to lead the majors. This year saw a home run production rate of 10.9, only the second time the rate topped the 10.0 level. Eddie Mathews of the National League Milwaukee Braves led all batters with 47 home runs as six sluggers hit at least 40 for the season, a first. Brooklyn's Duke Snider and Roy Campanella hit 42 and 41, respectively, and Ted Kluszewski of the Cincinnati Reds clouted 40. In the American League, Cleveland's Al Rosen led with 43 homers while Gus Zernial of the Philadelphia Athletics hit 42. Ralph Kiner, after leading the National League for seven consecutive years, hit 35 circuit drives to finish fifth in the league. When Kiner retired after the 1955 season, he placed second on the all-time list for most homers per 500 plate appearances. At the time, Babe Ruth led with a home run production rate of 33.6 while Kiner had hit 29.5 home runs for each 500 plate appearances.

The Braves had moved from Boston to Wisconsin during the winter of 1952–53, the first change in configuration of the American and National Leagues since 1903 when the American League's Baltimore club moved to New York. Eddie Mathews hit the last home run by a Boston Brave on September 27, 1952, when he smacked three in a game at Brooklyn's Ebbets Field. Roy Campanella of the Dodgers had hit the last homer at Braves

Field on September 21. On April 14, 1953, Bill Bruton hit a tenth-inning, game-winning home run in the first game at County Stadium in Bruton's second game in the big leagues for the first four-bagger by a Milwaukee Brave. The last National League homer in Milwaukee had been hit by King Kelly of the Chicago White Stockings, who had a two-home run game against the Providence Grays on September 25, 1885. Mike Grady of the Washington Senators had hit the last major league home run in Milwaukee in game two on September 8, 1901, during the one season in which the American League had a team there before 1954, as those Milwaukee Brewers became the St. Louis Browns in 1902. Only 51 major league home runs had ever been hit in the Badger State before the Braves relocated to Milwaukee.

On April 17, 1953, 21-year-old Mickey Mantle of the New York Yankees faced six-year veteran Chuck Stobbs, making his Senators debut, at Washington's Griffith Stadium. In the fifth inning with two out and a runner on first base, Mantle batted right-handed and hit the baseball over the 50-foot-high left center field wall behind the bleachers. The ball glanced off a beer sign at the top of the wall and flew out of sight. Yankees publicity man Arthur Patterson left the park to track down the ball and he determined that it first landed about 460 feet from home plate and eventually stopped rolling in the backyard of a house down the street, approximately 565 feet from home plate. A 10-year-old boy had picked up the ball and showed Patterson where he found it. The boy was given an undisclosed sum of money for the baseball and later received an autographed ball from Mantle. Patterson's effort on this day perhaps is the first example of what is now called "tape-measure home runs." The important fact to remember here is that the 565 feet is not how far the ball flew but where it stopped rolling, according to a 10-year-old boy. Mantle is also credited with many other long blasts, including multiple home runs that struck the façade of the roof at Yankee Stadium.

The move by the Braves started a series of such team transfers that expanded the major leagues into new cities and time zones. Before 1953, there were 16 teams in 10 cities, as Boston, Philadelphia, Chicago, and St. Louis had two each and New York claimed three clubs. In 1954, the St. Louis Browns moved to Baltimore, becoming the Orioles. In 1955, the Philadelphia Athletics moved west to Kansas City where they played through the 1967 season, so now the 16 teams occupied 13 cities. Clint Courtney hit the first home run for the new Baltimore Orioles in the home opener on April 15, 1954, and Bill Wilson clouted the initial four-bagger for the Kansas City Athletics on Opening Day in Kansas City on April 12, 1955. Finally, in 1958, the Dodgers and Giants moved from New York City to California, thus changing the baseball map far more greatly than it had ever changed before.

Ted Kluszewski of the Cincinnati Reds hit 49 homers in 1954 to lead the majors, thus becoming the first Cincinnati player to lead the National League since Fred Odwell in 1905. Big Klu hit his 49th homer in the 146th game of the season for the Reds and over the last eight games failed to hit the last one he needed to reach the 50 milestone. Larry Doby of the Cleveland Indians led the Junior Circuit for the second time with 32 home runs. From 1950 through 1954, Doby and Indians teammate Al Rosen led the American League four of five years with only Gus Zernial, who played for the White Sox and Athletics, breaking the streak in 1951. Two young New York center fielders, Willie Mays of the Giants and Mickey Mantle of the Yankees, appeared in the top five home run hitters in their respective leagues for the first time this season. Mays smacked 41 to tie Hank Sauer for third in the National League while Mantle stroked 27, good for third place in the American League. They would be among the leaders for many years and each would hit well over 500 career blasts.

On May 2, 1954, the New York Giants played a double header in St. Louis. In the first game, Stan Musial slammed three home runs to lead the Cardinals to victory, 10-6. In game two, Musial hit two more home runs but the Giants won, 9-7. Musial's five round-trippers in one day set a major league record. In 1972, Nate Colbert of the San Diego Padres would match the feat in Atlanta, and, in a strange twist of fate, St. Louis native Colbert attended the 1954 twin bill and watched Musial hit the five circuit clouts while sitting in the left field bleachers.

Joe Adcock of the Milwaukee Braves hit four homers off four separate Dodger pitchers on July 31, 1954, at Ebbets Field, using a teammate's bat. After the game, Adcock explained that he had broken his own bat the previous night and borrowed the cudgel of the Braves' back-up catcher, Charlie White, for the contest. White hit one homer in his short career, that coming on April 23, 1954, thus Adcock hit more four-baggers in one game with the bat than White did in his entire major league career. The Braves hit a total of seven that day, with Eddie Mathews contributing twice and Andy Pafko once. In addition, three Dodgers hit homers in a losing cause: Don Hoak, Rube Walker, and Gil Hodges (the last batter to clout four home runs in one game in 1950) as the Braves won, 15-7. The 10 total home runs in the contest tied the National League record for most clouts in one game by both teams and Adcock set a new total base record of 18 for one game by smacking a double to go with his quartet of round-trippers. Adcock's game was the seventh time a slugger had hit four homers in one contest and five of them had been in the National League to this point. As with most four-homer batters, Adcock's game came on the road; of the 15 batters to accomplish the feat, only four have hit them at home. (Refer to Appendix C for details of all four home run games.)

In 1955, major league batters hit homers 11.7 times in each 500 plate appearances, the first time the production rate had climbed above 11.0 for one campaign and the first of 10 consecutive years at that level. The Brooklyn Dodgers hit 201 home runs for the season, the second time in three years that the club had reached the 200 level and the third time in history for any club following the 1947 Giants. Willie Mays of the Giants led all hitters with 51 home runs for the season, only 22 of which were hit at home in the Polo Grounds. At the time, this was the lowest total of four-baggers hit at home for a 50-plus season but three batters have since hit fewer: Brady Anderson (19 of 50 in 1996), George Foster (21 of 52 in 1977), and Andruw Jones (21 of 51 in 2005). Mays broke the record set by Ralph Kiner in 1947, who had hit 28 of his 51 homers at Forbes Field in Pittsburgh. Mays is the youngest batter to hit at least 50 circuit drives in one season at 24 years and 137 days on the day he hit number 50 in 1955. (Refer to Appendix B for details of each home run number 50 in history.)

As part of his league-leading season, Mays hit at least one home run in six consecutive games from September 14 through September 20 to tie the record for most consecutive contests with a homer. Of the five players who held the mark, four of them played in New York with Mays, Walker Cooper, and High Pockets Kelly as members of the Giants, and Lou Gehrig playing for the Yankees. Only Ken Williams, who originally set the record, played in St. Louis. The record would be broken in 1956 by a player in Pennsylvania.

Robin Roberts set a new record for most home runs surrendered in one major league season in two consecutive years, 1955 and 1956. In the former season, the Philadelphia Phillies hurler watched 41 balls leave the yard, while in the latter year, Roberts gave up 46 homers. This record stood until 1986 when Bert Blyleven of the Minnesota Twins surrendered 50 home runs, the current mark. The 46 surrendered by Roberts in 1956 stood as the National League record until 2000 when Jose Lima of the Houston Astros gave up 48 gopher balls.

For the second consecutive year in 1956, a New York center fielder hit more than 50 home runs, as Mickey Mantle of the Yankees led the American League with 52 blasts. Mantle, the only switch-hitter to sock 50 homers in one season, had also led the league the previous year, hitting 37 homers. The Mick also led the league in batting average and runs batted in during the 1956 season to become the only switch hitter to win a Triple Crown. Mantle had broken the 1934 single-season record for switch hitters set by Ripper Collins, when he slugged 35 blasts. (See Table 7.1 for the progression of the season record for switch hitters.) Brooklyn's Duke Snider hit 43 to lead the National League in 1956, where all eight

Table 7.1 – Progression of the Switch-Hitters Season Record

Batter	Team (League)	Year	HR
Bob Ferguson	Troy (NL)	1881	1
Cliff Carroll (tie)	Providence (NL)	1884	3
Bill Greenwood (tie)	Brooklyn (AA)	—	—
Bill McClellan (tie)	Philadelphia (NL)	—	—
Tony Mullane (tie)	Toledo (AA)	—	—
Tommy Tucker	Baltimore (AA)	1887	6
Duke Farrell	Chicago (NL)	1889	11
Walt Wilmot	Chicago (NL)	1890	13
Duke Kenworthy	Kansas City (FL)	1914	15
Buzz Arlett	Philadelphia (NL)	1931	18
Ripper Collins	St. Louis (NL)	1932	21
Ripper Collins	St. Louis (NL)	1934	35
Mickey Mantle	New York (AL)	1955	37
Mickey Mantle	New York (AL)	1956	52
Mickey Mantle	New York (AL)	1961	54

teams in the circuit hit at least 100 homers each—a first. Only the American League's Baltimore Orioles failed to reach the century mark in home runs for the season, hitting 91. Willie Mays hit 36 home runs in 1956 to go with 40 stolen bases to become the second player in history to have 30 steals and 30 homers in the same season. Ken Williams in 1922 was the only other player to have a 30/30 season before Mays. Rookie Frank Robinson of the Cincinnati Reds hit 38 home runs to tie Wally Berger's record for most by a first-year player.

First baseman Dale Long of the Pittsburgh Pirates had a good week from May 19 through May 28, 1956, as he hit a home run in each of eight consecutive games over that span. Six of the eight games were played at Forbes Field, while two of the contests occurred at Connie Mack Stadium in Philadelphia. Long, a left-handed batter, hit exactly one round-tripper in each game during his streak, which set a new record for homering in the most consecutive games. The previous mark of six games had been held by five players. Two other left-handed sluggers, Don Mattingly and Ken Griffey Jr., would match Long's achievement.

On July 17, 1956, Ted Williams of the Boston Red Sox hit his 400th career home run, becoming only the fifth player in history to reach that milestone. It had been 15 years since Mel Ott had smashed his 400th drive and of the first four sluggers with 400 homers, only Lou Gehrig did not reach 500 in his illness-shortened career. Following on the increased home run production trend of 1955, the production rate climbed to the 12.0 mark for the first time in 1956 and the Cincinnati Reds hit 221 home runs for the season, thus matching the 1947 Giants for the top all-time mark for a year by a team to that point.

Murry Dickson, who had held the single-season record for most home runs surrendered in the early 1950s, set a new career record when he passed Red Ruffing's career total of 247 on June 12, 1956. Dickson would hold the mark for less than a year, as Robin Roberts of the Philadelphia Phillies passed him on June 29, 1957. Table 6.2 shows the complete progression of the career gopher ball record.

A new name appeared at the top of the National League home run leader list in 1957, Hank Aaron, who had made his debut in 1954 with the Milwaukee Braves. Aaron hit 44 homers, the first of eight times he would clout 40 in a season and the third of 20 consecutive years that Aaron would hit at least 20 homers. Aaron also hit at least 10 homers in 23 consecutive years (every season he played major league baseball). The latter two marks are major league records. Roy Sievers, the first Washington Senator ever to lead the American League, paced the circuit by hitting 42 homers. The only other member of the first American League club to play in the District of Columbia (the team that played in the nation's capital from 1901 through 1960) to top the league in home runs was Harmon Killebrew, who tied for the lead in 1959. Ted Williams provided one other notable home run feat in 1957 when he hit three circuit clouts in one game twice during the season, becoming the third batter and first American Leaguer to accomplish this. The next American League player to have two three-homer games in a season was Doug DeCinces of the California Angels in 1982. In 1957, Willie Mays repeated his 30/30 accomplishment of the previous year by hitting 35 homers and stealing 38 bases. Thus, there had been one 30/30 season before 1956, and Willie Mays then had performed the feat in consecutive seasons. Brooklyn's Duke Snider hit 40 home runs in 1957, his fifth consecutive year with at least 40. Only Babe Ruth with seven consecutive years from 1926 through 1932, and Ralph Kiner with five from 1947 through 1951 had previously achieved that record. Snider's 40 clouts all came off right-handed pitchers, the most home runs in a season all off a righty. (Ned Williamson's 27 in 1884 is the second-highest total with all homers hit off a right-handed hurler.) Pedro Ramos of the Washington Senators surrendered 43 home runs in 1957 to become the first American League hurler to give up 40 in one year. Table 5.1 (page 60) shows the complete progression of the American League gopher ball record.

Duke Snider, who played in the National League his whole career, hit 19 of his 407 home runs off fellow Hall of Famer Robin Roberts. Their National League careers intersected from 1948 through 1961, and from 1953 through 1957, Snider hit at least two homers off Roberts in each season. The 19 circuit clouts for the pair are the most by one batter off one pitcher in history.

On April 15, 1958, the Los Angeles Dodgers met the San Francisco Giants in the first major league game ever played west of Kansas City, Missouri. In the fourth inning of that contest held at Seals Stadium in

San Francisco, Giants' shortstop Daryl Spencer hit a 2-0 Don Drysdale pitch high into the left field seats for the first major league home run in California, a solo shot that plated the third run of the day for the Giants as they beat the Dodgers, 8-0. The first home run hit by a member of the Los Angeles Dodgers occurred the next day, April 16, in San Francisco when Dick Gray hit a two-run shot in the second inning. One inning later, Duke Snider hit another two-run home run for Los Angeles. San Francisco's Hank Sauer hit two homers in the first game played in Los Angeles on April 18 for the first multi-homer game in California. Dick Gray also homered that day for the Dodgers.

In 1958, for the first time, all 16 major league teams hit at least 100 home runs, although no squad hammered 200 homers for the year. The Chicago Cubs led the majors with 182 circuit drives while their cross-town rivals, the White Sox, finished last among the 16 teams with 101 home runs. The Cubs shortstop, Ernie Banks, led the majors with 47 homers—a career high. Mickey Mantle led the American League for the third of four times with 42 home runs. Frank Thomas of the Pittsburgh Pirates only hit nine of his 35 four-baggers at home in Forbes Field in 1958, which, at the time, was the lowest percentage for any batter with at least 30 home runs.

> *Joe Adcock lost a homer in Harvey Haddix's "perfect" game on May 26, 1959. In the bottom of the 13th inning, after Felix Mantilla reached on an error and was sacrificed to second, Hank Aaron was intentionally walked. Adcock then hit the ball into the left field stands. However, Aaron didn't know the ball left the park, so he returned to the dugout thinking the game was over when Mantilla scored and then Adcock was called out for passing Aaron, thus losing his home run but winning the game.*

A rule change enacted for the 1959 season stated that baseball fields built after June 1, 1958, must have a minimum distance of 400 feet to the fence in center field and 325 feet down the left and right field lines to the outfield fence. This change to the rule—the latest version of the statute first enacted in 1888 and modified in 1892 and 1926—was codified as a reaction to the 250-foot distance to left field at the Los Angeles Coliseum where the Dodgers had played in 1958. Two older ballparks still in use do not meet these standards, Fenway Park in Boston and New York's Yankee Stadium, but these were built before the 1958 cut-off.

Stan Musial, the long-time star of the St. Louis Cardinals, hit his 400th home run on May 7, 1959, becoming the sixth batter with that many four-baggers. He had hit at least 10 homers in 18 consecutive seasons from 1946 through 1963 and every season he played from 1942 through 1963 (he missed the 1945 season due to World War II)—21 seasons. The span includes 10 consecutive years from 1948 through 1957 with at least 20 circuit clouts and his career high came in 1948, when he hit 39. He held the mark for most career homers (475) without ever hitting 40 and without leading the league for a season for many years after he retired. Both Eddie Murray (504) and Fred McGriff (493) have since passed Musial in the former category, while Rafael Palmeiro (569) passed Musial in the latter. Since Musial had already collected 3,000 hits before attaining the 400 homer plateau, he became the first player to reach both these milestones, a feat since accomplished by seven other players.

On June 10, 1959 Rocky Colavito of the Cleveland Indians became the third American League player (and eighth overall) to slug four home runs in one contest. (Refer to Appendix C for details of all four home run games.) Rocky hit the four blasts in four consecutive at bats at Baltimore's Memorial Stadium on his way to slugging 42 homers for the season, which tied with Washington's Harmon Killebrew for the American League lead. On April 17, 1960, two days before the start of their seasons, the Indians traded Colavito to the Chicago White Sox in exchange for Harvey Kuenn, who had led the American League in batting during the 1959 season. Milwaukee's Eddie Mathews paced the 1959 National League with 46 home runs and Ernie Banks of the Cubs hit 45, good for second place. Mathews broke a tie with Banks in the second game of the pennant playoff between the Braves and the Dodgers. Milwaukee played one tie early in the season and, with the two playoff contests, a total of 157 games in 1959. Mathews hit 338 home runs in the decade from 1951 through 1960 to lead the majors.

In 1960, the last year with 16 teams in the two major leagues, the home run production rate held at approximately the same level as every season since 1955 with batters slugging homers 11.2 times in each 500 plate appearances, as shown in Figure 7.1. Three batters completed the

1960 campaign with 40 homers, as Ernie Banks of the Chicago Cubs led the National League with 41, and Hank Aaron of the Milwaukee Braves finished with 40. In the American League, Mickey Mantle of the New York Yankees led the circuit for the fourth time in six years and the last time in his career with his 40 home runs. Three other batters nearly reached that plateau: Roger Maris with 39 in his first year as a Yankee, Jim Lemon of the Washington Senators with 38, and Eddie Mathews of the Braves with 39.

◆   ◆   ◆

On June 17, 1960, Ted Williams of the Boston Red Sox hit his 500th home run at Cleveland's Municipal Stadium, also the site of Babe Ruth's 500th clout. A predominantly pull-hitting left-hander, Williams drove the ball the opposite direction over the left field fence into the Red Sox bullpen to become only the fourth player to join the 500 Home Run Club and the first since Mel Ott in 1945. The two-run homer by Williams broke a 1-1 tie in the game—which was won by the Red Sox, 3-1—and made him the oldest player to hit home run number 500. Williams's age that day, 41 years and 291 days, is more than a year older than anyone else who hit 500 home runs. Williams is the only member of the 500 Home Run Club who made his debut between 1927 and 1950. (Refer to Appendix A for details of each home run number 500.) The Splendid Splinter, who had suffered through his worst year in 1959, finished his career with a strong season in 1960, hitting 29 homers, including one on his last major league at bat, for a lifetime total of 521, and he retired with the third-most home runs in history, behind Babe Ruth (714) and Jimmie Foxx (534). Williams, who had passed Joe DiMaggio (361) for fifth place on the career home run list on September 3, 1954, passed Lou Gehrig (493) and Met Ott (511) during the 1960 season to move from fifth to third place on the career list. Stan Musial had hit 429 of his 475 lifetime total to place second on the active player list and sixth on the all-time list at the end of the 1960 season. Mel Ott with 511 and Lou Gehrig with 493 were the only other players to have hit at least 400 career homers at that point. Three of the four members of the 500 Home Run Club and five of the top six sluggers, including Williams, were left-handed; only Jimmie Foxx cracked the list batting right-handed at this point. In five of his first six seasons, Williams hit at least 30 home runs. He hit a combined 44 circuit clouts in the two-plus seasons after he turned 40 years old, which was at that time the most by any player. Stan Musial passed Williams in 1963 by hitting 46 after his 40th birthday and the current leader in the category is Carlton Fisk with 72. Williams is the career home run leader at Boston's venerable Fenway Park with 248. Williams, who smashed 30 home runs eight times in a career that twice was interrupted by wartime military duty, led the American League in homers four times, and the majors twice.

The next year would see dramatic changes on the major league landscape, as new teams would play major league baseball for the first time since 1915 when the Federal League shut down. These new clubs would be the first in either of the two current major circuits since the start of the American League in 1901.

8
EXPANSION

After the 1960 season, the Washington Senators, an original American League team, moved to Minneapolis and became the Minnesota Twins. The Junior Circuit also expanded by two teams in 1961 with a new team in Washington, confusingly called the Washington Senators, and one in Los Angeles, the Angels. These two teams became the first new clubs in either league since the American League started in 1901 and were the first of many waves of major league expansion that continued into the 1990s. The National League followed with its own initial expansion in 1962, also by adding two teams, one in Houston and one in New York to replace the departed Dodgers and Giants.

From 1961 through 1972, home run production decreased from the level of the late 1950s. As shown in Figure 8.1, only three years (1961, 1962, and 1970) matched the home run rate from 1956 through 1959, with the highest production in 1961. The period started with an increase in homer production from 11.2 per 500 plate appearances in 1960 to 12.0 in 1961. Although the team expansion took place in the American League, the larger increase in production took place in the National League, as it jumped from 11.0 in 1960 to 12.7 in 1961. The American League increase was from 11.4 to 12.3 in the same two years. The common perception that expansion dilutes pitching is not supported by the home run production rates of 1960 and 1961. In fact, David W. Smith published a research paper in 1999 titled

"Expansion: Does It Add Muscle or Fat?" that clearly shows pitching is not diluted by expansion and the changes in the level of offense from season to season have only a moderate relation to expansion. The Senior Circuit had had a higher production rate from 1947 through 1959 and some historians have tied this, at least partially, to the American League's slower pace in integrating during the 1950s. The National League's home run rate dropped below that of the American League in 1960, climbed above again in 1961 and then dropped back below the American League through 1971.

On April 30, 1961, Willie Mays of the San Francisco Giants hit four home runs in a game played at Milwaukee's County Stadium. Mays, the ninth batter to hit four in one game, led the parade of eight four-baggers by the Giants that tied the National League mark for most in a game by a team, set by the 1953 Milwaukee Braves and tied by the 1956 Cincinnati Reds. The 1999 Reds broke the league record by hitting nine home runs in one game. The New York Yankees held the American League record at the time, having hit eight in one game in 1939 but the Toronto Blue Jays broke that mark in 1987 when they hit ten homers in one game. In the 1961 contest between San Francisco and Milwaukee, Hank Aaron of the Braves hit two and the combined total of 10 homers tied the National League record for most in one game by both teams, which had been done five times previously. Mays became the first and only batter to hit four homers in one

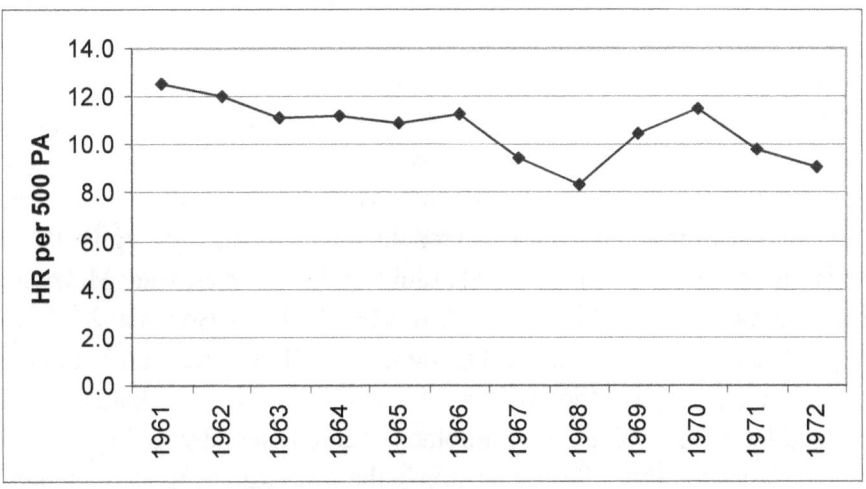

Figure 8.1 – Home Run Production Rate (1961–72)

game and 50 in one season, although he did not perform both feats in the same year. He also hit three home runs in a game on June 29, becoming the fourth batter to have two games in one season with three (or more) homers. (Refer to Appendix C for details of all four home run games.)

Jim Gentile of the Baltimore Orioles hit two grand slams in one game on May 9, 1961, at Metropolitan Stadium in Minneapolis. Gentile became the fourth player to perform the feat, all of whom did it in the American League on the road (Tony Lazzeri in 1936, Jim Tabor in 1939, and Rudy York in 1946). Gentile's slams came in the first and second innings of the contest, making him the first to hit the blasts in consecutive innings and in consecutive at bats, as he led the Orioles to a 13-5 victory.

Even though Mays and Gentile made news by smacking multiple homers, the main home run story of 1961 occurred in New York. For just the third time since 1927, a batter (or in this case, two) chased Babe Ruth's 60 home run single-season record. Mickey Mantle started the season strong by hitting 14 home runs by the end of May and his teammate, Roger Maris, kept pace with 12. Then in June they heated up the race when Maris hit 15 and Mantle hit 11 and the newspaper sports pages started writing about the race between the two Bronx Bombers for the American League leadership. As June turned into July, the talk turned from the 1961 home run race between Mantle and Maris to the race between them and the almost-mythical Babe Ruth and his 1927 record, one of the most recognizable numbers in all of sports. On July 25, Maris hit four homers in a double header to reach 40 for the season while Mantle hit his 39th the next day. At the end of July, Maris (with 40) and Mantle (with 39) were both well ahead of Ruth, who had hit 34 by the end of July 1927. Ruth had hit 41 home runs in 1928 before the start of August and Jimmie Foxx had also reached that number by August 1932. This was the record through the end of July until 1998 when Mark McGwire hit 45 home runs, and this new mark was tied by Barry Bonds in 2001.

On July 17, 1961, Baseball Commissioner Ford Frick, once a ghost writer for and personal friend of Babe Ruth's, declared that no batter would be credited with breaking the Bambino's record unless it was done in 154 games. (As part of the 1961 expansion in the American League, the schedule was expanded to 162 games to accommodate two more teams while

EXPANSION

maintaining a balanced schedule.) Frick's ruling stated, in part:

> Any player who may hit more than 60 home runs during his club's first 154 games would be recognized as having established a new record. However, if the player does not hit more than 60 until after his club has played 154 games, there would have to be some distinctive mark in the record books to show that Babe Ruth's record was set under a 154-game schedule and the total of more than 60 was compiled while a 162-game schedule was in effect.

An entire book could be written about this edict, its roots and its effects, but just a few facts will be listed here. First, Major League Baseball has no official record book. There are multiple record books produced by competing agencies and they print what they wish to print in their compilations without the oversight of Major League Baseball. On September 8, 1919, National League president John Heydler spoke out about Babe Ruth topping the single-season record of the day (see chapter 4) and stated that the league had "no official record" of the home run mark. This is probably an overstatement on Heydler's part but speaks to the fact that there are universally accepted numbers in many categories, although there is no single record book. Thus, Frick overstepped his authority by his statement, as what a particular publishing company prints in their version of a baseball record book is completely up to them. Second, this "distinctive mark" has come to be called an asterisk by most historians and writers, but an asterisk was never used in the publications. Instead, most record books simply listed Ruth's total of 60 in 1927 as having been set in a 154-game season and Maris's 61 as having been set in a 162-game season. Third, Ruth's 1927 Yankee team, ostensibly playing a 154-game schedule that year, actually played 155 contests because of one tie game on April 14. The Babe hit his 60th home run on the second to the last day of the season and had one more game in which to swat another ball over the fence but failed to do so. (Coincidentally, the 1961 squad also played one extra contest because of a tie in the second game of a doubleheader on April 22.) Fourth, the number of games matter less than the number of opportunities a batter has to hit a home run. In 1927, Ruth had 692 plate appearances and a home run production rate of 43.4 per 500 plate appearances, while in 1961, Maris had 698 plate appearances and a production rate of 43.7—a very close race between the two batters with Maris slightly ahead. Maris, when asked about his reaction to Frick's ruling, stated: "A season's a season."

As with the 1927 race, the eventual runner-up, Mantle, still led his teammate late in the season. On August 12, Roger Maris hit his 43rd homer of the season but Mickey Mantle had slugged his 44th the previous day. On August 15, Maris passed Mantle and led the rest of the year. Figure 8.2 shows how the race between the sluggers progressed. In August, Maris had his third consecutive month hitting at least 10 home runs, which included a span from August 11 through August 16 when he hit at least one home run in six consecutive contests. He reached 51 before September with Mantle three behind him at the start of the last month of the season. While Mantle stalled at 54 home runs for the season because of a viral infection and abscessed hip, the latter of which forced him to enter a hospital on September 28, Maris hit nine more homers in September to reach the magic 60 mark and tie Babe Ruth on September 26, thus becoming the second player to hit 60 in one major league season. His 59th home run came in game number 154 for the Yankees on September 20 and thus Frick's edict took away the drama of the chase to break the record. Maris tied Ruth with a solo homer off Jack Fisher of the Baltimore Orioles at Yankee Stadium with four games left in the year. On the last day of the season, October 1, only 23,154 fans showed up at Yankee Stadium to

Roger Maris following through on his swing after hitting home run number 61 on October 1, 1961; Maris held the single-season homer record from this date through September 1998. *AP Photos*

EXPANSION

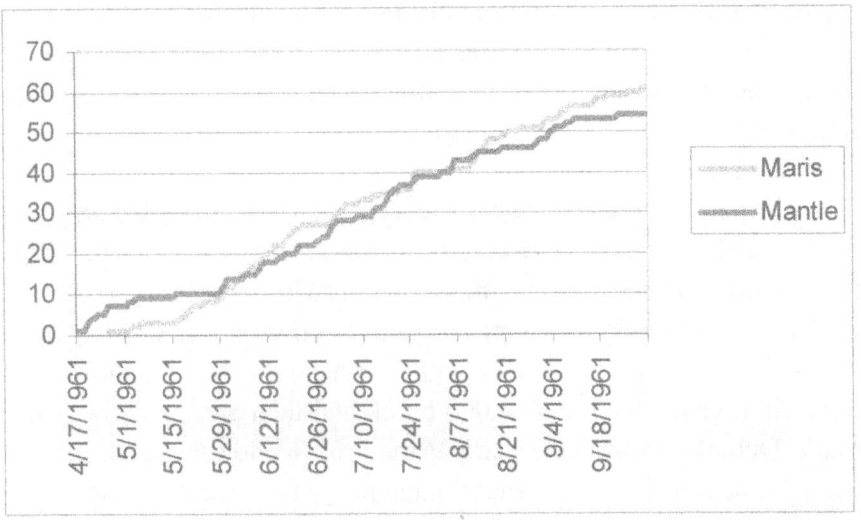

Figure 8.2 – The 1961 Home Run Race

see Maris hit his 61st circuit drive, because the commissioner declared that this did not break his friend Ruth's record. For the last month of the season, Maris had been under a severe nervous strain as he approached the Babe's record but on October 1, in his second trip to the plate, he hit a 2-0 pitch from Boston's rookie pitcher, Tracy Stallard, into the right field seats for the only run of the game. When he returned to the dugout, his teammates would not let the quiet slugger stay in the dugout until he acknowledged the applause. After four bows and a tip of his cap to the fans, the Yankee players allowed Maris, the youngest slugger to hit 60 home runs in one season by well over two and a half years, to enter the players' bench. Roger Maris still holds the American League record for most home runs in a season, as all the players who topped that number in the late 1990s played in the National League. Maris had hit 39 homers in 1960 and would hit 33 in 1963 but never hit more than 28 in any other season, as he finished his career with 275 circuit clouts.

One common misperception regarding Maris in 1961 is that he benefited from new, homer-friendly ballparks used by the expansion teams. However, he only hit one circuit drive at Metropolitan Stadium in Minneapolis and two at Wrigley Field in Los Angeles—the two new parks in the league. In fact, the big difference in 1961 was that evidently Maris learned how to hit at Yankee Stadium, as he clouted 30 of his 61 four-baggers there, whereas he had only hit 13 of 39 in New York the previous season. The increase of 17 at home accounts for most of the difference from one season to the next.

The young fan who caught the 61st home run ball, Sal Durante, was taken away by stadium police and brought to meet Maris during the game. Durante tried to give the ball to the slugger but Maris told him to collect the $5,000 prize offered by a Sacramento restaurant owner, Sam Gordon. Maris even offered to go to Sacramento with Durante. However, Gordon flew to New York, gave Durante a $5,000 check and then presented the ball to Maris. Durante also collected a trip to the 1962 World's Fair in Seattle and two 1962 season tickets to Yankee Stadium.

Maris and Mantle, called the "M-Boys" and the "M-Squad" in the press, became the third pair of hitters to each clout 50 home runs in one season and the first teammates to perform the feat. The previous pairs, Hank Greenberg and Jimmie Foxx in 1938 and Ralph Kiner and Johnny Mize in 1947, played in the same league but on different clubs. With their combined 115 homers, Maris and Mantle also set a mark for most home runs hit by a pair of teammates in one season, breaking the previous record of 107 set by Babe Ruth and Lou Gehrig in 1927. The record by the M-Boys still stands, although Barry Bonds (73) and Rich Aurilia (37) hit a combined total of 110 in 2001 for the San Francisco Giants to move into second place on the list and set a new National League record.

Mantle's second season with at least 50 homers made him the third American Leaguer, and fourth player overall, to have multiple 50-plus campaigns. Babe Ruth and Jimmie Foxx in the American League and Ralph Kiner in the National League had preceded Mantle, who also set a new record for switch hitters, breaking his own mark of 52 set in 1956. (Refer to Appendix B for details of each home run number 50 and number 60 in history.)

The Yankees as a team hit 240 home runs in 1961, the first American League club to top 200, to set a new single-season team record, beating the previous mark of 221 set by the 1947 New York Giants and the 1956 Cincinnati Reds. This team record would stand until 1996 when three teams would top it: the Baltimore Orioles with 257, the

Seattle Mariners with 245, and the Oakland Athletics with 243. That year was early in the period when home runs became much more common and the production rate reached record levels, so it is not a surprise that three teams all beat the mark in the same season. The Giants and Reds would hold the National League record until 1997 when the Colorado Rockies hit 239 circuit drives. The 1961 Yankees team hit 19.2 home runs for each 500 plate appearances for the season, setting a new record for a team by beating the former team home run production rate mark of the 1947 New York Giants of 18.7. The previous American League mark had been set in 1960 by the Yankees when their production rate reached 16.1. The new record by the Yankees would stand until 1996, when the Baltimore Orioles had a production rate of 19.8.

Eight different players hit at least 40 home runs in 1961, topping the previous mark of six set in each year from 1953 through 1955. Those eight, in addition to the M-Squad, are Jim Gentile (46) of the Baltimore Orioles, Harmon Killebrew (46) of the Minnesota Twins, Rocky Colavito (45) and Norm Cash (41), both of the Detroit Tigers in the American League, and National League leader Orlando Cepeda (46) and runner-up Willie Mays (40), both of the San Francisco Giants.

On June 8, 1961, four consecutive Milwaukee Braves batters homered in the seventh inning of a game at Crosley Field in Cincinnati. Eddie Mathews, Hank Aaron, Joe Adcock, and Frank Thomas hit home runs off two Reds hurlers but, even with two other Braves four-baggers, including another by Mathews and one by pitcher Warren Spahn, the Reds prevailed 10-8. This unprecedented event of hitting four consecutive homers has been duplicated only by the 1963 Cleveland Indians, the 1964 Minnesota Twins, and the 2006 Los Angeles Dodgers.

The San Francisco Giants thrashed the Cincinnati Reds 14-0 on August 23, 1961, at Crosley Field in Cincinnati. Joey Amalfitano had led off the game with a home run and the Giants scored a single run in the eighth inning. In the ninth, they hit five home runs and scored 12 runs to turn a pitching duel between Joey Jay and Juan Marichal into a rout. Orlando Cepeda and Felipe Alou hit back-to-back home runs and five batters later Jim Davenport hit an inside-the-park home run. Later in the inning, Willie Mays and John Orsino completed the quintet of round trippers. This was the third time that a club had hit five home runs in one inning, with the previous clubs to perform this feat being the 1939 New York Giants and the 1949 Philadelphia Phillies. In all three cases, the pitching staff of the Reds had taken the beating.

On August 28, 1961, Roy McMillan of the Milwaukee Braves hit a three-run home run at Connie Mack Stadium off Robin Roberts of the last-place Phillies. The Braves beat Roberts that day 7-1 but, more importantly, that homer was the 400th that Roberts had surrendered in his career. Roberts, who surrendered another four-bagger later that day, became the first hurler to surrender 400 home runs in a career and his mound opponent that day, Warren Spahn, placed second on the career list at the time with 332 gopher balls.

> *Don Demeter of the Phillies* hit two homers in the first game of a Polo Grounds twin bill on August 15, 1962, in the third and ninth innings. They were hit off two different pitchers for the Mets— both named Bob Miller.

In 1962, the National League expanded by two teams, thus creating two 10-team leagues, with the New York Mets, playing at the Polo Grounds, and the Houston Colt .45s joining the party. The first game played in the state of Texas featured four home runs. Houston's Roman Mejias hit the first four-bagger in the Lone Star State in the bottom of the third inning, followed three batters later by Hal Smith with another. Ernie Banks of the visiting Chicago Cubs hit a homer in the seventh frame, while Mejias hit his second of the contest in the eighth inning, as Houston won 11-2.

For the first time in 1962, two teams hit 200 home runs each in the same season. The Detroit Tigers led the American League with 209 blasts while the San Francisco Giants led the National with 204. Willie Mays of the Giants led the National League with 49 homers with Hank Aaron of the Milwaukee Braves the runner-up at 45. Harmon Killebrew of the Minnesota Twins hit 48 homers to lead the American League, followed by two Tigers, Norm Cash with 39 and Rocky Colavito with 37. Leon Wagner of the Los Angeles Angels also hit 37 playing home games at Dodger Stadium.

On June 24, 1962, the New York Yankees and Detroit Tigers played a 22 inning contest at Tiger Stadium. In the top of the last inning, Jack Reed, the third right fielder of the day for the Yankees, hit a two-run homer to score the winning runs in the 9-7 Yankee victory. Reed, who hit his only career homer this day, became the first batter in history to hit a home run after the 21st inning of a game. No one else homered this late in a contest for 22 years after Reed, but since then three batters have duplicated the feat: Harold Baines of the Chicago White Sox, who hit a home run in the latest inning in history (25th inning on May 8, 1984), Rick Dempsey of the Los Angeles Dodgers (22nd inning on August 23, 1989), and Pedro Munoz of the Minnesota Twins (22nd inning on August 31, 1993). In the 1962 game, there were no runs scored from the seventh inning through the 21st inning and the clubs left a combined 43 runners on base.

Before the 1963 season, rules makers enlarged the strike zone to try to cut down on the latest offense-happy era. The new zone was the area from the top of the shoulder to the bottom of the knee, which changed the previous definition, enacted in 1950, of the armpits to the top of the knee. This was a return to the strike zone that had been used through 1949. The home run production rate decreased from 1961 through 1968, the latter of which is generally referred to as the "Year of the Pitcher."

Harmon Killebrew of the Minnesota Twins led the American League in 1963 for the second of three consecutive years with 45 homers while Hank Aaron of the Milwaukee Braves and Willie McCovey of the San Francisco Giants tied for the National League lead with 44 blasts. Dick Stuart, in his first year in the American League with the Boston Red Sox, hit 42 homers, his career high. Stuart had hit 35 for the National League Pittsburgh Pirates in 1961. In addition to hitting 44 home runs, Hank Aaron stole 31 bases to become the third player with a 30/30 season, after Ken Williams and Willie Mays.

Willie Kirkland of the Cleveland Indians hit two extra-inning home runs in one game on June 14, 1963, repeating the feat first performed by Vern Stephens in 1943. Kirkland hit his two blasts in the second game of a double header with the Washington Senators at Cleveland's Municipal Stadium, having already singled in the bottom of the first inning to knock in the first run of the game for the Tribe. With the Senators ahead 2-1 Kirkland hit his first homer to lead off the bottom of the 11th inning. The two teams remained tied until the bottom of the 19th inning when Kirkland ended with game with a homer, again hit leading off the inning. Thus, Kirkland knocked in all three runs for the Indians in that game, in the first, 11th, and 19th innings.

Also on June 14, Duke Snider of the New York Mets, who had spent 16 years with the Dodgers in Brooklyn and Los Angeles, hit his 400th home run in the first inning at Cincinnati's Crosley Field. Snider, the career leader for the Dodgers with 389 homers, finished his career with the rival San Francisco Giants in 1964. His 407 total home runs placed him 10th on the all-time list when he retired and he hit the third-most homers in the majors for the period from 1951 through 1960 with 309 clouts. He smashed 40 home runs in five consecutive seasons from 1953 through 1957 and led the National League in 1956. Snider hit 19 round-trippers off fellow Hall-of-Famer Robin Roberts, the most by a batter off a single pitcher. Snider and longtime Dodger teammate Gil Hodges homered in the same game 67 times, the fourth-highest total of any pair.

> *On September 11, 1963,* Cincinnati's right-handed-hitting Don Pavletich homered in the fourth inning off lefty Denny Lemaster of the Milwaukee Braves with one man on base. The Reds batted around in the inning, scoring nine runs and by the time Pavletich's spot came up again, the Braves had changed pitchers to right-hander Ron Piche so lefty Gordy Coleman pinch hit for Pavletich with the bases full and hit a home run. That's two homers from the same lineup spot in one inning by two different batters.

On July 31, 1963, the Cleveland Indians repeated a feat first performed by the Braves in 1961. In the sixth inning of the second game of a double header against the Los Angeles Angels in Cleveland, Woodie Held, pitcher Pedro Ramos, Tito Francona, and Larry Brown hit four consecutive home runs, all off Paul Foytack, who had been traded by the Tigers to the Angels on June 15. The four batters seemed an unlikely group to perform such a feat, as they hit a total of only 35 home runs during the 1963 season. Joe Adcock, part of the Braves quartet who had hit four consecutive blasts in 1961, watched from the Indians bench. Unlike the Braves, the Indians won this game 9-5.

In 1964, Harmon Killebrew hit 40 home runs for the fourth consecutive season and for the fifth time in six years. Killebrew's 49 clouts led both leagues while Willie Mays hit 47 to lead the National League. On May 2, the Twins beat the Kansas City Athletics in Kansas City 7-3. In the top of the 11th inning, the first four batters homered: Tony Oliva, Bob Allison,

Jimmie Hall, and Killebrew. Both Oliva and Killebrew had hit home runs earlier in the game. This was the third time that a team had socked four consecutive homers in an inning, but the first time it had happened in extra innings. The Athletics pitching staff, victims of the Twins quartet in May, surrendered 220 gopher balls during the 1964 season, breaking their own record of 199 set in 1964, and making them the first team to surrender at least 200 homers in one season.

Warren Spahn of the Milwaukee Braves became the second member of the 400 Home Runs Surrendered Club on July 22, 1964, when he gave up a gopher ball to Bobby Wine of the Philadelphia Phillies. The solo shot in the seventh inning broke a 1-1 tie on the way to a 4-1 Philadelphia victory at Milwaukee's County Stadium. Robin Roberts led all hurlers with 463 home runs surrendered on this day and Early Wynn, who had retired the previous year, placed third with 339 homers surrendered. At the end of the 1965 season, Spahn retired as an active player having surrendered 434 home runs in his career. The long-time hurler for the Braves in Boston and Milwaukee had pitched for the New York Mets and San Francisco Giants in his last season at the age of 44. When he retired, Spahn had surrendered the second-most gophers ball of any major league pitcher, behind only Robin Roberts, but has since been passed by four others. Spahn hit 35 homers in his career, tied for second among pitchers with Bob Lemon behind Wes Ferrell's 37 as a pitcher. Ferrell also hit one in his career as a pinch hitter.

The Houston Astros moved into a new park for the 1965 season, baseball's first indoor ballpark, named the Astrodome in honor of the U.S. space program centered in the Houston area. Dick Allen of the Philadelphia Phillies slugged the first home run in the park (and thus the first major league homer indoors) on Opening Day, when he hit a two-run shot in the third inning off Bob Bruce to drive in all the game's runs in a 2-0 Phillies victory. Willie Mays hit 50 home runs for the second time in his career in 1965, as he led the majors with 52. Having become the youngest slugger to clout 50 in a season when he hit 51 for the New York Giants in 1955, Mays had his second 50 campaign with the Giants in San Francisco, thus making him the only batter to have two seasons of 50 or more home runs for one franchise but in two different cities. Mays became the fifth player with multiple seasons of at least 50 home runs and the second National Leaguer. Babe Ruth, Jimmie

Foxx, and Mickey Mantle had performed the feat in the Junior Circuit, while Ralph Kiner had done it in the National League. Willie McCovey, a teammate of Mays's, placed second in the National League with 39 homers in 1965. A Giants player had led the league in home runs for five consecutive seasons, starting in 1961. Mays led three times, Orlando Cepeda once, and McCovey had tied in 1963. In the American League, Boston Red Sox center fielder Tony Conigliaro hit 32 to lead the circuit. (Refer to Appendix B for details of each home run number 50 in history.)

Willie Mays passed Lou Gehrig on August 29, 1965, when he hit his 494th home run to move into fifth place all-time. The three-run clout came off Jack Fisher of the New York Mets at Shea Stadium in New York. Mays became the fifth member of the 500 Home Run Club on September 13, 1965, when he smashed his 47th long ball of the season at the Astrodome in Houston. Mays was the second National Leaguer and the first African American to join the club when he led off the fourth inning by hitting the 3-1 pitch of Don Nottebart into the center field seats to tie the game at one run each and he remains the only player to hit his 500th home run indoors. (Refer to Appendix A for details of each home run number 500.)

◆ ◆ ◆

In exactly six years to the day from September 13, 1965, through September 13, 1971, seven batters joined the 500 Home Run Club. From 1876 through the beginning of the 1965 season, a period of 89 years, only four batters had hit a 500th career home run (Ruth, Foxx, Ott, and Williams), and each of those four sluggers had played at least part of his career before World War II. More batters joined the club in the six-year period from 1965 through 1971 than in any other six-year period in the history of the game, including the start of the twenty-first century. The six batters to follow Mays were Mickey Mantle, Eddie Mathews, Hank Aaron, Ernie Banks, Harmon Killebrew, and Frank Robinson, and they all made their major league debuts from 1951 through 1956. Of these seven batters, five were primarily National Leaguers and four of the seven were African American. Those latter four played most or all of their careers in the National League, which had been quicker to integrate in the 1940s and 1950s.

EXPANSION

The 1965–66 off-season saw three important moves. The Milwaukee Braves relocated to Atlanta after only 13 years in Wisconsin. Eddie Mathews, who had made his debut when the club was still in Boston, hit 16 home runs for the Georgia version of the team and is the only player to play and homer for the Braves in all three cities. The second important move during the off-season helped decide the American League pennant in 1966 as the Cincinnati Reds traded Frank Robinson, who was 20th on the all-time list with 324 home runs at the time, to the Baltimore Orioles. In 1966, Robinson led the American League with 49 homers, his career high, while leading the Orioles to victory in their first World Series appearance. He became the eighth American Leaguer to win the Triple Crown that season, the first in 10 years and the only African American. Hank Aaron of the Braves topped the National League with 44 home runs and Dick Allen of the Philadelphia Phillies placed second with 40 clouts. The third relocation occurred in California as the Los Angeles Angels moved down the freeway to Anaheim and into their own ballpark.

> **Hank Aaron hit** *a Curt Simmons pitch in the seventh inning of a tie game on top of the pavillion roof at Busch Stadium in St. Louis for an apparent homer on August 18, 1965. However, umpire Chris Pelekoudas called Aaron out for having one foot out of the batter's box when he connected. It would have been Aaron's 394th home run.*

Willie Mays continued his assault on the home run record book in 1966, after hitting more than 50 for the second time in 1965 and reaching the 500 mark during that season. On May 4, 1966, Mays hit his 512th home run, all of which had come in the National League, off Claude Osteen of the Los Angeles Dodgers in San Francisco, and became the career leader for the Senior Circuit. Mel Ott, the only other National Leaguer with 500 home runs at the time, had been the league leader since 1937, and Mays would hold the mark until 1972, when Hank Aaron took the lead. Before the end of August, Mays would pass Ted Williams and Jimmie Foxx to claim the No. 2 spot on the all-time list. Foxx held second place on the career list from August 16, 1940, to August 17, 1966. On May 8, 1966, in the first inning of the second game of a double header, Frank Robinson hit a home run in Baltimore off Luis Tiant of the Cleveland Indians that sailed over the left field seating area and the outer wall of the park, the only time that a batter hit a ball completely out of Memorial Stadium.

The Minnesota Twins became the first American League team, and fourth overall, to hit five home runs in one inning on June 9, 1966, against the Kansas City Athletics at Metropolitan Stadium in Minnesota. Harmon Killebrew hit a two-run homer in the sixth inning to bring the Twins within one run at 4-3. In the seventh inning, pinch hitter Rich Rollins hit a two-run shot and Zoilo Versalles hit one back-to-back with Rollins. After a pitching change and one out, Tony Oliva and Don Mincher also hit back-to-back shots and then, after another pitching change, Killebrew hit the fifth of the inning (and the third in a row for the team) and his second of the game. The next batter after Killebrew, Jimmie Hall, hit a double to right field that missed clearing the wall for the sixth home run of the inning by a few feet. This would have been the second time that the Twins had hit four consecutive homers, as they had performed the feat on May 2, 1964, against these same Athletics.

On July 3, 1966, Atlanta Braves pitcher Tony Cloninger pitched a complete-game victory against the Giants at Candlestick Park in San Francisco. In the top of the first inning with two outs, Cloninger hit a grand slam to put his team ahead 7-0. In the fourth inning, Cloninger did what no other pitcher has ever done by hitting a second grand slam in the same game. This one also came with two outs in the inning and the Braves eventually won the contest 17-3. Cloninger's second blast came off Ray Sadecki, who hit a solo homer off Cloninger in the bottom of the fifth inning. Cloninger, the first National League player to hit two slams in one game, continued the trend by the four previous players to perform the feat by doing it on the road. Only one other National Leaguer has hit two slams in one game, Fernando Tatis of the St. Louis Cardinals, who hit both of his in the third inning on April 23, 1999, off Chan Ho Park of the Dodgers in Los Angeles.

Robin Roberts of the Chicago Cubs, who had pitched in the big leagues since 1948, surrendered his 500th career home run on August 2, 1966, to Hank Aaron at Wrigley Field. Roberts is the only hurler to surrender 500 home runs in his career, finishing with 505 gopher balls. On this day, Warren Spahn held second place on the career list, having retired with 434 home runs surrendered. Roberts led the National League in home runs surrendered five times, including four in succession from 1954 through 1957, and surrendered 20 or more in 11 consecutive years from 1950 through 1960. He held the single-season record for most home runs surrendered for 31 years. Duke Snider hit 19 homers off Roberts, the most of any one batter off one pitcher in history.

The Pittsburgh Pirates and the Cincinnati Reds played a 13-inning contest at Crosley Field on August 12, 1966, in which 11 home runs were hit. Art Shamsky, who entered the game in the top of the eighth inning as part of a double switch, hit a two-run homer in the bottom of that frame to put the Reds in front 8-7. After the Bucs tied the game in the ninth, Willie Stargell hit a solo homer in the top of the 10th inning but Shamsky also hit a solo shot to tie the game again in the bottom of the inning. The Pirates scored twice in the top of the 11th inning but Shamsky hit his third home run of the game and second in extra innings in the bottom of the 11th to tie the contest once again. In the 13th inning, the Pirates scored three times and won the game 14-11. Shamsky became the third player and first National Leaguer to hit two home runs in extra innings of the same game in the only three-homer game of his career. In his next game, on August 14, Shamsky pinch hit a home run, thus clouting homers in four consecutive at bats over two games.

The home run production rate dropped in 1967 from 11.3 the previous season to 9.4, a decrease of 1.9 home runs per 500 plate appearances, which represents the fourth largest decrease from one season to the next in the history of the sport. At the time, the largest drop in one season had occurred from 1930 to 1931 when the production rate dropped 2.4 homers. Since 1967, there have been two other times when the rate dropped more than the 1.9, from 1977 to 1978 (2.0) and 1987 to 1988 (3.8). The drop in 1967 was part of a general decrease in offense in baseball that bottomed out in 1968.

◆　　◆　　◆

The summer of 1967 produced one of the greatest pennant races in the history of the American League as the Minnesota Twins, the Detroit Tigers, and the Boston Red Sox were all within one game of each other at the top of the league standings with two days left in the season. The Sox swept a two-game set with the Twins while the Tigers split a pair of double headers to catapult Boston into the World Series. Carl Yastrzemski of the Red Sox hit 44 home runs to tie with Twins slugger Harmon Killebrew at the top of the American League home run list. They each hit their last homer of the season in the first game of the battle between the two pennant contenders. Yaz also led the league in batting average and runs batted in, thus winning the Triple Crown, the most recent player to do so in the major leagues and the second in two years, as Frank Robinson had led in all three categories in 1966. Yastrzemski only led the league in homers once in a career in which he hit 452 home runs but he placed in the top five in two other seasons, 1969 and 1970. During Yastrzemski's time in the major leagues, only Harmon Killebrew and Reggie Jackson hit more home runs in the American League than Yaz. Hank Aaron led the National League for the fourth and last time with 39 homers.

That summer also produced two more members of the 500 Home Run Club as Mickey Mantle and Eddie Mathews joined two months apart, the first time that two players had hit home run number 500 in the same season. On May 14, 1967, Mantle smacked his 500th homer in front of his home-town fans at Yankee Stadium to become the sixth member of the club. The solo shot, off Stu Miller of the Baltimore Orioles, produced the game-winning run, as the Yankees won 6-5. Mantle joined Mel Ott as the only two of the six to hit his milestone homer in his own ballpark. Mantle, who played his entire career for the Yankees, led the American League in home runs four times, including 1956 when he won the Triple Crown. He hit at least 20 homers in 11 consecutive seasons, a streak that was broken in 1963 when Mantle played only 65 games, and hit more than 50 on two occasions. He passed Jimmie Foxx to move into third place on the all-time list on September 19, 1968, with a homer off 1968 American League Cy Young Award winner Denny McLain at Tiger Stadium in the game where the latter won his 31st game of the season. McLain grooved a fast ball for Mantle and The Mick deposited the ball in the upper deck just inside the right field pole. He hit one more homer the next day at Yankee Stadium off Boston's Jim Lonborg, the 1967 American League Cy Young Award winner, and retired third on the all-time home run list behind Babe Ruth and Willie Mays, who had 587 homers at the end of the 1968 season. Mantle remains at the top of the home run list for switch hitters and only Eddie

Murray has also hit 500 home runs among the switchers. Mantle smashed 18 home runs in World Series competition, more than any other batter in history, and his 256 homers at Yankee Stadium top the list for "The House That Ruth Built."

On July 14, 1967, Eddie Mathews, who had hit 493 home runs for the Braves in three cities, smacked his 500th career homer as a member of the Houston Astros at Candlestick Park in San Francisco off Juan Marichal. Mathews joined with Willie Mays and Mickey Mantle as the three active players with 500 home runs, the first time this had occurred in history. Marichal, the only Hall of Fame pitcher to surrender a 500th home run, lost the game to Houston 8-6. Mathews was the first player in National League history to hit at least 30 homers in nine consecutive years (1953 through 1961), as the only previous players to achieve this feat, Jimmie Foxx (12 years from 1929 through 1940) and Lou Gehrig (nine years from 1929 through 1937) played in the American League. Like Mantle, Mathews retired after the 1968 season, finishing sixth on the all-time list with 512 home runs but had the third-highest total for a left-handed swinger behind Babe Ruth and Ted Williams. Mathews hit 338 home runs from 1951 through 1960 to lead the majors in that 10-year span. He teamed with Hank Aaron on the Braves for 13 years, and the duo homered in the same game 75 times, two more than the more famous Yankee pair of Babe Ruth and Lou Gehrig. Mathews managed the Atlanta Braves from mid-1972 through mid-1974, including the day that Aaron hit his 715th home run to pass Babe Ruth. (Refer to Appendix A for details of each home run number 500.)

Pitching brothers Phil (Braves) and Joe (Cubs) Niekro faced each on July 4, 1967, at Atlanta Stadium and each surrendered a home run in the game. Lee Thomas hit one off Phil in the sixth inning, while Mack Jones and Rico Carty each clouted one off Joe. The Niekros would repeat this feat on September 26, 1969, as Joe, now with the San Diego Padres, surrendered a blast to Orlando Cepeda, while Tommy Dean and Al Ferrara each hit a four-bagger off Phil. They would perform this feat once more on May 29, 1976, which is discussed in chapter 10.

The Year of the Pitcher, 1968, had the lowest home run production rate since 1948 at 8.3 and in two years, the rate had dropped a full three points. Since that time, only one year has had a lower rate than 1968, 7.6 in

1976. Pitchers dominated the season, with Bob Gibson leading the National League in ERA at 1.12 and Denny McLain winning 31 games in the American League. These and other pitchers benefited greatly from the enlarged strike zone implemented in 1963. Also in 1968, a third team moved to California, giving the state four clubs, as the Kansas City Athletics (who had moved from Philadelphia in 1955) relocated across the bay from the San Francisco Giants and played at Oakland-Alameda County Coliseum. The Athletics joined the Dodgers and Giants, as well as the expansion team, the Angels.

Frank Howard of the Washington Senators led the American League in 1968 with 44 home runs, the first of three consecutive years in which Hondo hit over 40 homers. Runner-up Willie Horton of the Detroit Tigers hit 36, his career high, while Willie McCovey of the San Francisco Giants led the National League, also hitting 36. These totals were the lowest for the two league leaders since 1952 when Larry Doby led the American League with 32 and Ralph Kiner and Hank Sauer tied for the National League lead with 37. As part of Howard's league-leading total, he hit 10 round-trippers in one week from May 12 through May 18, breaking the record of nine in a week held by many batters. Barry Bonds and Shawn Green would tie Howard's mark in the twenty-first century.

Even though home run production was down in 1968, there were still some exciting moments during the season. On June 24, 1968, Jim Northrup, Willie Horton's teammate on the Tigers, hit two grand slams in the same game, becoming the sixth player and fifth American Leaguer to accomplish this. The Tigers beat the Indians in Cleveland that day 14-3, behind Denny McLain's complete game for the 13th of his 31 wins that year. Northrup's blasts came in the fifth and sixth innings and only Jim Gentile had hit his two slams in consecutive innings before Northrup. Northrup continued the pattern of all six two-slam batters as he slugged his on the road.

Hank Aaron of the Atlanta Braves clouted his 500th career home run on July 14, 1968, one year to the day after his former teammate, Eddie Mathews, joined the 500 Home Run Club. Hammerin' Hank missed hitting the milestone in the first inning when his drive curved foul past the left field pole. After a one-hour rain delay in the second inning, the rest of the game was played in the rain. Aaron homered over the left center field fence in the third inning off Mike McCormick of the San Francisco Giants to break a scoreless tie, but the continuing rain threatened to wash out the game. He became the eighth batter to slug 500 home runs and the fourth active player with that many, a list that also included Willie Mays (second on the all-time list at 577), Mickey Mantle (fourth at 529), and Eddie Mathews (sixth at 512). There had never been four active players with 500 home runs before in history but Mantle and Mathews both retired at the end of the season, making this a short-lived event. There have been two other times when there were at least four active players with 500 home runs: the end of the 1971 season with five (Mays, Aaron, Banks, Killebrew, and Robinson) and starting in July 2004 through the end of the 2005 season with four (Bonds, Sosa, Palmeiro, and Griffey). (Refer to Appendix A for details of each home run number 500.)

More expansion took place in 1969, as each league added two teams and split into two divisions of six clubs each. The National League welcomed the San Diego Padres, the fifth team in California, and the Montreal Expos, expanding Major League Baseball outside the United States for the first time, while the American League added the Kansas City Royals and the Seattle Pilots. In the first game played in Canada on April 14, 1969, Mack Jones of the Expos hit the first major league home run (*le circuit* in French) outside the United States in the bottom of the first inning at Jarry Park in Montreal. The three-run shot gave the home team a lead, which they surrendered in the top of the fourth to the National League champion St. Louis Cardinals as the Redbirds scored seven runs in the inning. Four of those tallies came from the first grand slam (*grand chelem*) in Canada clouted by the light-hitting shortstop of the Cardinals, Dal Maxvill, who hit six total home runs in his career and only one grand slam.

Other changes that occurred in the 1969 season included a redefinition of the strike zone back to the rule that existed before 1963: from the armpits to the top of the batter's knees. The pitcher's mound was also lowered this year to a maximum of 10 inches in height. Both of these changes were made to counteract the dearth of offense that had plagued the game in the previous few years. The home run rate reflected the increased offense as it jumped from 8.3 in 1968 to 10.5, the second largest increase in one year in history, the largest being the 3.7 jump from 1976 to 1977.

Harmon Killebrew of the Minnesota Twins led the majors in 1969 by hitting 49 home runs, which tied his career high set in 1964. Frank Howard of the Senators, the previous year's leader in the American League, placed second with 48 clouts (his career high) and Reggie Jackson of the Oakland Athletics hit 47. Jackson had hit 29 home runs by the end of June but his pace slowed considerably after that with only 18 in the second half of the season. Willie McCovey of the Giants hit 45 home runs to lead the National League, and Hank Aaron of the Braves finished second with 44. McCovey's teammate, Bobby Bonds, hit 32 homers in 1969 and paired that with 45 stolen bases, thus becoming the fourth player to accomplish a 30/30 season. Bonds would achieve this level of production four more times in his career, in 1973, 1975, 1977, and 1978. Through 2005, the only player who has matched Bonds in 30/30 seasons is his son, Barry, who also accomplished the feat five times. Bobby Bonds is also one of four players to hit 300 homers and steal 300 bases in his career, along with Willie Mays, Andre Dawson, and Barry Bonds. (See chapter 14 for an update from the 2006 season for both of these achievements.) Bobby stole 461 bases and hit 332 circuit clouts in his career.

On June 2, 1969, Hank Aaron hit home run number 522 off Gary Waslewski of the St. Louis Cardinals at Busch Stadium to pass Ted Williams and move into the top five on the career homer list. By the end of July, Aaron had also passed Jimmie Foxx and Mickey Mantle to claim third place on the list. He passed Mantle in game one on July 30 with a solo homer off Grant Jackson of the Phillies at Connie Mack Stadium in Philadelphia.

◆ ◆ ◆

For the second time in history, a player reached 600 career home runs, on September 22, 1969, as Willie Mays hit a ball into the left center field seats at San Diego Stadium off Mike Corkins. Pinch hitting for rookie George Foster in the seventh inning, Mays broke a 2-2 tie to win the game for the Giants 4-2. Mays, the oldest player to hit number 600, received a sports car from his bat company as a tribute for the milestone homer. (Refer to Appendix A for details of each home run number 600.) Mays, who retired after the 1973 season with 660 homers, hit 30 in a season 11 times and 50 twice. Of those 660 four-baggers, 22 of them came in extra innings, which is the record. Also, he hit 18 homers off fellow Hall of Famer Warren Spahn, the second-highest total for one batter off one pitcher. Mays led the National League four times, including two consecutive seasons (1964–65), and finished in the top five in the league 10 times. He hit 30 home runs and stole 30 bases in the same season twice in consecutive years (1956–57), and was the first player to hit 300 homers and steal 300 bases in a career. Mays also became the second player of four to hit 500 home runs and collect 3,000 hits in a career in 1970, with only Hank Aaron, Eddie Murray, and Rafael Palmeiro also accomplishing this feat. Mays had joined the list of the top five home run sluggers in 1965 and gradually moved to number two on the list on August 17, 1966, when he passed Jimmie Foxx. Hank Aaron passed Mays on June 10, 1972, and the top three sluggers remained the same until 2004, although Aaron moved ahead of Ruth.

Another team relocated in 1970, continuing the unstable franchise trend of the period. The Seattle Pilots, a 1969 expansion team, moved to Milwaukee after a bankruptcy court referee ruled on March 31, 1970, that the team could be sold. The club, now known as the Brewers, played their first game one week later on April 7 at County Stadium, which had been the home of the Braves when they played in Milwaukee. The home run rate went up a full point in 1970 to 11.5, a further reversal of the mid-1960s downward trend.

Frank Howard led the American League for the second time in three years in 1970, hitting 44 for the Washington Senators. Harmon Killebrew of the Twins and Carl Yastrzemski of the Red Sox also topped the 40 mark, with 41 and 40 homers, respectively. In the National League, Cincinnati catcher Johnny Bench led the league with 45 dingers, while Billy Williams of the Chicago Cubs hit 42 and Tony Perez of the Reds hit 40. Tommy Harper of the Milwaukee Brewers hit 31 homers and stole 38 bases for the year, becoming the fifth player with a 30/30 season.

On May 12, 1970, Ernie Banks slugged his 500th home run, the ninth player to accomplish this, when he lined a 1-1 fast ball into Wrigley Field's left field seats off Pat Jarvis, in a game eventually won by the Cubs over the Braves in 11 innings 4-3. Banks's entry into the 500 Home Run Club brought the active number of players in that august body up to three, as Willie Mays (with 606 homers that day) and the gentleman playing right field for the

Braves, Hank Aaron (568), already had passed that milestone in their careers. Banks had hit at least 40 home runs in four consecutive seasons and five of six years in the late 1950s, leading the National League twice in that span. He split his career evenly between playing shortstop early on and then moving to first base later, with 277 homers at the former position and 210 at the latter. Until the 2006 season, only Babe Ruth had hit at least 200 home runs at each of two positions with 313 as a left fielder and 354 as a right fielder. (Refer to Appendix A for details of each home run number 500.)

Just a few weeks after Banks joined the 500 Home Run Club, the Giants entertained his Cubs in a day game at Candlestick Park. In the contest, played on June 17, Banks hit a three-run homer in the top of the eighth inning, his 504th. Then, in the bottom half of the same frame, Willie Mays hit a solo-home run, his 615th career blast. Two members of the 500 Home Run Club had never homered in the same game before, a feat that would be repeated three times.

On June 26, 1970, at Robert F. Kennedy Memorial Stadium in Washington, DC, Frank Robinson of the Baltimore Orioles slugged two grand slams in one game. The clouts came in consecutive innings, the fifth and sixth, off a pair of Joes, Coleman and Grzenda, and propelled the Orioles to a 12-2 victory. Robinson became the seventh batter to perform this feat, all of whom had done it on the road. His slams were the last hit at RFK Stadium until August 2005, as the stadium did not host baseball from 1972 through 2004.

In 1971, home run production dropped again to 9.8 homers per 500 plate appearances, a level approaching the 1967 rate. In the National League, Willie Stargell of the Pittsburgh Pirates led with 48 home runs, his career high, and Hank Aaron placed second with 47. In the American League, Bill Melton hit 33 home runs for the second consecutive year as a member of the Chicago White Sox. In 1970, Melton, who only hit 160 career homers, placed sixth in the league, but in 1971 he led it, becoming the first White Sox player to lead the league. Melton's 160 career home runs is the lowest total for a season league leader since 1945, when Tommy Holmes of the Boston Braves led the war-depleted National League. Holmes, who hit 28 that season, only hit 88 in his career and no league leader since 1920 hit fewer career clouts than Holmes. Norm Cash of the Detroit Tigers and

Reggie Jackson of the Oakland Athletics tied for second place in the 1971 American League with 32 home runs each.

As part of his league-leading performance, Willie Stargell had two three-homer games in April 1971. On April 10, he hammered Braves pitchers in Atlanta and then on April 21, he duplicated the feat against the same team, this time at Three Rivers Stadium in Pittsburgh. Stargell became the fifth batter to have two three-homer games in the same season.

The third member of the 600 Home Run Club joined on April 27, 1971, when Hank Aaron of the Atlanta Braves hit his milestone homer. In the game against the San Francisco Giants in Atlanta, Aaron connected in the third inning off Hall of Famer Gaylord Perry to give the Braves a temporary lead, in a contest they later lost 6-5 in 10 innings. The first batter to hit 600 homers, Babe Ruth, had retired in 1935, but the second to accomplish this, Willie Mays, patrolled center field for the Giants that night. This is the only time that two active players had each hit 600 home runs in their careers, a pairing that lasted until Mays retired in 1973. (Refer to Appendix A for details of each home run number 600.)

Eleven days later, on May 8, Aaron and the Braves played the Giants at Candlestick Park in San Francisco. In the bottom of the sixth inning, Mays hit a solo home run to score the first run of the game. As part of a five-run eighth inning, Aaron hit a three-run shot that put the Braves ahead, as they beat the Giants 5-2. This was the second time in history that two sluggers with 500 home runs each hit one in the same game. Mays hit his 634th while Aaron smacked his 604th for a combined total of 1,238 home runs. The feat has been accomplished three other times, once each in 1970, 2004, and 2005, and the Mays/Aaron combined total is the most of the quartet of pairings.

On May 17, 1971, Ralph Garr of the Atlanta Braves became the fourth player to hit two home runs in extra innings of the same game. With the New York Mets playing in Atlanta, the visitors scored a run on a Donn Clendenon 10-inning home run, his second of the game, but with two outs in the bottom of the inning, Garr hit a solo shot off Tom Seaver to tie the game. Two innings later, Garr hit another two-out, solo homer off Ron Taylor to win the contest for the Braves 4-3.

Rick Wise pitched for five teams in his big league career and hit 15 home runs in that time, enough to make the top 20 list for pitchers. In 1971,

Wise smacked six home runs for the Philadelphia Phillies, his career high, including two in one game twice that season. On June 23, he hit home runs in two consecutive at bats off Ross Grimsley and Clay Carroll of the Reds at Cincinnati's Riverfront Stadium. The four-baggers came in the fifth and eighth innings and provided three of the four runs in the 4-0 victory. Meanwhile, Wise threw a complete game in which he walked one batter, Dave Concepcion in the sixth inning, struck out three, and allowed no hits. Wise is the only hurler to throw a no-hitter and hit two home runs in the same game. Only four other pitchers hit one homer in their no-hit performance: Frank Mountain of the Columbus Colts (June 5, 1884), Wes Ferrell of the Cleveland Indians (April 29, 1931), Jim Tobin of the Boston Braves (April 27, 1944), and Earl Wilson of the Boston Red Sox (June 26, 1962).

> *Former Baltimore Orioles* manager *Earl Weaver has been widely quoted as having said: "Baseball is pitching, three-run homers, and fundamentals." However, in the history of the game, three- and four-run homers account for less than fifteen percent of major league round-trippers. Weaver obviously didn't wait around for that three-run home run, as he won many more ballgames than he lost as a skipper.*

Just as in 1967, two batters hit their 500th home runs in 1971. On August 10, Harmon Killebrew of the Minnesota Twins hit a solo shot off Mike Cuellar of the Baltimore Orioles in the first inning of a game at Metropolitan Stadium in Minneapolis to become the 10th member of the club. In the sixth inning, Killebrew clouted another home run to become the first player to hit two homers in the game in which he hit number 500. Mark McGwire also hit two blasts in his number 500 game in 1999. Killebrew made his major league debut six days before his 18th birthday in 1954 with the Washington Senators but played very little until he became an every-day player in 1959. He hit at least 40 home runs in eight seasons, including four in a row from 1961 through 1964, topping out at 49, and he had six consecutive years with 30. Killebrew led the American League six times (second only to Babe Ruth's 12 seasons on top of the Junior Circuit) and placed in the top five 11 times in his career. From 1961 through 1970, he hit 403 home runs, becoming the third batter to hit at least 400 in a decade after Babe Ruth (462 from 1921 through 1930) and Jimmie Foxx (414 from 1931 through 1940). When he retired at the end of the 1975 season, Killebrew had hit 573 home runs, placing him fifth on the all-time list and second in the American League behind Babe Ruth's 708 homers in the Junior Circuit, a spot that Killebrew still holds. Killebrew hit more in the American League than any other right-handed batter. Also at the time of his retirement, he had the third best home run production rate of any batter at 29.1, behind Ruth (33.6) and Ralph Kiner (29.5). Killebrew and his long-time teammate, Bob Allison, hit home runs in the same game 61 times, the sixth best total for that achievement all-time. Killebrew hit at least 140 home runs at each of three positions: first base (210), third base (191), and left field (143). No other player has hit that many homers at three positions.

A month after Killebrew hit homer number 500, Frank Robinson did likewise. Still with the Orioles, Robinson connected on September 13, 1971, at Memorial Stadium in Baltimore. He had hit number 499 in the first inning of the first game of a double header and then hit number 500 in the ninth inning of the second game off Fred Scherman as the Orioles and Detroit Tigers split the twin bill. In his career, Robinson hit 30 homers in one season 11 times and was the first batter to hit 200 home runs in both the National (343) and American (243) Leagues. He is the only player to homer for each league in the All-Star Game and the only batter to hit a ball completely out of Baltimore's Memorial Stadium. On April 8, 1975, he managed his first game for the Cleveland Indians, becoming the first African American manager in the major leagues. In the first inning of the game, Robinson, also serving as the team's designated hitter, hit a home run, thus becoming the first player/manager to hit a four-bagger since Eddie Joost of the Philadelphia Athletics on June 1, 1954. Pete Rose homered as player/manager of the Cincinnati Reds twice in 1985 to become the most recent manager to do so. Robinson, who won the Triple Crown in 1966, hit at least 10 home runs for 19 consecutive seasons and at least one home run for 21 consecutive seasons. When he retired as a player after the 1976 campaign, Robinson had hit 586 home runs, good for fourth place on the all-time list, a spot he held until June 5, 2002, when Barry Bonds passed him. Robinson's joining the 500 Home Run Club brought the number of active players in the group to five: Mays, Aaron, Banks, Killebrew, and Robinson. This is the only time in history with five active players who had hit 500 or more home runs and the second with at least four, duplicating the end of the 1968 season. (Refer to Appendix A for details of each home run number 500.)

Another team relocated for the 1972 season, as the second Washington Senators moved to Arlington, Texas, a suburb of Dallas. Frank Howard hit the last home run by the Senators in 1971 on September 30, which was also the last four-bagger hit at RFK Stadium until 2005. Three Yankees also homered earlier in the contest, which was forfeited to the Yankees when fans poured onto the field and order could not be restored. Howard hit the first four-bagger for the new Texas Rangers on April 21, 1972, in the first American League game played in Texas.

For the second consecutive year, the home run production rate decreased in 1972 to 9.1 homers per 500 plate appearances and, in general, the 1970s saw a lower production rate than the 1960s. Johnny Bench, the Cincinnati Reds catcher, led the majors for the second time by hitting 40 home runs while Nate Colbert of the San Diego Padres hit 38. In the American League, Dick Allen, in his first year in the Junior Circuit with the Chicago White Sox, led the league with 37 blasts. Allen had now hit at least 20 homers in nine consecutive seasons.

◆ ◆ ◆

On June 10, 1972, Hank Aaron hit his 649th career homer off Wayne Twitchell of the Philadelphia Phillies at Veteran's Stadium in Philadelphia to give him sole possession of second place on the all-time home run list behind Babe Ruth. Aaron passed Willie Mays that day and became the top home run hitter in National League history, a title he held until 2006, with 733 hammered in the Senior Circuit.

Nate Colbert of the San Diego Padres, who placed second in the 1972 National League in home runs, hit five of his 38 on one day. In the first game of a double header on August 1 in Atlanta, Colbert had four hits in five at bats, including two home runs, as the Pads beat the Braves 9-0. In the second game that night, Colbert had three hits in four at bats, all of them homers, as the Padres swept the Braves 11-7. Colbert's five home runs in a double header matched the feat first accomplished by Stan Musial in 1954. They are the only two batters who have hit for the circuit five times in a double header, and Colbert had attended the 1954 games when Musial had set the mark. Colbert also broke the major league record for most runs batted in for a double header with his 13. The previous record of 11 had been set by Earl Averill of the Cleveland Indians in 1930, Jim Tabor of the Boston Red Sox in 1939, and Boog Powell of the Baltimore Orioles in 1966. With his two singles in the first game, Colbert collected 22 total bases in the twin bill to break Musial's record of 21.

On August 17, 1972, Harmon Killebrew moved into fifth place on the all-time home run list when he smacked number 535 to pass Jimmie Foxx in the first game of a double header. The blast came off Woodie Fryman of the Detroit Tigers at Tiger Stadium. On September 5, Killebrew moved into fourth place by passing Mickey Mantle with a two-run homer off Eddie Fisher of the White Sox at Comiskey Park. Killebrew would remain in the top five until 2001 when Mark McGwire passed him on the list.

When each league expanded into two six-team divisions in 1969, there was a side effect that changed post-season baseball. Two divisions meant no champion for the league at the end of the season, so baseball created a second round of post-season play and called it the League Championship Series. The next chapter talks about the post-season and then we will get back to the chronology.

9
POST-SEASON HOME RUNS

Home runs are prominent events in the baseball post-season, since the level of competition is higher in the post-season, making those four-baggers harder to hit and, perhaps, more important. Also, through the years post-season baseball has drawn more attention from the media and the general public than the regular season, so an important home run hit in post-season will be remembered far longer than one hit in May or June. This effect has been heightened beginning in the last part of the twentieth century by the television coverage of post-season games because viewers see those homers repeated often in October and, in fact, at other times of the year.

The first meeting between the champions of the rival National and American Leagues was held in 1903, as the Boston Americans (now Red Sox) defeated the Pittsburgh Pirates five games to three in a best-of-nine competition. Jimmy Sebring of the Pirates hit the first World Series home run, an inside-the-park clout off Cy Young in the seventh inning of the first game played on October 1 at Boston's Huntington Avenue Baseball Grounds. In game two the next day, Patsy Dougherty of Boston hit the first leadoff homer in Series history (an inside-the-park drive) and then in the sixth inning hit his second of the day over the left field wall, thus becoming the first batter to have a multi-homer game in the World Series. There have been 12 inside-the-park home runs in World Series competition, the most recent by Mule Haas of the Philadelphia Athletics on October 12, 1929.

In true Deadball Era fashion, four World Series before 1920 had no home runs, these being the years 1905 through 1907 and 1918. The two leagues did not compete in a post-season series in 1904. The short length of the World Series and the small total of plate appearances for the teams make the home run production rate less accurate than during the regular season. Therefore, it will not be used as a measure for post-season home run prowess. It is evident, however, that the batters during the Deadball Era hit fewer home runs in the Series than have later generations of players, mirroring the regular season production rate.

The next home run in the World Series after Patsy Dougherty in 1903 occurred when Joe Tinker hit a circuit clout in game two of the 1908 Series. Davy Jones of the Detroit Tigers hit a leadoff homer in game five of the 1909 Series, the second time a batter had performed this feat. No more leadoff home runs occurred in the World Series until 1942 when Phil Rizzuto of the New York Yankees would start game five with a round-tripper. The two homers by Frank "Home Run" Baker in the 1911 Series, the second of which provided the first late-inning heroics in World Series history, have been chronicled in the chapter on the Deadball Era. Baker became the first player to hit three World Series home runs in his career on October 7, 1913, when he hit a two-run shot at the Polo Grounds. This blast came off Rube Marquard, the victim of his first World Series home run in 1911.

Larry Gardner of the Boston Red Sox hit 27 homers in a 17-year career from 1908 through 1924. He hit a ball that bounced into the overflow crowd in right field for a ground rule home run in the second inning of game seven of the 1912 Series, on October 15. This was the first World Series home run hit at Fenway Park, which had opened that April. Larry Doyle of the New York Giants also bounced a homer into the right field crowd in the sixth inning of that game. In 1916, Gardner hit two more home runs in consecutive games to tie Home Run Baker with three career World Series homers.

On October 12, 1914, in game three of a four-game set, Hank Gowdy of the Boston Braves hit the first extra-inning homer in Series history. Gowdy connected on a bounce home run to lead off the bottom of the 10th inning and the Braves later scored another run in that inning to tie the score with the Philadelphia Athletics, 4-4, in a game eventually won in 12 innings by the Braves, 5-4.

In game five of the 1920 World Series, played on October 10, Elmer Smith of the Cleveland Indians hit the first grand slam in Series history in the first inning of a game played at Cleveland's Dunn Field (later called League Park). Later in the game, Indians hurler Jim Bagby, who pitched a complete-game victory that day, hit a three-run blast to center field to become the first pitcher to homer in post-season competition. Coincidentally, in that same game Bill Wambsganss of the Indians executed the only triple play in World Series history, putting out all three runners by himself for an unassisted triple play.

Emil Frederick "Irish" Meusel of the New York Giants, older brother of Bob Meusel of the New York Yankees, hit his third career World Series home run in the second inning on October 11, 1923, to tie Home Run Baker and Larry Gardner at the top of the career list for the Series. Babe Ruth, who had swatted his first World Series home run on October 9, 1921, to become the first New York Yankee to homer in the World Series, hit two home runs in consecutive at bats in the fourth and fifth innings on October 11 to win the game for the Yankees and tie for the career lead in Series homers with three. Four days later, Ruth hit a solo shot in the first inning of game six to set a new career record for the World Series with four circuit clouts.

Ruth hit all four of those home runs at the Polo Grounds in New York, the Yankees' home field through 1922, but his favorite post-season ballpark was Sportsman's Park in St. Louis, where he swatted six home runs. Ruth's first post-season homer at Yankee Stadium did not come until October 10, 1926, three years after the park opened, and he only hit three World Series home runs at Yankee Stadium in his career. Ruth hit 15 home runs in the Series, all for the Yankees, to place second on the all-time list behind Mickey Mantle, who hit 18 in World Series competition. In 1923, Ruth became the first batter to hit three home runs in one World Series and three years later he hit four in one Series.

On two occasions, Ruth clouted three homers in one Series game. The first of these three-homer games came on October 6, 1926, and he repeated the feat on October 9, 1928. Both of these games were played in St. Louis, accounting for all six home runs Ruth hit at Sportsman's Park in the World Series. Only one other batter, Reggie Jackson also of the Yankees, has hit three home runs in one Series game.

On October 10, 1923, Casey Stengel, center fielder of the New York Giants, hit an inside-the-park home run in the ninth inning for the deciding run in a game won by the Giants 5-4. This was the first World Series home run hit at Yankee Stadium, and two days later on October 12, 1923, Stengel hit a solo homer in the seventh inning to knock in the only run of the game, the first time a batter had accounted for all the runs in a World Series contest with one home run. This round-tripper was the second hit at Yankee Stadium.

Joe Harris of the Washington Senators played in his first World Series in 1925. In the top of the second inning of game one, played at Forbes Field in Pittsburgh, Harris homered in his first Series at bat, the first player to accomplish this feat. With the scene shifted to Griffith Stadium for game four, the Senators scored four runs in the third inning on back-to-back home runs by Leon Allen "Goose" Goslin and Harris. This was the first time that two batters had hit consecutive homers in the Series.

Goose Goslin hit three home runs in the 1924 World Series for the Washington Senators against the New York Giants. The following year, he homered in game three against the Pittsburgh Pirates at Washington's Griffith Stadium to tie Babe Ruth for the career lead in Series homers with four. In the next game, on October 11, 1925, Goslin's home run, the first of the back-to-back with Joe Harris, made him the career leader and he later added to his total with a sixth homer on October 13, 1925. Ruth hit four more homers in the 1926 World Series to reclaim the lead from Goslin, a lead which the Babe did not surrender until 1964, when Mickey Mantle clouted his 16th Series blast.

Lou Gehrig hit 10 homers in his World Series career, including two games of two each on October 7, 1928, and October 1, 1932. Gehrig, the regular-season grand-slam leader, never hit a bases-loaded home run in the Series but he did smack an inside-the-park hit, one of the two home runs he hit on October 7, 1928. Two days later, Ruth and Gehrig hit back-to-back homers in St. Louis in the seventh inning. They repeated the feat in the fifth inning on October 1, 1932 at Wrigley Field, Chicago. Both sluggers hit two home runs in that contest, all four blasts coming off Charlie Root, who was the first pitcher to surrender four home runs in one Series contest, a feat repeated by Junior Thompson of the Cincinnati Reds in 1939 and Dick Hughes of the St. Louis Cardinals in 1967. Ruth and Gehrig are the only pair of batters to hit back-to-back World Series homers more than once.

The 1928 New York Yankees, who swept the St. Louis Cardinals in the Series, hit nine home runs in the four games. Lou Gehrig hit four homers, Babe Ruth swatted three, and Bob Meusel and Cedric Durst contributed the other two. The Yankees were the first club to hit nine homers in one World Series, a record that stood until 1952 when the Yankees hit 10. Five of the nine 1928 home runs came in one game, on October 9, also setting a new record, which was tied by the 1989 Oakland Athletics. This 1928 game is the contest in which Ruth and Gehrig hit two blasts each, including back-to-back once. Gehrig homered in three consecutive games in that Fall Classic to set a new record in that category that has since been tied by many players. Bob Meusel's home run on October 4, 1928, when paired with the homers that his older brother Irish hit earlier in the decade, made them the first brothers to each hit a round-tripper in World Series competition.

Hazen Shirley "Kiki" Cuyler of the Chicago Cubs homered in the game on October 1, 1932, in which Babe Ruth and Lou Gehrig each hit two home runs. Cuyler had also hit a four-bagger on October 8, 1925, as a member of the Pittsburgh Pirates, thus becoming the first player to hit a home run in the World Series for two different teams. These two homers are Cuyler's career output in the Series.

Tony Lazzeri, who had hit two grand slams in one game on May 24, 1936, hit a bases-loaded home run in the third inning of game two of the 1936 World Series, played on October 2 at the Polo Grounds. The slam was part of a seven-run inning in a game won by the New York Yankees 18-4 over the New York Giants. Lazzeri joined Elmer Smith of the 1920 Cleveland Indians as the only two batters to hit a grand slam in World Series competition at that time.

Jimmy Ripple of the New York Giants hit a fifth-inning solo home run on October 3, 1936, to tie game three at one run each. Four years later, on October 3, 1940, Ripple, now a member of the Cincinnati Reds, homered to become the second player in history to hit a home run for two different teams in the World Series. This 1940 home run by Ripple was the first hit by a Cincinnati Reds player in the World Series. Junior Thompson of the Reds threw four gopher balls in one game on October 7, 1939, at Crosley Field in Cincinnati. The four Yankee home runs were hit by Charlie Keller (with two), Joe DiMaggio, and Bill Dickey. Thompson became the second hurler to surrender four home runs in one World Series game.

In the 1946 World Series, Rudy York of the Boston Red Sox accomplished two feats with one home run. In the first game of the Series, played on October 6 at Sportsman's Park in St. Louis, York won the game with a solo homer in the top of the 10th inning. This was the third extra-inning home run in Series history, all coming in the 10th inning of a game, and the first for York as a member of the Red Sox squad. On October 4, 1940, York had homered at Briggs Stadium for the Detroit Tigers. York was the third batter to homer for two teams in the World Series, and the first American Leaguer to accomplish the feat. Yogi Berra, who hit 12 home runs in World Series games to place third all-time, hit his first on October 2, 1947, in his third Series game. In the seventh inning, Berra pinch hit for Sherm Lollar and clouted the first pinch-hit home run in World Series history.

At Braves Field in Boston on October 11, 1948, Joe Gordon homered to lead off the sixth inning for the Cleveland Indians, thus breaking a 1-1 tie. He had hit a home run for the 1938 New York Yankees in the World Series, thus becoming the fourth player to homer for two teams in the Series. Game one of the 1949 World Series featured a pitching duel between Don Newcombe of the Brooklyn Dodgers and Allie Reynolds of the New York Yankees, played on October 5. After eight innings, the teams had combined for no runs and six hits at Yankee Stadium. In the bottom of the ninth inning, Tommy Henrich led off the frame and hit a 2-0 curve ball into the right field seats for the first game-ending home run in World Series history. This was also the fourth time that a hitter had driven in all the runs in a game with one homer. Joe DiMaggio of the New York Yankees, who hit eight home runs in the World Series from 1937 through 1951, became the first batter to homer in three decades of World Series play, a feat only achieved by three other batters: Yogi Berra, Eddie Murray, and Matt Williams.

On October 3, 1952, Johnny Mize of the New York Yankees hit a solo homer in the bottom of the ninth inning as a pinch hitter, the second pinch homer in Series history. Mize hit round-trippers in three consecutive games of that Fall Classic to become the second batter in history to accomplish this after Lou Gehrig in 1928. Duke Snider of the Brooklyn Dodgers hit a home run in the first game of the Series and another in game five. Then in the sixth game he socked two homers to become the third player to hit four in one World Series. The Yankees hit 10 home runs in the Series, thus breaking the record of nine set by the 1928 Yankees.

The 1954 World Series featured a home run by Dusty Rhodes of the New York Giants that qualifies as one of the most memorable Series homers of all time. Game one, played on September 29 at the Polo Grounds, was tied 2-2 in the bottom of the 10th inning with one out and Willie Mays and Bobby Thomson on base when Rhodes hit a three-run, pinch-hit, extra-inning, game-ending home run. The Giants won the first of a four-game sweep over the Cleveland Indians. The home run by Rhodes was the fourth pinch-hit, fifth in extra innings, and second game-ending homer in World Series history. In the fourth and final game of the Series, Hank Majeski of the Indians hit a three-run, pinch-hit home run in the bottom of the fifth inning. This was the first time that two pinch-hit home runs were hit in the same World Series, a feat that would be repeated in 1959.

Duke Snider of the Dodgers smashed two solo home runs on October 2, 1955, at Ebbets Field in Brooklyn, the third and fourth homers of the Series for the Duke. Combined with his four-homer performance in the 1952 Series, Snider became the only batter to hit four round-trippers in each of two different World Series. At this time, only Babe Ruth and Lou Gehrig had also hit four in one Series, a record that would be broken by Reggie Jackson when he hit five in the 1977 World Series.

◆   ◆   ◆

For the first time in a World Series, two batters hit grand slams in the same year in 1956. In game two, Yogi Berra of the Yankees hit the first of the pair in the second inning in a losing cause, as the Dodgers won the game 13-8. In the seventh game, Bill Skowron helped the Yankees win the Series with his seventh inning homer with the bases full, one of four home runs hit by the Yankees as they won the game, 9-0. The Yankees hit 12 homers in the Series, breaking the old record of 10 set by the 1952 Bronx Bombers. The record of 12 stood until 2002, when the San Francisco Giants hit 14 circuit clouts. Enos Slaughter homered for the Yankees in game three and became the first player in history to clout a round-tripper for a National League team and an American League team in the World Series. He had homered for the St. Louis Cardinals in the 1942 and 1946 Series.

For the second consecutive year, the New York Yankees and Milwaukee Braves competed in the 1958 World Series. Bill Bruton of the Braves led off game two with a home run, the first of seven runs in the inning, as the Braves won the contest 13-5. Lew Burdette hurled a complete game for Milwaukee and helped his own cause with a three-run homer to cap off the scoring in the first inning. Burdette started three of the seven games and surrendered five homers in the Series, breaking the old record for homers surrendered in one Series of four, held by many pitchers. Hank Bauer hit four home runs in the Series, becoming the fourth different batter to accomplish this. Bauer's round-trippers came in three consecutive games to make him the third player to accomplish this feat after Lou Gehrig and Johnny Mize. On October 8, 1958, Gil McDougald of the Yankees hit a solo homer to lead off the top of the 10th inning and the Yankees scored another run in the inning on the way to a 4-3 victory. McDougald had hit a grand slam as a rookie in the 1951 World Series, to become the only batter to hit a slam and an extra inning homer in World Series play.

Chuck Essegian of the Los Angeles Dodgers hit two pinch-hit homers in the 1959 World Series, becoming the first batter to accomplish this feat. In game two, played on October 2 at Chicago's Comiskey Park, Essegian hit for pitcher Johnny Podres in the seventh inning and hit a 3-1 pitch into the left field upper deck seats for a solo homer to tie the score at 2-2. Charlie Neal, who had homered in the fifth, making him the first Los Angeles Dodger and first player for a California team to hit a four-bagger in the World Series, hit his second home run of the game in the seventh inning to give the Dodgers a victory and tie the Series at one game each. Six days later in the sixth and deciding game of the Series, the Dodgers hit three home runs to win the game and Series. In the top of the ninth inning with the Dodgers ahead 8-3, Essegian batted for Duke Snider, who had homered earlier in the game, and socked the first pitch into the left field seats. Thus, two different batters hit home runs in the same batting order slot in the game, one pinch hitting for the other.

The Pittsburgh Pirates played the New York Yankees in the 1960 World Series, the first Pittsburgh appearance in the Fall Classic since 1927. On

October 13 at Forbes Field in Pittsburgh, the two teams had each won three games. In the top of the ninth inning, the Yankees scored two runs to erase the lead that the Pirates had taken a half inning earlier. Bill Mazeroski stepped to the plate to lead off the bottom of the ninth inning with the score tied at 9-9 and hit Ralph Terry's 1-0 pitch over Yogi Berra's head and over the brick wall in left field to end the game and the Series. This was the fourth game-ending home run in World Series competition but the first to also end the Series. Only one other batter has ended a World Series with a home run, Joe Carter of the Toronto Blue Jays in 1993.

In 1962, the San Francisco Giants played in the Series for the first time since moving from New York and Willie McCovey hit the first home run for the California version of the club on October 5, in the seventh inning of game two against the Yankees. Three days later, Chuck Hiller of the Giants hit a seventh-inning grand slam that put the game out of reach, as the Giants won 7-3. Hiller became the eighth player and first National Leaguer to hit a slam in the World Series.

Yogi Berra hit 12 home runs for the Yankees in nine World Series from 1947 through 1961, thus becoming the second player to hit round-trippers in three decades of Series play, after Joe DiMaggio. Bill Skowron, who had hit seven home runs for the New York Yankees in the World Series between 1955 and 1961, became the second player in history to homer for both leagues in the Series by slugging one for the Los Angeles Dodgers on October 3, 1963, at his old stomping grounds, Yankee Stadium.

In game four of the 1964 Series, played October 11 at Yankee Stadium, Ken Boyer hit a sixth inning grand slam to provide the winning margin for the Redbirds in a 4-3 victory. Boyer became the second National Leaguer in three years to hit a slam in the Series, after seven consecutive American Leaguers had performed the feat. In game six, Joe Pepitone hit a grand slam, thus teaming with Ken Boyer as the second pair of batters to each hit a slam in the same World Series, and the first pair of opponents to do so. In the sixth inning, Roger Maris and Mickey Mantle hit back-to-back drives, only the fourth such pair of consecutive homers in the Series. In game seven, played on October 15, Mickey Mantle hit his third homer of the Series and 18th of his career, which is the record for one batter. Also that day, Ken Boyer of the Cardinals hit a seventh inning homer and his brother Clete of the Yankees hit a home run in the ninth inning to become the only pair of brothers to homer in the same World Series game.

The Baltimore Orioles made their first World Series appearance in 1966 and swept the Los Angeles Dodgers. In the top of the first inning of game one played on October 5, Frank and Brooks Robinson hit back-to-back homers, the first home runs for the Orioles in the Series, to provide the winning margin for Baltimore. Three days later in Baltimore, Paul Blair hit a solo homer in the bottom of the fifth inning to score the only run of the game. The next day, in game four, Frank Robinson drove in the only run of the game by hitting a solo homer in the fourth to win the game and the Series. These were the fifth and sixth times that a batter drove in all the runs of a World Series game with one four-bagger and the only time it has happened twice in the same Series. Frank Robinson, by homering for the Orioles, became the third player to hit a home run for teams in both leagues in the World Series, since he had already hit one for the Cincinnati Reds in 1961.

Jose Santiago of the Boston Red Sox started and lost the first game of the 1967 World Series. In his first at bat in the third inning, Santiago homered off Bob Gibson of the St. Louis Cardinals for the only run Boston scored that day in a 2-1 loss. Santiago became the first pitcher to homer in his first World Series at bat. In game six, played on October 11, Carl Yastrzemski of the Red Sox led off the fourth with a home run and, three batters later, Reggie Smith and Rico Petrocelli hit back-to-back solo homers, the sixth time this feat had been accomplished in the World Series, all by American League players. The Red Sox are the only team to clout three homers in one inning of a World Series game and Dick Hughes, who surrendered the three clouts, also gave one up to Petrocelli in the second inning, to tie Charlie Root in 1932 and Junior Thompson in 1939 with the record for most home runs surrendered in one game in the Series. Hughes had also been taken deep in game two by Yaz, and his total of five surrendered in the Series tied Lew Burdette in 1958 for the most given up in one Series. Roger Maris, who had hit five homers for the New York Yankees in the Series, smacked one for the St. Louis Cardinals on October 9, 1967, to become the fourth player to homer for both leagues in the World Series.

Pitchers Mickey Lolich of the Detroit Tigers and Bob Gibson of the St. Louis Cardinals each hit a home run in the 1968 World Series. For Lolich, it came on his first Series at bat, the second and most recent pitcher to accomplish this, and was his only home run in a 16-year major league career. For Gibson, it was his second career circuit clout in the Series to become the first hurler to hit two in World Series play. This feat is not a surprise, since Gibson hit 24 regular season home runs in his career, the seventh highest total for a hurler all-time.

The post-season changed in 1969, as one of the side effects of that year's expansion into four divisions was to force a second round of games to determine the champion of each league. On the first day of League Championship Series (LCS) play, October 4, 1969, the American League game in Baltimore started at one o'clock, while the National League game in Atlanta started at four o'clock. Frank Robinson of the Orioles hit the first League Championship Series home run while Tony Gonzalez of the Atlanta Braves hit the first round-tripper in the National League Championship Series. In the World Series that year, both Don Buford of the Orioles and Tommie Agee of the New York Mets hit leadoff home runs, the first time that two batters hit leadoff clouts in the same World Series. For Buford, it was his first at bat in the World Series.

On October 3, 1970, Mike Cuellar hit the first grand slam in the history of the League Championship Series while pitching for the Baltimore Orioles, becoming the only pitcher to hit a home run with the bases loaded in the LCS and the first of five pitchers to clout a four-bagger in a League Series. Don Buford followed with a back-to-back homer, the first time that had happened in League Championship Series play. Cuellar hit seven homers in his career but no grand slams and this was his only post-season homer. Dave McNally, who had homered in the fifth and final game of the 1969 World Series, hit a grand slam in the 1970 Series to become the second pitcher to hit two home runs in his World Series career, along with Bob Gibson, and the only pitcher to clout a grand slam in the history of the Fall Classic.

On October 3, 1971, Bob Robertson of the Pittsburgh Pirates hit three home runs off three different San Francisco Giants hurlers in game two of the National League Championship Series, thus becoming the first player to hit three in one LCS game. Robertson hit one more home run in that National League Series and two in the World Series. This record of six in one post-season stood until 2002 when both Troy Glaus of the Anaheim Angels (with seven) and Barry Bonds of the San Francisco Giants (with eight) topped Robertson. Al Kaline hit the first extra inning home run in League Championship Series history on October 7, 1972, in the 11th inning of game one of the American League Series. In the 1972 World Series, Gene Tenace of the Oakland Athletics hit home runs in each of his first two World Series at bats, becoming the first player to accomplish the feat, which was duplicated by Andruw Jones of the Atlanta Braves in 1996.

In game one of the 1973 National League Championship Series, Tom Seaver of the New York Mets had driven in the only run of the game after seven innings. In the bottom of the eighth, Pete Rose of the Cincinnati Reds hit a solo homer off Seaver to tie the score and in the bottom of the ninth, Johnny Bench hit another solo shot to win the game 2-1. Bench's blast was the first game-ending homer in League Championship Series history. In game two of the American League Championship Series, Bert Campaneris of the Oakland Athletics hit the first leadoff home run in the history of LCS play, in a game won by his team 6-3. Two days later, on October 9, Campaneris hit another solo homer, this time in the bottom of the 11th inning, the first time an American Leaguer had ended an LCS game with a four-bagger. On October 8, 1974, Sal Bando of the Athletics won the third game of the American League Championship Series with a solo homer off Baltimore's Jim Palmer and became the first batter to drive in all the runs in League Championship Series game with one home run. Eight days later, Ken Holtzman of the Athletics became the most recent hurler to hit a home run in the World Series when he smacked one in the third inning of game four to provide the first run in a game that he won 5-2.

In game one of the 1975 National League Series, Don Gullett of the Cincinnati Reds pitched a complete-game victory and hit a two-run homer in the fourth inning, his only homer in a nine year major league career. That year's World Series between the Reds and the Boston Red Sox featured two extra-inning games and five one-run contests in one of the most exciting Series in history. In game three of the battle, Bernie Carbo of the Red Sox (who had made his big league debut with Cincinnati) hit a pinch homer in the seventh inning, followed by a two-run blast by Boston's Dwight Evans in the top of the ninth to tie the game at 5-5, which was won in the 10th by the Reds on an unearned run. On October 21, in game six at Fenway Park, Carbo again hit a homer in a pinch, this time a three-run blast into the center field seats that tied the game at six runs each. Carbo was the second and most recent player to hit two pinch homers in one World Series, following Chuck Essegian in 1959. In the bottom of the 12th inning, Boston catcher Carlton Fisk hit a 1-0 pitch down the left field line, and, as the ball flew, Fisk stood near home plate applying body English and waving with his hands, willing the ball to be fair as it reached the wall, and then leaped into the air when it hit the pole for a game-ending home run. This scene was captured accidentally by the television cameraman stationed in the left field scoreboard, as he had been instructed to follow the path of the ball but did not pay attention to that instruction because he was watching a rat at his feet, and kept the camera trained on Fisk and his gyrations, thus providing one of the most famous moments in World Series history. At the time, the 12th inning homer was the latest for a home run in World Series history, a feat surpassed by Geoff Blum of the Chicago White Sox in the 2005 Series with a four-bagger in the 14th inning of game three.

On October 14, 1976, Chris Chambliss of the New York Yankees hit a homer to lead off the bottom of the ninth inning to win the American League Series over the Kansas City Royals. Many in the Yankee Stadium crowd surged onto the field as Chambliss ran the bases, and before he reached the plate, Chambliss, the other players, and the umpires all abandoned the field. Thus, Chambliss hit a home run on which he never completed the circuit as required by the rules. However, American League Vice-President Robert Fishel explained after the game that the umpires did not expect Chambliss to step on home plate under the circumstances, so the run counted and the Yankees went on to the World Series. Only Chambliss and Aaron Boone in 2003 have ended a League Championship Series with a home run. (See chapter 14 for a 2006 update to this note.)

The 1977 National League Series featured grand slams on consecutive days by teammates. In game one on October 4, Ron Cey of the Los Angeles Dodgers hit a game-tying slam in the seventh inning but the Philadelphia Phillies scored two runs in the ninth to win 9-7. This was the first grand slam in National League Championship Series history. The next night, Dusty Baker hit a home run with the bases loaded in the fourth inning that gave the Dodgers a lead that they did not surrender, as they tied the Series with a 7-1 win.

In the 1977 World Series, Reggie Smith of the Dodgers hit three home runs in a losing cause. Combined with the two he hit for the Boston Red Sox in the 1967 Series, Smith became the fifth player to homer for both leagues in the World Series. Another Reggie, named Jackson, hit three homers in one game on October 18. The blasts came on the first pitch Jackson saw in each of three consecutive at bats off three different pitchers, propelling the Yankees to a victory in the Series. His third of the day landed in the center field bleachers, estimated at 450 feet from home plate. Jackson had homered in his last at bat the previous day and walked in his first trip to the plate this day, so he hit four homers in four consecutive at bats over two days. He hit five homers in the Series, which is the record for one World Series, earning the nickname "Mr. October" with this performance. He had also homered for Oakland in the World Series, so his first home run in this Series added his name to the list of players who have homered for two teams in the World Series. Jackson hit round-trippers in three consecutive games in 1977 to tie a record held by many players.

In 1978 Jerry Martin hit the first pinch hit homer in the short history of the League Championship Series on October 4. Martin's teammate on the Philadelphia Phillies, Bake McBride, also hit a homer in a pinch three days later. In game three of the American League Series, October 6, George Brett hit a leadoff homer for the Kansas City Royals. He followed that with two more home runs to become the second player—and first in the American League—to hit three homers in one League Championship Series game. On October 3, 1979, John Lowenstein of the Baltimore Orioles hit the first American League pinch-hit home run in League Championship Series history. The three-run home run, on Lowenstein's first at bat in post-season, was a pinch-hit, extra-inning game-ender, as the Orioles won 6-3.

Graig Nettles of the New York Yankees hit the first inside-the-park home run in post-season since 1929 on October 9, 1980 in game two of the American League Championship Series. Nettles, who had been out of action since July with hepatitis and was playing only his third game since coming back, hit the ball off the right field wall where John Wathan, a catcher playing in the outfield, tried to catch it and then could not retrieve the ball in time to catch Nettles at the plate. In game one of the World Series, played on October 14, Willie Aikens of the Royals in his first Series game hit two

two-run home runs on his birthday. In game four, on October 18, Aikens hit two more homers to become the only player to hit multiple home runs in multiple games of the same World Series. In fact, the only other batters to have more than one multiple-homer game in the World Series are Babe Ruth, Lou Gehrig, Duke Snider, and Mickey Mantle. This was the only time Aikens played in the World Series.

Because of the player strike in 1981, the season was divided into two parts and the division winners of each half played each other in an extra round of playoffs before the League Championship Series. On October 6, the first game of the division playoffs between the Los Angeles Dodgers and the Houston Astros ended with a two-run home run hit by Alan Ashby of Houston in the ninth inning. On October 10, game four between the Montreal Expos and the Philadelphia Phillies was tied at 5-5 in the 10th inning. In the bottom of that frame, George Vukovich pinch hit for Tug McGraw and hit an extra-inning, pinch-hit, game-ending homer.

On October 6, 1982, Paul Molitor hit the second and most recent inside-the-park home run in League Championship Series history when Fred Lynn of the California Angels attempted a shoe-top catch and missed the ball, which rolled to the center field wall. Mike Schmidt of the Philadelphia Phillies hit a solo homer in the first inning on October 4, 1983, that plated the only run of the first game of the National League Championship Series. He was the second player and first National Leaguer to perform this feat in the LCS. Joe Morgan of the Philadelphia Phillies homered in the 1983 World Series having already homered in 1976 for the Cincinnati Reds in the Series to join the list of batters who have homered for two teams in World Series play. The Chicago Cubs hit five home runs in game one of the 1984 National League Championship Series to become the only team to hit five in one LCS game.

Ozzie Smith, the light-hitting shortstop of the St. Louis Cardinals, hit one of the most improbable game-ending home runs of all time on October 14, 1985, in game five of the National League Series. The switch-hitting Smith hit the ball batting left-handed for the first lefty homer of his eight-year career and he had only hit 13 total home runs to that point in his career. On October 8, 1986, Glenn Davis of the Houston Astros hit his only post-season home run with a solo shot that won the first game of the National League Series on his first post-season at bat. Four days later in the American

League Series, it appeared that the California Angels, up 3-1 in the Series over the Boston Red Sox, were going to win and make their first World Series appearance. After eight innings, the Angels led 5-2, but a two-run home run by Don Baylor brought the Red Sox within one run. With two out and a runner on first base, California's relief ace Donnie Moore came out of the bullpen to get the last out, but Dave Henderson, the first batter to face Moore, hit a homer to put the Red Sox in front 6-5. The Angels tied the game but Boston won in 11 innings on a sacrifice fly by Henderson off Moore. Boston won two more games to beat California and Moore never got over the pain of Henderson's home run. On October 15, 1986, Billy Hatcher of the Houston Astros hit a solo homer in the 14th inning of the sixth and final game of the National League Series to tie the contest 4-4. This is the latest inning for a home run in League Championship Series history. The New York Mets won the game in 16 innings, 7-6.

On October 7, 1987, Gary Gaetti hit a home run in his first League Championship Series at bat, which also happened to be his first post-season at bat. Gaetti had also hit a four-bagger in his first major league at bat on September 20, 1981, and he is the only player in history to homer in his first big league at bat and his first post-season at bat. Gaetti smacked another homer in his second at bat in post-season later in the same game. The 1987 World Series featured grand slams by teammates for only the second time in history. On October 17, the Minnesota Twins beat the St. Louis Cardinals in game one 10-1, and Dan Gladden hit a bases-loaded home run in the fourth inning. Seven days later, Kent Hrbek hit a sixth-inning grand slam as part of another one-sided Twins victory. This is the most recent occasion when two teammates each hit a grand slam in the same World Series.

The Los Angeles Dodgers and the Oakland Athletics traded game-ending home runs in the 1988 World Series. In the first game, Oakland was leading 4-3 in the bottom of the ninth inning with two out and a runner on base. Kirk Gibson, the Dodgers' team leader, limped to the plate on two bad legs to pinch hit. Gibson did not start the game because of his ailments and was unlikely to play the next day. It was painful to watch him move from the dugout to home plate. Dennis Eckersley, the closer for the Athletics, took Gibson to a 3-2 count when Gibson hit a line drive into the right field seats with nothing more than an upper-body and arm swing to win the game

5-4 in very dramatic fashion. As he limped around the bases, Gibson continually pumped his arms in celebration of the victory, one of the most memorable World Series moments of all time and Gibson's only appearance in the Series that year. He had already hit home runs for the 1984 Detroit Tigers, thus Gibson became the sixth player in history to homer in the World Series for both leagues. In game three of the 1988 Series, Mark McGwire of the Athletics ended the only game won by Oakland with a solo home run, McGwire's only World Series homer.

Will Clark of the San Francisco Giants hit two home runs in one game on October 4, 1989, off Greg Maddux of the Chicago Cubs. Clark's homers in consecutive at bats in consecutive innings, the second with the bases loaded, came in game one of the National League Championship Series and turned a close contest into a one-sided game. That year's World Series between the Giants and the Oakland Athletics was interrupted for 12 days by a severe earthquake that struck the Bay Area. On October 27, the first game after the delay, Oakland hit five home runs in the game to become the second and most recent team to clout five in one World Series game after the 1928 New York Yankees. In game four of the Series, swept by Oakland, Rickey Henderson of the Athletics led off the game with a round-tripper. Henderson is the career regular-season leader for leadoff home runs with 81, but this is his only post-season leadoff blast. Dave Henderson hit two homers in the 1989 World Series for Oakland having already hit two circuit drives for the Boston Red Sox.

Lonnie Smith of the Atlanta Braves hit home runs in three consecutive games in the 1991 World Series to tie a record held by six other players. In the sixth game of that Series, Kirby Puckett of the Minnesota Twins hit a game-ending home run at the Metrodome in Minneapolis as the first batter to face Charlie Leibrandt of the Atlanta Braves to start the 11th inning. This tied the Series at three games each and the Twins won game seven 1-0 with a bases-loaded single in the 10th inning the next day. This was the third extra-inning contest in the 1991 Series. In the 1992 World Series, Smith became the third and most recent National League player to hit a grand slam in the Series. The fifth-inning blast broke up a close game and helped the Braves beat the Blue Jays 7-2. Lenny Dykstra hit four home runs for the 1993 Philadelphia Phillies in the World Series, having already hit two in

1986 for the New York Mets. In game six of the 1993 Series, Dykstra clouted a home run as part of a five-run seventh inning in which the Phillies took the lead 6-5. In the bottom of the ninth inning, the Toronto Blue Jays had two runners on base and one man out when Joe Carter hit a 2-2 slider off Mitch Williams over the left field fence to end the game and the World Series, the second time a batter had hit a Series-ending home run. As he jumped up and down while running to and past first base, he missed the bag and had to back up to touch it before continuing on his joyous journey.

◆   ◆   ◆

In 1994, baseball added a third round to the playoff structure by creating three divisions and a wild card in each league, but when the season was cancelled on August 11, the new playoff format had to wait until 1995 for its first appearance. Tony Pena of the Cleveland Indians hit an extra-inning game-ending homer in the 13th inning on October 3, 1995, to beat the Boston Red Sox and the next day Jim Leyritz of the New York Yankees hit a game-ender in the 15th inning to beat the Seattle Mariners. Mark Lewis of the Cincinnati Reds hit the first grand slam and the first pinch-hit home run in Division Series play on one swing in the sixth inning on October 6 as part of a 10-1 Reds victory. Ken Griffey Jr. of the Mariners hit five home runs in the five game series with the Yankees, including two in the first game. That Mariners/Yankees series turned into a slugfest as each team clouted 11 home runs, the record for one Division Series. The Houston Astros also hit 11 in their 2004 Division Series. In game six of the 1995 World Series, David Justice of the Atlanta Braves hit a sixth-inning solo home run to plate the only run of the game and win the Series for the Braves over the Indians. The last time one homer had driven in all runs of a World Series game was in 1966 when Paul Blair and Frank Robinson performed the feat on consecutive days and Justice is the most recent player to do this. Eddie Murray hit a two-run homer in the second game of the World Series for the Indians, thus becoming the 15th player to hit a circuit clout for two different teams in the Series. Murray also became the third player to homer in three decades of World Series competition, as he had homered for the Baltimore Orioles in 1979 and 1983. Ryan Klesko of the Braves homered in three consecutive games of the World Series to tie a record held by six other players.

In the four-game 1996 Division Series between the Texas Rangers and the New York Yankees, Juan Gonzalez of the Rangers hit five home runs to tie Ken Griffey Jr. for the most homers in a Division Series. Gonzalez homered in all four games with two home runs in game two. Nineteen-year-old rookie Andruw Jones of the Atlanta Braves made his first World Series appearance just two months after his major league debut in 1996. On his first Series at bat, he hit a two-run homer in the second inning and then batted again in the third inning when he hit a three-run home run. Jones became the second and most recent batter to hit home runs in each of his first two World Series at bats.

When Sandy Alomar of the Cleveland Indians homered in the 1997 post-season, he joined his brother, Roberto, to become the third pair of brothers to each hit home runs in the post-season. On September 30, 1997, in game one of an American League Division Series, Tim Raines, Derek Jeter, and Paul O'Neill of the New York Yankees hit three consecutive home runs. This is the only time that three batters hit home runs in any post-season game back-to-back-to-back. After 10 innings in game six of the American League Championship Series on October 15, the Cleveland Indians and Baltimore Orioles had not scored any runs in the game. In fact, the Indians had been held to two hits in the contest. In the top of the 11th inning, Tony Fernandez of Cleveland hit a solo home run to plate the only run of the game and win the series for the Indians. In the 1997 World Series, both Darren Daulton and Jim Eisenreich hit a home run in game three for the Florida Marlins. They had each hit a four-bagger for the Philadelphia Phillies in the 1993 World Series and so became part of the short list of players who have hit home runs in the Series for two teams. The next day, Matt Williams of the Cleveland Indians clouted a homer to go with the home run he had hit for the San Francisco Giants in 1989. Williams became the seventh batter to hit a home run in the World Series for both leagues and the 18th player to homer for two different clubs.

In 1998 the Atlanta Braves, in the midst of their perennial post-season appearance string, hit two grand slams in the Division Series against the Chicago Cubs. In game one, Ryan Klesko put the game out of reach with his seventh-inning blast, and in the last game of the three-game sweep, Eddie

Perez hit a home run with the bases loaded in the seventh inning. On October 13, 1999, Bernie Williams of the New York Yankees hit a 10th-inning, game-ending home run in the first game of the American League Series, the second time that Williams had hit a game-ender in a League Championship Series game. In game one of the 1996 American League Series, Williams had smacked an 11th-inning solo shot. He is the only batter who has hit two game-ending homers in League Championship play and only David Ortiz of the Boston Red Sox has also hit multiple game-enders in post-season, both in 2004.

In the 2001 American League Championship Series, Stan Javier homered for the Seattle Mariners. His father, Julian Javier, had hit a round-tripper in the 1967 World Series for the St. Louis Cardinals. On October 28, 2001, at Bank One Ballpark in Phoenix, Matt Williams of the Arizona Diamondbacks accomplished a feat that no other batter in history has performed before or since by hitting a World Series home run for his third different team. In 1989, Williams homered for the San Francisco Giants and in 1997 he clouted one for the Cleveland Indians. Williams hit just three home runs in World Series competition for three different teams and is one of four to homer in three decades of World

> *In game five of the 1999 National League Championship Series, the Braves had taken a 3-2 lead in the top of the 15th inning. However, after an intentional walk to load the bases in the bottom of the inning, Todd Pratt walked to push across the tying run for the Mets and Robin Ventura came to the plate with a chance to win the game. Ventura hit a Kevin McGlinchy pitch over the right-centerfield fence for an apparent game-ending grand slam. However, once each base runner had advanced one base, thus scoring the winning run, Pratt turned and ran toward Ventura to give him a big hug.*
>
> *Ventura had rounded first base and was advancing toward second in his home run trot and kept motioning to the other runners to keep going. Since each runner only advanced the one bag, Ventura is officially credited with an RBI-single. It would have been the first game-ending grand slam in the history of post-season play.*

Series games along with Joe DiMaggio, Yogi Berra, and Eddie Murray.

In 2002, Adam Kennedy of the Anaheim Angels hit three home runs in the fifth and deciding game of the American League Championship Series to match the record total for one League Championship Series game of Bob Robertson in 1971 and George Brett in 1978. In the National League Series that year, the St. Louis Cardinals recorded pinch-hit home runs on consecutive days. The first came in game one off the bat of J. D. Drew and the second in game two was hit by Eduardo Perez. Neither solo shot affected the outcome of the game, as the San Francisco Giants won both contests and the Series. This was the second and most recent time that a team hit two pinch homers in the same League Championship Series, as the Philadelphia Phillies had first accomplished this in 1978. The Giants lost to the Angels in the World Series in 2002 while hitting 14 home runs in the Fall Classic. Barry Bonds of the Giants hit a home run in his first Series at bat and in each of the first three games to tie a record held by many players. He hit eight homers for the entire 2002 post-season, setting a record for one year. The Giants as a team hit 27 in the three 2002 post-season series, also a record.

On October 4, 2003, in game three of an American League Division Series, the Boston Red Sox and the Oakland Athletics were tied 1-1 in the bottom of the 11th inning at Fenway Park. Trot Nixon pinch hit and clouted the 1-1 pitch into the center field seats to win the game with a pinch-hit, extra-inning, game-ending home run. In the seventh game of the American League Championship Series, the New York Yankees tied the contest with the Boston Red Sox in the bottom of the eighth inning and forced the game into extra innings. In the bottom of the 11th frame, Aaron Boone poked the first pitch down the left field line and into the seats at Yankee Stadium to win the game and Series. Boone became the second and most recent batter to end a League Series with a home run and made the Boone family the most prolific home run family in post-season. Bob Boone had homered in two different League Championship Series and Aaron's older brother, Bret, had socked one in the 2001 LCS. They are the only family with three members who have each hit a home run in post-season. (See chapter 14 for a 2006 update concerning ending an LCS with a home run.) In the 2003 National League Championship Series, the Chicago Cubs hit 13 home runs but lost to the Florida Marlins in seven games. The Cubs set a record for most home runs in one League Championship Series by a team, beating the previous mark of 10 set by the 1992 Toronto Blue Jays and the 1996 New York Yankees. The record would fall again in 2004 when the Houston Astros hit 14. Carlos Beltran of the Astros hit eight home runs in the 2004 post-season to tie the record set by Barry Bonds in 2002. David Ortiz, the designated hitter of the Boston Red Sox, hit an extra-inning, game-ending, and series-ending home run on October 8, 2004, in the Division Series against the Anaheim Angels that completed a three-game sweep by Boston. Nine days later, Ortiz hit another extra-inning, game-ending homer, this time in the 12th inning of game four of the American League Championship Series against the New York Yankees. Ortiz is the only batter to hit two game-ending home runs in the same post-season, and they both came in extra innings. In the World Series, Manny Ramirez of the Red Sox homered in game three of the four-game sweep of the St. Louis Cardinals to become the 19th player to hit a World Series home run for two different clubs. Ramirez had hit three homers for the Cleveland Indians in 1995 and 1997.

The 2005 post-season featured home runs in late innings. In the Division Series between the Houston Astros and the Atlanta Braves, Brad Ausmus of the Astros hit a two-out solo home run in the bottom of the ninth inning of game four to send the contest into extra innings. Nine innings later, Chris Burke hit a home run into the left field seats at Minute Maid Park to end the 18-inning contest in the latest inning a post-season home run has ever been hit and win the League Division Series for Houston. In game three of the World Series, Geoff Blum of the Chicago White Sox entered the game in the 13th inning as part of a double-switch. In the top of the 14th frame in his first World Series at bat, Blum hit a solo shot that eventually won the game for the Pale Hose. Blum, who had had only one at bat in the previous two series that post-season, set the record for the latest home run in World Series competition, breaking the old mark of the 12th inning set by Carlton Fisk in 1975 and Alex Gonzalez in 2003. The record for League Championship Series play is also the 14th inning, set by Billy Hatcher in 1986.

10
THE DESIGNATED HITTER ERA

On January 11, 1973, at a joint meeting in Chicago, the owners of the 24 major league clubs voted the most radical change to the game of baseball since 1903 when the foul ball was ruled a strike. The American League teams would, for three years starting in 1973, use a "designated pinch hitter," whose only duty would be to hit for the pitcher without that pitcher having to be removed from the lineup. This, in effect, changed the American League lineup from nine to 10 players, contrary to the definition of the game in the official rules. It also meant that the two leagues would play the game using different rules on the field, a difference that is still in place because the three-year experiment has turned into a permanent situation. This change has affected the home run greatly, as many of the regular designated hitters through the years have been sluggers who might not have played without the creation of the "10th man" in the Junior Circuit.

This rule substitutes a strong-hitting player for a weak-hitting pitcher, with the effect of increasing offense in general and home runs in particular from that place in the batting order. In general, the designated hitter has been a slugger rather than a singles hitter, as shown by the fact that, since 1973, only first basemen have had a higher home run production rate among the various defensive positions (understanding that designated hitter is not a defensive position). Table 10.1 shows the breakdown of the production rate by position. For the period 1973 through 2005, first basemen have the highest home run production, hitting 16.4 home runs for each 500 plate

Table 10.1 – Home Run Production Rate by Position (1973–2005)

Position	Production
1B	16.4
DH	15.8
RF	15.6
LF	14.1
3B	13.0
C	11.4
CF	10.9
PH	8.6
2B	7.0
SS	6.5
P	1.8

appearances, while designated hitters place second with 15.8 homers.

The top four defensive positions in the table (first base, right field, left field, and third base) are the players positioned along either foul line, and the positions in the bottom half of the list (shortstop, second base, center field, and catcher) are positioned in the center of the field. Baseball people traditionally consider the players in the latter positions primarily defensive rather than offensive, and the accuracy of this conventional wisdom shows in the table. Of course, there is the question of which of these concepts caused the other. Plate appearance numbers by position back to 1876 for players are not available, so a complete analysis of this type cannot be done at this time.

Another note of interest in the table is the 8.6 home run production rate for pinch hitters. This means that a pinch hitter has a better chance to clout a four-bagger than a second baseman or shortstop and certainly has more chance than a pitcher.

One strange quirk in the interpretation of the scoring rules creates an occasional player who bats without having a defensive position. This is not a batter who comes to the plate in the top of the first inning, as he is assumed to have the position listed on the lineup card. There have been 10 times in history in which a pinch hitter has batted twice in the same inning and homered the second time. Such a batter is considered officially to have no defensive position because he pinch hit the first time at bat but bats for himself the second. Table 10.2 lists these batters with the indicator "(H)" before their names. The other way to hit without a position is to pinch run and then bat later in the same inning. Table 10.2 also lists the eight batters in this category who have homered with the indicator "(R)" before their names.

The first home run by a designated hitter came on April 6, 1973, the first day of the season, when Tony Oliva of the Minnesota Twins hit a two-run blast with one out in the top of the first inning at Oakland-Alameda County Stadium off Catfish Hunter. The Twins never surrendered that lead,

Table 10.2 – Players Who Homered with No Defensive Position

Date	Batter	Team (League)
04/14/1925	(R) Pat McNulty	Cleveland (AL)
06/10/1952	(R) Al Zarilla	Chicago (AL)
06/06/1953	(R) Johnny Temple	Cincinnati (NL)
07/18/1953	(H) Wayne Belardi	Brooklyn (NL)
07/29/1953	(R) Fred Marsh	Chicago (AL)
04/21/1958	(H) Frank House	Kansas City (AL)
07/13/1959	(R) Gene Stephens	Boston (AL)
07/22/1970	(H) Von Joshua	Los Angeles (NL)
07/04/1971	(H) Jim Lefebvre	Los Angeles (NL)
07/01/1973	(R) Dave Kingman	San Francisco (NL)
05/31/1975	(H) Cliff Johnson	Houston (NL)
08/14/1982	(H) Bill Robinson	Philadelphia (NL)
07/06/1986	(H) Jeff Stone	Philadelphia (NL)
04/08/1993	(H) Alvaro Espinoza	Cleveland (AL)
06/25/1995	(H) John Cangelosi	Houston (NL)
05/09/1996	(H) Willie McGee	St. Louis (NL)
09/30/2000	(R) Ryan Christenson	Oakland (AL)
04/18/2001	(R) Darren Lewis	Boston (AL)

(H) – pinch hit earlier in the inning
(R) – pinch ran earlier in the inning

and they won the game, 8-3, over the eventual World Series champions. Frank Robinson of the California Angels hit the most home runs as a designated hitter in 1973 with 26 (he also hit three as a left fielder and one as a pinch hitter that season to tie for second in the league), and Orlando Cepeda hit the second-most as a designated hitter that season with his 20 for the Boston Red Sox, his complete season output. Robinson led the league again in 1974 with 20 homers as a designated hitter, with none at any other position. Jim Rice of the Boston Red Sox hit 31 home runs as a designated hitter in 1977 out of 39 total, the first player to reach the 30 mark as a DH and the first to lead the league while primarily a designated hitter. David Ortiz, also of the Red Sox, hit 43 of his 47 as a DH in 2005 to become the first designated hitter to top 40 in one season. Edgar Martinez of the Seattle Mariners hit 243 of 309 career clouts as a DH, the most of any player, and is a clear case of a player who might not have played as long as he did without the DH. Martinez played 1,403 of his career 2,055 career games as a designated hitter, with 563 at third base, and 28 at first base.

Figure 10.1 shows the home run production rate for the first 21 years of the designated hitter era. The rate is generally between 8.9 and 10.7 home runs per 500 plate appearances for the major leagues during this time, which is about the same as that for the late 1960s and early 1970s, after the higher offensive period that ended in 1966. However, the 1973

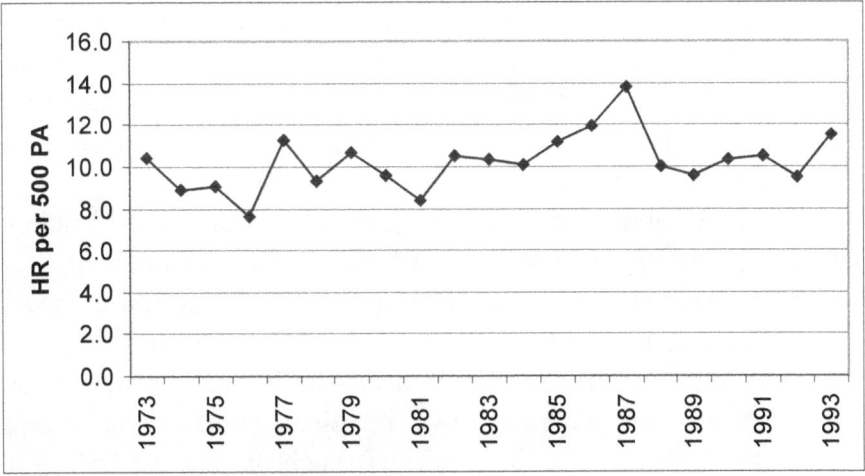

Figure 10.1 – Home Run Production Rate (1973–93)

rate of 10.4 reflected a jump from the previous year's 9.1 production rate, a fairly large increase but not nearly the largest increase between two seasons, which was the 3.7 increase from 1976 to 1977. The American League, with its new designated hitters, showed a larger increase in 1973 than their colleagues in the National League, as the Junior Circuit hitters increased production from 8.5 to 10.4, while the National League hitters increased from 9.6 to 10.4. The American League rate matched that of the National League in 1973 and then was higher than the NL rate every year through 2000.

In 1973 Willie Stargell of the Pittsburgh Pirates led the majors with 44 home runs. He was followed by three Atlanta Braves: Davey Johnson (43), Darrell Evans (41), and Hank Aaron (40). The three Atlanta sluggers became the first trio of teammates to each hit 40 home runs in the same season, a feat duplicated by the 1996 and 1997 Colorado Rockies. Reggie Jackson of the Oakland Athletics led the American League with 32 clouts. On July 13, 1973, Hal Breeden of the Montreal Expos pinch hit for Boots Day in the first game of a double header and hit a solo home run. In game two he again smacked a pinch-hit homer, this time hitting for the pitcher, to become the second and most recent batter to hit pinch homers in both games of a twin bill. Joe Cronin had accomplished this feat in 1943. Bobby Bonds of the San Francisco Giants hit 11 leadoff home runs in 1973 to set a new single-season record in that category, which would stand until 1996, when Brady Anderson would top it. Bonds broke the record of six held by many players. On July 3, 1973, the Cleveland Indians hosted the Detroit Tigers at Municipal Stadium, and the opposing starting pitchers were brothers, Jim (Tigers) and Gaylord (Indians) Perry. Norm Cash hit two home runs off Gaylord, while Jim surrendered four-baggers to Charlie Spikes and Oscar Gamble. Frank Robinson passed Mickey Mantle on July 17, 1973, to take fifth place on the career home run list, and on August 17 he passed Harmon Killebrew for fourth place. Robinson would remain fourth on the all-time list until June 5, 2002.

Hank Aaron became the second player to hit 700 career home runs on July 21, 1973, when he clouted a two-run drive into the left center field seats at Atlanta Stadium. An 18-year-old fan caught the ball, and the Braves gave him 700 silver dollars in exchange for the sphere, which the fan presented to Aaron. Babe Ruth, the only other player to hit 700 home runs to this point, had hit his on July 13, 1934, when Aaron was five-months old. Ruth hit his 700 homers in 8,173 at bats while it took Aaron 11,145 at bats to reach the mark. (Refer to Appendix A for details of each home run number 700.) Aaron had joined the list of top-five home run sluggers on June 2, 1969, by passing Ted Williams and moved into third place by the end of July. He moved past Willie Mays in 1972 to take second place on the list. At 9:07 p.m. on April 8, 1974, Hank Aaron hit his 715th career home run into the left center field bullpen at Atlanta Stadium off Al Downing of the Los Angeles Dodgers to pass Babe Ruth on the all-time career list. During his pursuit of 715, Aaron had received hate mail and death threats from people who did not want a black player to break Ruth's record, but Aaron went about his work as he always had, quietly and efficiently. After he touched home plate, his parents came out of the seats to greet him, and his mother hugged him and would not let go, fearing that someone might try to kill her son at that moment. Even the baseball commissioner had caused Aaron some trouble, when, after the Braves announced that he would not play in the opening series in Cincinnati (to give him the chance to tie Ruth at home in Atlanta), Bowie Kuhn ordered the Braves to play him in approximately two of every three games as they had in 1973. Aaron hit number 714 in Cincinnati on Opening Day to tie the Babe, sat out the second game, and played in the third game as ordered, but without hitting the record-breaking homer. In the Atlanta home opener, before a national television audience, Aaron slugged his homer in the fourth inning, with politicians and entertainers in attendance to celebrate, but no commissioner present.

On October 2, 1974, Aaron hit his 733rd and final National League home run, all of them slugged for the Braves in Milwaukee and Atlanta. The next two seasons he hit 22 home runs for the Milwaukee Brewers in the American League, returning to the city in which he started his career. All of his American League four-baggers came as a designated hitter. Babe Ruth, whom Aaron passed on the all-time career list for homers, also returned to his initial big league city to finish his career in the other league. The Babe started with the Boston Red Sox in the American League and ended with the Boston Braves in the National League. (Jimmie Foxx also ended in the same city but the other league.) Aaron hit 245 home runs after his 35th birthday to top Babe Ruth's record in that category, just as his 755 topped Ruth's 714. Among the 245 homers, Aaron hit 40 in 1973 at the age of 39. He hit at least 20 home runs in 20 consecutive seasons from 1955 through 1974, which is the record, and he hit at least 10 homers in 23 consecutive years from 1954 through 1976, also a record. Aaron led the National League in home runs four times and hit 17 round-trippers off pitcher Don Drysdale, which is the third highest total for one batter off one pitcher, behind Duke Snider's 19 off Robin Roberts and the 18 Willie Mays hit off Warren Spahn. Aaron collected his 3,000th hit on May 17, 1970, and, combined with his 500 home runs, he became the first to reach these two milestones. Willie Mays joined Aaron on July 18, 1970, and they remained the only two to achieve this feat until 1996, when Eddie Murray joined them. Rafael Palmeiro has since also accomplished this.

For the first time since 1952, no batter hit 40 home runs in 1974, as Mike Schmidt of the Philadelphia Phillies led the National League with 36 and Dick Allen of the Chicago White Sox hit 32 in the American League. This lack of a 40-homer hitter continued through 1976, the year that tallied the lowest production rate since 1946. In 1975, Schmidt again led the Senior Circuit by hitting 38 homers and Reggie Jackson of the Oakland Athletics and George Scott of the Milwaukee Brewers led the American League with 36. Dave Kingman of the New York Mets placed second in the National League with 36 circuit drives.

Mike Schmidt led the National League for the third consecutive season in 1976 by smacking 38 home runs with Dave Kingman one behind at 37. In the American League, Graig Nettles of the New York Yankees hit 32 to lead that circuit. No one had led the National League for three consecutive seasons since Ralph Kiner from 1946 through 1952. Schmidt hit four home runs in one game at Chicago's Wrigley Field on April 17, 1976. He had already had two at bats in the game before he hit his first homer, and then he hit the quartet in the fifth, seventh, eighth, and 10th innings as Schmidt became the third and most recent batter to use extra innings to complete a four-homer game, following fellow Phillie Chuck Klein in 1936 and Pat Seerey in 1948. The first two homers came off Rick Reuschel and the last off his brother, Paul. The Phillies overcame a 12-1 deficit to beat the Chicago Cubs, 18-16, as the teams combined for nine home runs among the 43 hits that day.

When the Reuschels each surrendered home runs to Schmidt on April 17, they became the second pair of brothers to surrender homers to the same batter in the same game. The only previous time this had happened was in 1922, when Rogers Hornsby of the St. Louis Cardinals hit a pair off Virgil and Jesse Barnes of the New York Giants. On August 26, 1976, the Reuschels surrendered home runs in the same game for the second time in the season. However, this time different batters took them deep. The Reuschels performed this feat a third time on May 5, 1977, again to different batters. On May 29, 1976, Phil (Atlanta Braves) and Joe (Houston Astros) Niekro faced each other in a game at Fulton County Stadium in Georgia. Jim Wynn of the Braves hit a round-tripper off Joe Niekro in the eighth inning in a losing cause. In the seventh frame, Joe had hit his only career home run off brother Phil to tie the game, won by the Astros (and Joe), 4-3. This was the third time that the Niekros had each surrendered a home run in the same game, and each time Joe pitched for a different team. While Phil continued with the Braves, Joe had pitched for the Chicago Cubs, the San Diego Padres, and the Astros. Rick and Paul Reuschel also performed this feat three times in their career.

At the end of the 1976 season, Billy Williams retired with 426 home runs to place 15th on the all-time list and eighth among left-handed batters. Williams hit at least 20 homers in 13 consecutive seasons from 1961 through 1973, and although he never led the league, he placed in the top five seven times, including second three times. He and teammate Ron Santo hit home runs in the same game 64 times, the fifth-highest total for any pair of teammates.

In 1977 the largest increase in home run production in one year occurred, as the rate jumped from 7.6 home runs per 500 plate appearances in 1976 to 11.3 in 1977, an increase of 3.7. The primary reason for this increase likely is the fact that the Rawlings Sporting Goods Company became the official supplier of baseballs to the major leagues for that season, replacing the Spalding Company, which had supplied baseballs since the start of the National League in 1876 (although Rawlings manufactured the balls for Spalding from 1968 through 1973). Figure 10.1 shows that for the three years that Spalding made their own baseballs from 1974 through 1976, the home run production rate dropped from the rate during the short period when Rawlings made the Spalding major league ball to the lowest level in 30 years. Spalding machine-wound the yarn onto the core at their plant in Massachusetts and then shipped the balls to Haiti to have the covers stitched on by hand. Shipping the half-completed baseballs from New England to the Caribbean evidently affected the quality of the product, which lost some of its tightness in the yarn winding during the trip to the island, likely because of the radical change in climate. Rawlings performed the entire manufacturing process in Haiti, thus preventing the decompression of the ball caused by travel and producing a livelier baseball that met the Major League specifications. The last years of Spalding balls were below standards, with manufacturing defects, such as loose covers and softer overall composition, often noted by players. This drop in ball quality probably caused the drop in home run production during that period, and Rawlings, eager to prove themselves with their new contract, used exact quality control standards to ensure that the baseball met the specifications of Major League Baseball, thus producing a livelier ball than the last few years of Spalding-manufactured balls.

The American League expanded by two teams in 1977, as the Seattle Mariners and Toronto Blue Jays joined the circuit, thus increasing the league to 14 teams. The Mariners played indoors at the Kingdome and Joe Rudi of the California Angels hit the first American League home run indoors in the third inning on Opening Day off Diego Segui, as the Angels beat the Mariners, 7-0. For the first time since 1965, a batter slugged 50 home runs in a season in 1977, as George Foster of the Cincinnati Reds hit 52 to lead the National League. (Refer to Appendix B for details of each home run number 50 in history.) Jeff Burroughs of the Atlanta Braves hit 41 home runs to place second in the league, while Jim Rice of the Boston Red Sox led the American League with 39 circuit drives. Dave Kingman started the season with the New York Mets, his team for the past two years. After hitting nine home runs for the National League East Division team, the Mets traded Kingman to the San Diego Padres on June 15. While playing in the National League West Division, Kingman socked 11 homers but then, on September 6, he was claimed by the California Angels on waivers. While with the American League West Division team, he hit two more home runs and then on September 15, the Angels sold his contract to the New York Yankees. Kingman clouted four home runs for the American

League East Division club, thus homering in all four divisions in one season, the only player to accomplish this feat during the 25 years of four-division play.

Willie Stargell, who played his entire career with the Pittsburgh Pirates, hit his 400th home run on June 29, 1977, at Busch Stadium in St. Louis, to become the 17th player to reach that mark. Stargell, who finished his career 14th on the all-time list tied with Stan Musial with 475 home runs, led the National League in home runs twice. From 1971 through 1980, Stargell hit the third-most homers in the majors with 276, behind Reggie Jackson (310) and Mike Schmidt (283). Stargell hit the first home run at Shea Stadium, New York, and is tied with Schmidt as the all-time leader among visitors at Shea with 26 clouts. He led the 1979 Pirates with three homers as they won the World Series, hitting the go-ahead home run in game seven against the Baltimore Orioles.

The same two batters led their respective leagues again in 1978, as Jim Rice hit 46 and George Foster hit 40. On September 12, 1978, Ron Fairly of the California Angels hit the 215th and last home run of his career at Arlington Stadium in Texas.

> *Two families* have had three generations hit home runs in the major leagues. Gus Bell and his son, Buddy, have been joined by Buddy's two sons, Mike and David, as big league home run hitters. Mike's first home run on October 2, 1990 made the Bells the first family to achieve the distinction. Ray Boone and his son, Bob, have been joined by Bob two's sons, Bret and Aaron on the major league home run list. Each of the Boones have hit at least 100 home runs in the big leagues.

Fairly had hit his first major league four-bagger 20 years to the day earlier as a member of the Los Angeles Dodgers at Forbes Field in Pittsburgh.

On June 30, 1978, Willie McCovey hit his 500th career home run to become the twelfth slugger to join the exclusive club and the first since 1971. McCovey had played most of his career for the San Francisco Giants, with whom he hit homer number 500, but had also played for the San Diego Padres and 11 games in the American League with the Oakland Athletics, for whom he hit no home runs. He finished with 521 home runs, at the time the third most in the National League, to tie Ted Williams in eighth place on the career list and was the active home run leader at his retirement in July 1980. McCovey and Williams had hit the second-most home runs of any left-handed slugger in history, behind only Babe Ruth at that time. McCovey had hit more home runs as a San Francisco Giant than any other player, with 469, a mark that was topped by Barry Bonds. On April 12, 1973, McCovey hit two home runs in one inning of a game, a feat that he repeated on June 27, 1977. At the time, he was the only player to have accomplished this twice in his career, but Andre Dawson has since done this on July 30, 1978, and September 24, 1985. McCovey led the National League in home runs three times in his career and hit at least 30 homers in six consecutive years from 1965 through 1970. He hit 18 grand slams, second only to Lou Gehrig at the time but since passed by Eddie Murray and Manny Ramirez. However, those 18 are still the most in National League history. He and long-time teammate Willie Mays hit home runs in the same game 68 times, third best behind Hank Aaron/Eddie Mathews and Babe Ruth/Lou Gehrig.

The Boston Red Sox hosted the New York Yankees at Fenway Park in a one-game playoff to determine the champion of the American League East Division on October 2, 1978. Carl Yastrzemski had hit a homer down the right field line that just stayed fair in the second inning to give Boston an early lead. With two out and two runners on in the top of the seventh inning, Bucky Dent faced Mike Torrez. Dent fouled the second pitch off his foot, and while he was treated by the trainer, on-deck hitter Mickey Rivers noticed a crack in the bat and retrieved another for Dent. Dent hit a wind-aided fly ball that barely cleared the top of the left field wall into the netting atop it to put the Yankees in front, 3-2. One batter later, Bob Stanley came into the game for Boston and gave up two more runs, including an eighth-inning homer to Reggie Jackson, that the Red Sox could not overcome with their late-inning rally as the Yankees won the game and the division, 5-4. Years later Dent ran a baseball school in Florida where the left field fence on the main field had a green wall with a painted scoreboard that showed the exact game situation when Dent hit his home run, one of only 40 in his career. That fly ball earned Dent an unprintable nickname throughout New England that persists to this day.

Dave Kingman vaulted to the top of the National League home run list in 1979 while playing for the Chicago Cubs as he hit 48 long balls.

Mike Schmidt of the Philadelphia Phillies placed second with 45, and Gorman Thomas of the Milwaukee Brewers led the American League with 45 home runs. As part of Kingman's league-leading total, he hit three home runs in one game twice during the season to become the sixth player to achieve this, although Johnny Mize had done this twice in his career.

On August 18, 1979, Fergie Jenkins of the Texas Rangers surrendered two home runs in a 7-3 win over the Milwaukee Brewers at County Stadium. The first of the pair, a solo shot in the third inning by Don Money, made Jenkins the third hurler in history to surrender 400 gopher balls. In his career, Jenkins surrendered a total of 484 homers to place second on the all-time list and led his league seven times. He hit 13 of his own, including six in 1971 for the Chicago Cubs.

Mike Schmidt led the National League again in 1980 by hitting 48 home runs, his career high, for the Phillies. Schmidt broke Eddie Mathews's record for most home runs in a season by a third baseman, set in 1953. Reggie Jackson of the New York Yankees and Ben Oglivie of the Milwaukee Brewers each hit 41 homers to lead the American League. In the strike-shortened 1981 season, only Mike Schmidt hit over 30 home runs, as he led the National League for the fifth time with 31 clouts. Four players in the American League tied for the lead with 22 homers: Tony Armas of the Oakland Athletics, Dwight Evans of the Boston Red Sox, Bobby Grich of the California Angels, and Eddie Murray of the Baltimore Orioles. After a home run production rate in 1981 lower than any since 1976, the production increased to above 10.0 in 1982, where it remained for seven years. Reggie Jackson, in his first year with the California Angels, and Gorman Thomas of the Milwaukee Brewers led the American League with 39 homers, while Dave Kingman of the New York Mets topped the Senior Circuit with 37. Jackson's teammate, Doug DeCinces, had two three-homer games in a six-day period in August. Bob

> *On May 28, 1981,* Steve Henderson of the Cubs singled to center field in the fourth inning of a game at Wrigley Field. Shortly after that, Pirates catcher Tony Pena picked him off first base and while diving back to the bag, Henderson broke his right hand. In the fifth inning, he homered to left with one man on, two men out, and one broken hand.

Horner of the Braves hit 25 of his 32 homers at Atlanta-Fulton County Stadium, the second highest percentage at home for any batter with 30 in a season. Only Ken Williams in 1922 had a higher percentage.

Mike Schmidt hit 40 in 1983 to top the National League again, while runner-up Dale Murphy of the Atlanta Braves, who hit 36 for the season, also stole 30 bases, to become the sixth player to have a 30/30 season. Carl Yastrzemski of the Red Sox retired after the 1983 season with 3,419 hits and 452 home runs. In 1979 he hit his 400th homer and collected his 3,000th hit to become the fourth player (and first in the American League) with those career totals, joining Stan Musial, Hank Aaron, and Willie Mays in that group. Yaz hit home runs in 23 consecutive seasons from 1961 through 1983 and won the Triple Crown in 1967. When he retired, he was 17th on the career home run list.

◆ ◆ ◆

On July 24, 1983, one of the strangest dramas ever involving a home run played out at Yankee Stadium in New York. With two out in the top of the ninth inning, George Brett of the Kansas City Royals hit a two-run homer off Rich Gossage to give the visitors a 5-4 lead. Minutes later, while Brett sat in the dugout after running the circuit, New York skipper Billy Martin protested that the bat was illegal, and the umpires, after consultation, called Brett out for having pine tar on his bat higher than is allowed by rule 1.10. Thus the score reverted back to 4-3 and the game was over, with the Yankees as the winners. Home plate umpire Tim McClelland, while holding the bat, called Brett out for violating the rule, and Brett charged out of the dugout to confront McClelland, who is 6'6" tall. Umpire crew chief Joe Brinkman, as well as other umpires and players, had to restrain Brett during his tirade. Pitcher Gaylord Perry, the wily 44-year-old veteran not in the game, grabbed the bat and tried to take it to the clubhouse, but Brinkman retrieved it. Brett, Perry, manager Dick Howser, and coach Rocky Colavito were ejected, even though the game was over. On July 28 American League president Lee McPhail overruled the umpires when he upheld the protest of the Royals. McPhail acknowledged that the pine tar was too high on the bat but stated that "games should be won and lost on the playing field—not through technicalities of the rules." He further stated that pine tar is not a substance that increases distance potential, and the rule was instituted to prevent baseballs from being soiled by the pine tar and thus having to be removed from the game. McPhail left the four ejections in place. Because of McPhail's decision, the game's situation reverted to a 5-4 Royals lead with two out in the top of the ninth inning and had to be completed. The game was resumed on August 18 (an off-day for both teams), and Martin, in a childish move, placed left-handed Don Mattingly at second base in place of Bert Campaneris, who was on the disabled list, and pitcher Ron Guidry in center field to replace Jerry Mumphrey, who had been traded to Houston the previous week. Before the first pitch of the resumption, pitcher George Frazier tossed to first base to appeal that Brett had missed the base and Tim Welke, the umpire at that bag, signaled "safe." Then Frazier threw to second base and Dave Phillips signaled "safe." Martin came out of the dugout to discuss with the umpires (a different crew from the start of the game in July) his contention that Brett missed first base, but Phillips produced a notarized letter from the original crew stating that Brett and UL Washington both had touched all of the bases and the runs counted. After all the theatrics were finished, four batters made four outs and the second part of the contest was completed in nine minutes and 41 seconds. The Royals, who had flown from Kansas City to New York that afternoon, went back to the airport and continued on to Baltimore to start the scheduled part of their road trip.

In 1984, Tony Armas of the Boston Red Sox led the American League by hitting 43 home runs, and Dale Murphy of the Atlanta Braves and Mike Schmidt of the Philadelphia Phillies tied atop the National League list with 36 each. Harold Baines of the Chicago White Sox hit a home run in a game played on May 8, 1984, more than 24 hours after the contest started. The White Sox played host to the Milwaukee Brewers at Comiskey Park and the teams were tied, 3-3, at the end of the ninth inning. After 17 innings, the game was suspended to the next night, and in the 21st inning, each club scored three runs, with the Brewers tallying on Ben Oglivie's three-run home run. With one out in the bottom of the 25th inning at 9:13 p.m. on May 9, Baines hit a 2-0 pitch off Chuck Porter of the Brewers into the center field bullpen to win the contest, 7-6. This is the latest inning for a home run in major league history.

Later that season Baines and Greg Walker of the Chicago White Sox hit back-to-back homers off Phil Niekro of the New York Yankees on July 27 at Comiskey Park. The second of the consecutive blasts off the knuckleball pitcher made Niekro the fourth hurler to surrender 400 home runs in his career. He finished his career with 482 long balls in 1987 and is third on the all-time home runs surrendered list behind fellow Hall-of-Famers Robin Roberts and Fergie Jenkins. Niekro led his league in gopher balls in four seasons and hit seven of his own during his 20 years with the Braves in Milwaukee and Atlanta.

On September 17, 1984, Reggie Jackson of the California Angels joined the 500 Home Run Club as its 13th member with a solo homer into the right center field terrace at Anaheim Stadium that came on the 17th anniversary of his first major league home run, which also was hit at Anaheim Stadium. Jackson led the American League in home runs four times and hit at least 10 homers in 20 consecutive seasons from 1968 through 1987, tied for second with many other players behind Hank Aaron, who hit 10 in 23 straight years. When he retired with 563 long balls, Jackson placed third on the all-time list of American League home runs hitters and had hit more home runs than any other left-handed batter except Babe Ruth, but he has since been passed by Barry Bonds and Rafael Palmeiro. From 1971 through 1980, Jackson led the major leagues in homers with 310 and became the first slugger to clout at least 100 round-trippers for three different teams, as he hit 268 for the Athletics in Kansas City and Oakland, 144 for the New York Yankees, and 123 for the Angels. Only Darrell Evans has matched this feat. Jackson is the only twentieth-century batter to lead his league while playing for three different teams: the Oakland Athletics (1973 and tied in 1975), the New York Yankees (tied in 1980), and the California Angels (tied in 1982). Harry Stovey led his league with three teams in the nineteenth century. Reggie hit 10 home runs in the World Series (including three in consecutive at bats in 1977), six in League Championship Series play, and one in a 1981 League Division Series game, and his post-season performance earned him the nickname, "Mr. October." Jackson's home run in the 1971 All-Star Game came as a pinch hitter, and the ball struck the light tower on the Tiger Stadium right field roof.

On June 11, 1985, in a game at Philadelphia's Veteran's Stadium, the New York Mets got two hits in the top of the first inning but both runners were out on the bases. Von Hayes led off the bottom of the frame for the Phillies by hitting a home run. Four runs and two outs later, Hayes came to the plate for the second time in the inning, this time with the bases loaded, and hit his second round-tripper of the inning. Although many players had hit two home runs in one inning before Hayes, none of them had done this in the first inning. The Phillies scored nine runs in the frame on the way to a 26-7 drubbing of the Mets, as Hayes hit the only two four-baggers of the contest.

The New York Mets played the Braves in Atlanta on July 4, 1985, a game that featured four home runs and a batter hitting for the cycle. The start of the game was delayed 90 minutes by rain and the action stopped in the bottom of the third for another 41-minute delay. First baseman Keith Hernandez of the Mets hit an eighth-inning round-tripper as part of a four-hit day that included one of each type, a cycle of hits. The game went into extra innings tied at eight runs each, and in the top of the 13th, Howard Johnson, who had entered the game in the ninth and scored the tying run, hit a two-run homer to put the Mets in front, 10-8. However, in the bottom of the frame, Terry Harper hit his own two-run clout to tie the score again. In the top of the 18th inning, the Mets scored an unearned run after an error by hurler Rick Camp. With two outs in the bottom of the inning, Camp batted and hit the only home run of his career over the left field fence to tie the game again. The Mets scored five runs in the top of the 19th inning and won the game, 16-13. Since this game was part of a Fourth of July celebration, the Braves shot off the planned fireworks at the completion of the contest, even though the game ended at 3:55 a.m.

◆ ◆ ◆

On August 10, 1985, Dave Kingman of the Oakland Athletics hit home run number 400 of his career indoors at Seattle's Kingdome. Kingman, who twice led the National League in home runs, played for seven different teams in both leagues during his big league career, including four teams in 1977. His 270 homers from 1971 through 1980, more than half his career total of 442, placed him fourth in the majors for that period, and he retired 19th on the career home run list. Kingman hit three home runs in one game five times in his career, the second highest total in history, as he performed that feat once with the New York Mets, three times with the Chicago Cubs, and once with the Athletics. Only Johnny Mize before him and Alex Rodriguez after him have had three-homer games for three different clubs. Kingman also hit 100 home runs for two different franchises, with 154 as a member of the Mets and 100 with the Athletics. When he retired, Kingman's home run production rate of 29.7 placed him second all-time behind Babe Ruth, just ahead of Ralph Kiner's 29.5.

> **On July 4, 1976,** *Tim McCarver of the Phillies hit a grand slam in the first game of a doubleheader at Pittsburgh. The 375-foot homer barely cleared the right field wall. However, after rounding first base, McCarver passed Garry Maddox, who was returning to first, and was called out. He received credit for a single and three runs batted in.*

The home run production rate started a three-year increase in 1985, when the rate climbed from 10.1 in 1984 to 11.2. As was discussed previously, there is a natural rhythm to the balance between hitting and pitching, and for three years the batters had more control of that dance. Darrell Evans of the Detroit Tigers led the American League home run chase in 1985 by hitting 40 circuit blasts, while Dale Murphy of the Atlanta Braves led the National League with 37. For the second consecutive season in 1986, the American League leader, this time Jesse Barfield of the Toronto Blue Jays, hit 40 home runs. Mike Schmidt of the Philadelphia Phillies led the National League for the eighth and final time by hitting 37 homers. Bert Blyleven of the Minnesota Twins surrendered a record 50 homers in 1986, breaking the old mark of 46 set by Robin Roberts in 1956. Blyleven still holds the major league record. On July 6, 1986, Bob Horner, a teammate of Dale Murphy on the Braves, hit four home runs in one game at Fulton County Stadium in Atlanta. Three of the four were solo shots and all that power did nothing for the Braves, as they lost to the Montreal Expos, 11-8, only the second time that a four-homer-game team lost the contest. The first time had been in 1896 when Ed Delahanty hit four home runs for the Philadelphia Phillies. (Refer to Appendix C for details of all four-home-run games.)

In 1986, because of political unrest in Haiti, Rawlings moved its baseball manufacturing plant to Costa Rica, where the company continues to make baseballs today. Moving the plant meant new workers were hired to hand-stitch the ball covers, and the 1987 baseball evidently did not meet the specifications of Major League Baseball, causing offense in general and home runs in particular to increase that season. The home run production rate that year rose to 13.8, a record high for the time and the first time the rate had been higher than 12.0 since 1961, when sluggers pounded homers at a rate of 12.5 per 500 plate appearances. From 1988 through 1993, the production rate decreased to pre-1987 levels, but then the level jumped again, with every year from 1994 through 2005 having a rate of 13.0 or higher.

On April 15, 1986, Don Sutton of the California Angels surrendered the 400th home run of his career to Ivan Calderon in a 9-4 loss to the Seattle Mariners at Anaheim Stadium. Sutton surrendered 325 homers in the National League and 147 in the American, and his 472 total homers surrendered places him fourth on the all-time list.

Rookie Mark McGwire of the Oakland Athletics led the American League in homers in 1987, hitting 49 to set a new rookie record, breaking the mark of 38 set by Wally Berger in 1930 and Frank Robinson in 1956. Berger and Robinson still hold the mark in the National League. George Bell of the Toronto Blue Jays finished second with 47 homers. In the National League, Andre Dawson of the Chicago Cubs topped the list with 49 round-trippers and Dale Murphy of the Atlanta Braves hit 44. The Baltimore Orioles pitching staff set a new record for home run futility as they surrendered 226 long balls during the 1987 season, thus

A young Mark McGwire swinging for the fences in Oakland; McGwire held the single-season homer record from September 8, 1998 through October 2001. *National Baseball Hall of Fame Library, Cooperstown, New York*

becoming only the second team to surrender 200 gopher balls in one season and beating the old record set by the 1964 Kansas City Athletics.

◆ ◆ ◆

Mike Schmidt joined the 500 Home Run Club on April 18, 1987, with a three-run blast at Three Rivers Stadium, Pittsburgh, the club's first new member in nine years. Schmidt, the 14th member of the club, played his entire career with the Philadelphia Phillies. He led the National League in home runs eight times (the most of any batter in the Senior Circuit), including three consecutive years from 1974 through 1976, and hit 40 homers three times. Schmidt hit 30 home runs in nine consecutive years from 1979 through 1987 and hit the second-most homers in the decade from 1971 through 1980, with 283. Schmidt also placed third from 1981 through 1990 by hitting 265 circuit clouts. Dale Murphy (299) and Eddie Murray (268) are the only sluggers to hit more in that decade. Schmidt hit four homers in one game in 1976 and had two three-homer games in his career. He hit 50 round-trippers at Chicago's Wrigley Field to tie with Hank Aaron for second place among visitors to Wrigley. Willie Mays leads all visitors with 54 homers in the "Friendly Confines." When one considers that both Aaron and Mays played many more games in the ballpark because fewer teams were on the schedule during their careers, Schmidt's accomplishment is even more outstanding. He tied with Willie Stargell with 26 home runs at Shea Stadium, the most of any visitor in Flushing, and led outright at Busch Stadium, St. Louis, with 27 as a visitor. (Refer to Appendix A for details of each home run number 500.)

On April 13, 1987, the San Diego Padres surrendered two runs in the top of the first inning to the San Francisco Giants. In the bottom half of the inning, Marvell Wynne led off with a home run and Tony Gwynn followed with his own solo shot to tie the game. The third hitter, John Kruk, hit the third consecutive homer to start the game for the Padres. This had never happened before in the major leagues. Three Atlanta Braves duplicated the event in 2003, when Rafael Furcal, Mark DeRosa, and Gary Sheffield hit back-to-back four-baggers. The three Padres hit only 275 combined home runs in their careers, with Wynne hitting 40, Gwynn hitting 135, and Kruk

100, but they were the premier sluggers that day. On May 28, 1987, Mike Young of the Baltimore Orioles pinch hit for designated hitter Jim Dwyer after a pitching change in the fifth inning to take advantage of the left/right matchup between pitcher and batter. Although Young struck out in that pinch appearance, he remained in the game and, with the California Angels ahead, 6-5, led off the bottom of the 10th inning with a home run. The Angels scored a run in the top of the 12th frame, but Young clouted a two-run homer in the bottom of the inning to win the game for Baltimore, 8-7. Young became the fifth and most recent player to hit two extra-inning home runs in one game, following in the footsteps of Vern Stephens in 1943, Willie Kirkland in 1963, Art Shamsky in 1966, and Ralph Garr in 1971. All batters except Stephens performed the feat at home.

From July 8 through July 18, 1987, Don Mattingly of the New York Yankees hit at least one home run in eight consecutive games, thus matching the record set by Dale Long in 1956. Both sluggers were left-handed first basemen not known as power hitters during their careers. Mattingly hit 10 long balls during the span, with six at Yankee Stadium and four at Arlington Stadium in Texas. During the course of the 1987 season, Mattingly hit six grand slams for the Yankees, setting a record for most home runs with the bases loaded in a season. Curiously, Mattingly hit no other slams in his career.

Steve Carlton of the Cleveland Indians became the sixth pitcher to surrender 400 home runs, but only the second left-hander to do so, on July 30, 1987, in a game played at Cleveland's Municipal Stadium. Carlton surrendered three round-trippers in that game, but reached the milestone with the first of the trio, a blast hit by Floyd Rayford of the Baltimore Orioles in the fifth inning. Carlton spent most of his Hall-of-Fame career in the National League, which he led in this category during the 1978 season. Carlton surrendered 379 of his 414 career homers in the Senior Circuit and is eighth all-time among hurlers.

Before 1987 six different batters had hit 30 home runs and stolen 30 bases in one season, with Bobby Bonds accomplishing this four times and Willie Mays twice. In 1987 four batters each reached those totals, as Eric Davis of the Cincinnati Reds stole 50 and hit 37, Joe Carter of the Cleveland Indians stole 31 and hit 32, Howard Johnson of the New York Mets stole 32 and slugged 36, and Johnson's teammate Darryl Strawberry stole 36 and hit 39. The 30/30 season became commonplace at this time, but Jose Canseco of the Oakland Athletics raised the bar on this accomplishment the following season by stealing 40 bases and clouting 42 home runs. Canseco, who led the American League in home runs in 1988, established a new standard, the 40/40 Club, which has since been joined by only three other players, Barry Bonds in 1996, Alex Rodriguez in 1998, and Alfonso Soriano in 2006. Darryl Strawberry of the New York Mets hit 39 homers for the second consecutive year in 1988 to lead the National League after finishing third in 1987.

Kevin Mitchell of the San Francisco Giants led the National League with 47 home runs in 1989, while Fred McGriff of the Toronto Blue Jays led the Junior Circuit with 36. Joe Carter of the Cleveland Indians, who finished second to McGriff with 35 clouts, hit three homers in one game on June 24 and again on July 19. On August 23, the Los Angeles Dodgers and the Montreal Expos battled for 22 innings at Olympic Stadium in Montreal. In the bottom of the eighth inning, Rick Dempsey entered the game as the Dodger catcher and caught the rest of the game. In the 22nd inning, Dempsey led off against his former battery-mate with the Baltimore Orioles, Dennis Martinez, and homered for the only run of the game. This is the latest inning in history for a home run that provided all the runs of a game. When Dempsey was asked years later if the many times he caught Martinez helped him know what pitch to expect, he laughed and admitted that it did. There have been four occasions when a batter hit a home run in the 22nd inning or later. In the other three games, at least nine runs were scored by the two teams, making Dempsey's 1-0 game even more special.

At the end of the 1989 season, Darrell Evans retired with 414 home runs, to place 21st on the all-time list and 11th among left-handed batters. He had hit 60 after his 40th birthday, second to Carlton Fisk's 72. Evans hit at least 30 in one season for three different teams, the Atlanta Braves, the San Francisco Giants, and the Detroit Tigers. He also slugged at least 100 homers for each of those same teams, only the second player to achieve this after Reggie Jackson. Evans hit at least 10 homers for 19 consecutive seasons from 1971 through 1989. He led the American League once and placed in the top five in the National League twice in his career.

Bert Blyleven of the California Angels surrendered home run number 400 of his career in the first inning on April 14, 1990, to Kent Hrbek of the Minnesota Twins in Anaheim. Blyleven retired after the 1992 season having surrendered 430 home runs in his career, placing him seventh on the career list. He holds the single-season record for homers surrendered with 50 in 1986 and led the American League twice in gopher balls.

Cecil Fielder of the Detroit Tigers, who had played in Japan in 1989, led the 1990 American League by hitting 51 home runs, to become the first batter to slug 50 in a season since George Foster in 1977 and the first American Leaguer to accomplish this since Roger Maris and Mickey Mantle in 1961. As part of his career-high output, Fielder hit three homers in one game twice that season, exactly a month apart on May 6 and June 6. Ryne Sandberg of the Chicago Cubs led the National League with 40 home runs. In 1991, Fielder and Jose Canseco of the Oakland Athletics tied for the American League lead, each slugging 44 homers, while Howard Johnson of the New York Mets led the National League list with 38 home runs. The 1992 American League home run sluggers were led by Juan Gonzalez of the Texas Rangers with 43 and Oakland's Mark McGwire, who hit 42. Fred McGriff, who had led the American League in 1989, topped the National League in 1992 by hitting 35 long balls for the San Diego Padres, the first Friar to lead the league in homers. McGriff became the fifth player to lead two different major leagues in home runs for a season.

> *On May 26, 1993*, in a game at Cleveland Stadium, Indians designated hitter Carlos Martinez hit a fly ball to deep right field to lead off the bottom of the fourth inning. Jose Canseco, never considered an adequate outfielder but patrolling right field for the Rangers, chased down the ball. At the last second he turned his head to look for the fence, the ball flew past his glove, bounced off his head and over the wall. The scoring on the play? A home run for Martinez and a "run butted in" for Canseco.

On April 18, 1992, Jeff Tackett of the Baltimore Orioles homered off Frank Tanana of the Detroit Tigers in the third inning of an Oriole win at Camden Yards in Baltimore. With this four-bagger, Tanana became the eighth and most recent pitcher to surrender 400 home runs in his career but only the third lefty to join the club. He finished his career in 1993 with 448 gopher balls to place fifth on the all-time list for that category.

During the 1993 season, the home run production rate increased a full two points to 11.5 over the 1992 rate. Juan Gonzalez led the American League for the second consecutive year by hitting 46 homers, the first repeat leader in the league since Jim Rice topped the circuit in 1977–78, and Barry Bonds, in his first season with the San Francisco Giants, matched JuanGon's total and led the National League. Ken Griffey Jr. was a close runner-up in the American League with 45 clouts. Griffey had a great week for home runs from July 20 through July 28 as he hit a homer in eight consecutive games to tie the record held by Dale Long and Don Mattingly. Griffey hit the blasts in three ballparks with two at Yankee Stadium, four at Cleveland's Municipal Stadium, and the final two at home in Kingdome. All three sluggers who hold this mark hit left-handed.

◆ ◆ ◆

Two teams were added to the National League in 1993: the Florida Marlins and the Colorado Rockies. Tim Wallach of the Los Angeles Dodgers hit the first major league home run in Florida off Charlie Hough on April 5. Eric Young of the Rockies hit the first home run in the Mountain Time Zone on April 9 in the opening game at Mile High Stadium in Denver when he led off the bottom of the first inning off Kent Bottenfield of the Montreal Expos. This game in Denver meant that Major League Baseball now had teams in all four time zones in the continental United States for the first time.

In the second inning on August 6, 1993, Reggie Sanders of the Cincinnati Reds homered off Ramon Martinez of the Dodgers in Los Angeles. Chris Sabo hit a four-bagger off Ramon's brother and teammate, Pedro, in the eighth inning. Ramon and Pedro became the third pair of teammate brothers to each surrender a home run in the same game, following in the footsteps of Virgil and Jesse Barnes and Rick and Paul Reuschel. On August 31 Pedro Munoz of the Minnesota Twins led off the bottom of the 22nd inning at the Metrodome by hitting a 2-2 pitch by Jason Grimsley of the Cleveland Indians to right center for a game-ending solo homer. He had entered the game in the 20th inning as a pinch hitter and his four-bagger made him the fourth and most recent player to homer in the 22nd inning or later in a game. On September 7, Mark Whiten of the St. Louis Cardinals hit four home runs in the second game of a double header at Cincinnati's Riverfront Stadium. He hit his initial blast in the first inning with the bases loaded to become the only four-homer slugger to hit a slam as part of his big day. Whiten drove in 12 runs on the four home runs to tie the major league record for most RBIs in one game set in 1924 by Jim Bottomley of the Cardinals. Whiten led the Redbirds to a 15-2 victory after the Reds had won the first game, 14-13.

The home run production rate would increase to record levels during the next 10 years, producing many never-before-seen individual totals and eventually drawing a lot of negative attention and criticism from observers.

11
THE ALL-STAR GAME

The All-Star Game provides fans the opportunity to watch each league's best players compete against each other, thus creating some classic batter/pitcher matchups. Whether it is Babe Ruth facing Carl Hubbell in 1934 or Greg Maddux pitching to Cal Ripken in 1998, this popular annual game has provided many memorable pairings. The All-Star Game started as a one-time event—part of the 1933 World's Fair held in Chicago and has grown into one of baseball's premiere events. In the 1990s, Major League Baseball added another event the day before the game, the Home Run Derby, which has grown in popularity to the point that it now rivals the game itself for the most attention each year.

The National and American Leagues met in the first All-Star Game at Chicago's Comiskey Park on July 6, 1933, and, appropriately, Babe Ruth of the New York Yankees swatted the first All-Star homer, a two-run blast off Bill Hallahan of the St. Louis Cardinals in the third inning that put the American Leaguers up 3-0, on the way to an eventual 4-2 win. Frankie Frisch of the St. Louis Cardinals hit the first National League home run in the sixth inning that day. Frisch hit his second home run in the Midsummer Classic when he led off the bottom of the first inning at New York's Polo Grounds on July 10, 1934, to take an early lead on the career list. Frisch was the first batter to lead off the first inning of an All-Star Game with a four-bagger, an achievement duplicated by four other batters in the Midsummer Classic. Joe Medwick of the St. Louis Cardinals hit a third-inning homer to go with the homer he hit in the World Series later that year to become the first player to hit four-baggers in both those events in the same year. Lou Gehrig hit round-trippers in consecutive All-Star Games in 1936 and 1937 to match Frisch's career total and also hit World Series home runs in those two years. The American League won for the fifth time in seven games in 1939, as Joe DiMaggio of the New York Yankees hit his only home run in All-Star competition at Yankee Stadium, thus becoming the first player to hit a home run in his own ballpark. "Joltin' Joe" later homered in the World Series that year as well. In the 1940 Classic, Max West of the Boston Bees (as the Braves were called then) played in his only All-Star Game. He hit for the first and only time in the bottom of the first inning with two runners on base and whacked a homer to right center field. He hurt himself in the top of the second inning and left the game after becoming the first player to homer in his first All-Star at bat. On July 8, 1941, Arky Vaughan of the Pittsburgh Pirates homered into the right field upper deck seats at Detroit's Briggs Stadium (later called Tiger Stadium) to give the National League a 3-2 lead in the seventh inning. In the next inning, he hit another two-run blast into the right field upper deck to extend the lead, making Vaughan the first of five batters to hit two home runs in one All-Star Game. In the bottom of the ninth inning with the National League's lead now at 5-4, Ted Williams of the Boston Red Sox came to bat with two runners on base and two out. Williams hit the 2-1 pitch by Claude Passeau of the Chicago Cubs off the facing of the right field roof to win the game for the American League, 7-5. "The Kid" in Ted showed through as he joyously romped around the bases

Ted Williams, who hit a game-ending home run in the 1941 All-Star Game and two more four-baggers in the 1946 game. *National Baseball Hall of Fame Library, Cooperstown, New York*

after hitting the four-bagger to become the first of three players to end an All-Star Game with a home run.

Lou Boudreau, player/manager of the Cleveland Indians, led off the 1942 All-Star Game, the first played at night, with a homer, and four batters later, Rudy York of the Detroit Tigers hit a two-run shot. This was the first time a team hit two homers in one inning of an All-Star Game, though this has been done many times since. In the bottom of the eighth inning, Mickey Owen of the Brooklyn Dodgers hit the first pinch-hit home run in the Midsummer Classic and all four runs scored by the two teams were knocked in by the three home runs. Vince DiMaggio of the Pittsburgh Pirates collected three hits in three at bats in the 1943 game, including a ninth-inning home run. His younger brother, Joe, had homered in the 1939 contest, and they became the first pair of brothers to each hit a home run in All Star-competition. In 1946, after a year off because of World War II, the All-Star Game was held at Fenway Park in Boston and the star of the day was home-town hero, Ted Williams. Williams collected four hits, including two home runs, in four at bats in his own ballpark in the 12-0 American League victory. "The Thumper's" second homer was hit off a blooper pitch by Rip Sewell, called the "Eephus Pitch," and these two circuit clouts gave Williams three in his All-Star career to set a new record in that department. Two years later, in 1948, Detroit's Hoot Evers homered in his first All-Star at bat off Brooklyn's Ralph Branca to score the first run of the day for the American League, as the Junior Circuit won, 5-2. Stan Musial of the St. Louis Cardinals also homered in that game played at Sportsman's Park, Musial's home field, making Stan the Man the third player to hit one in his own park. After the 1949 win by the American League, the Junior Circuit had won 12 of the 16 games played but the National League won the next four and six of the next seven contests. The American League seemed to be headed for yet another victory in 1950 when Ralph Kiner of the Pittsburgh Pirates hit a solo shot in the top of the ninth inning to tie the score, 3-3. The NL victory was secured when Red Schoendienst of the St. Louis Cardinals hit the first extra-inning homer in All-Star Game history in the 14th frame of the first-ever, extra-inning All-Star contest.

The 1951 Midsummer Classic featured four round-trippers by the National League, the first time a squad had hit that many in one game. The four sluggers who cleared the fences at Detroit's Briggs Stadium were Stan

Musial of the Cardinals, Bob Elliott of the Boston Braves, Gil Hodges of the Brooklyn Dodgers, and Ralph Kiner of the Pirates. Both Musial and Kiner hit their third career homers in All-Star competition in this game, thus tying Ted Williams for the all-time mark. Two American Leaguers hit homers in the game, and they both played for the hometown Tigers, as Vic Wertz and George Kell each hit a solo shot off Sal Maglie of the New York Giants. The combined six home runs in the game set a new record for one contest, which has been tied twice. The next summer, the National League took a first-inning lead on Jackie Robinson's home run at Philadelphia's Shibe Park. Robinson also homered in the 1952 World Series to become the fourth batter to accomplish that pair of home runs. In 1954 at Cleveland's Municipal Stadium, the American League team hit four home runs. Cleveland infielder Al Rosen hit two homers in a three-for-four day, and Larry Doby of the Tribe knocked a pinch-hit homer in the eighth inning to tie the score in an eventual American League victory. Former Indian and current Tiger Ray Boone hit the fourth home run by the Junior Circuit back-to-back with Rosen in the third inning, the first time that two batters had hit consecutive blasts in an All-Star Game. Gus Bell of the Cincinnati Reds hit a pinch homer in the game, the first of two times that multiple home runs were socked by pinch hitters in one game. The two squads hit six total homers to tie the 1951 record for most in one contest.

The National League won for the fifth time in six games in 1955, powered by Stan Musial's extra-inning, game-ending home run. The American League squad had taken an early lead at Milwaukee's County Stadium with five unanswered runs in the first six innings, three of which were scored on Mickey Mantle's first-inning home run to center field, but the National League tied the contest with five runs of their own in the seventh and eighth innings. Musial led off the bottom of the 12th frame with a home run into the right field seats, the second time a batter had hit an extra-inning clout and also the second time for a game-ender. Musial took sole possession of the top spot on the career leader board for All-Star homers with this, his fourth round-tripper in the Midsummer Classic, hit in his 12th game, also a record at the time. Another National League victory in 1956 featured home runs by Willie Mays of the New York Giants and Musial. Mays clouted a two-run, pinch-hit four-bagger in the fourth inning while Musial extended his record total to five All-Star homers with his seventh-inning solo shot. Ted Williams of the Boston Red Sox and Mickey Mantle of the New York Yankees hit back-to-back homers in the sixth inning off Milwaukee Braves hurler Warren Spahn. Both Williams and Mantle hit more than 500 homers while playing their entire careers for one club (and rival teams, at that) and having them smack consecutive home runs could only happen in the All-Star Game. Mantle had now homered in consecutive All-Star Games and also in the World Series in the same two years, a feat that only Lou Gehrig had also accomplished.

◆ ◆ ◆

In 1959, the Midsummer Classic went to California for the first time. Baseball expanded the event to two games in 1959, an experiment that lasted through 1962, and the second 1959 game was played at Los Angeles Memorial Coliseum, the temporary home of the Dodgers. The visiting American League team won, 5-3, behind the power of three home runs by Frank Malzone of the Boston Red Sox, Yogi Berra of the New York Yankees, and Rocky Colavito of the Cleveland Indians, who also won the 1959 American League home run championship with 42 for the season. Jim Gilliam of the hometown Dodgers hit a solo homer in the seventh inning in his first All-Star at bat, the third batter to accomplish this feat. Gilliam also became the eighth batter to hit an All-Star home run in his own ballpark. In the second 1960 game, played on July 13 at Yankee Stadium, the National League scored all six runs on four home runs as they shut out the American League. The four sluggers who left the yard represented three different teams: Eddie Mathews of the Milwaukee Braves, Willie Mays of the San Francisco Giants, Ken Boyer of the St. Louis Cardinals, and Boyer's teammate, Stan Musial, who smacked a seventh-inning homer as a pinch hitter, Musial's sixth and final All-Star Game home run, which is still the career record.

San Francisco's Candlestick Park, which had opened in 1960, hosted the first 1961 All-Star Game, played on July 11. Each team hit a pinch homer in the contest, as Harmon Killebrew of the Minnesota Twins hit one in the sixth inning and George Altman, in his first All-Star at bat, hit a home run in a pinch in the eighth inning. The All-Star Game traditionally features batters as substitute hitters, in an attempt by the managers to allow as many players as possible to see action in the contest, and as a result, many pinch-hit homers have been clouted in the Midsummer Classic. Pete Runnels of the Boston Red Sox hit one in the third inning of the second 1962 game, played on July 30 at Chicago's Wrigley Field, to score the first run in an eventual American League victory, 9-4. On July 7, 1964, the National League came from behind in the bottom of the ninth inning at New York's Shea Stadium to win, 7-4. They hit three homers, including a solo shot by Billy Williams of the Chicago Cubs in the fourth and another solo homer by Ken Boyer three batters later in the inning. (Boyer also homered in the 1964 World Series, the sixth player to achieve this pair.) In the bottom of the ninth, after scoring a run to tie the game, Johnny Callison became the first Philadelphia Phillies player to homer in an All-Star Game when he hit a game-ending, three-run homer to right field, the third and most recent game-ending home run in the Midsummer Classic. The very next All-Star batter, Willie Mays, who led off the 1965 game in Minneapolis, hit a home run, the third leadoff homer in All-Star history. Harmon Killebrew of the Minnesota Twins hit a two-run home run in the fifth inning, the ninth hitter to clout an All-Star home run in his own ballpark, and he also hit a home run in the World Series that season. The All-Star game returned to California in 1967, as Anaheim Stadium was the scene for the most pitcher-dominated All-Star Game in history, a 2-1 National League victory which saw 30 batters strike out in 15 innings, partly because of the late-afternoon starting time and the resultant poor visibility for the batters. All three runs scored on solo home runs, with Dick Allen of the Philadelphia Phillies hitting one in the second and Brooks Robinson of the Baltimore Orioles matching Allen in the sixth frame. In the top of the 15th inning, Tony Perez of the Cincinnati Reds, who had replaced Allen at third base in the 10th inning, hit the game-winning homer, the latest inning ever for a home run in the All-Star Game.

On July 23, 1969, the All-Stars came to RFK Stadium in Washington, D.C., and the National League won 9-3, scoring all nine runs in the first four innings. Willie McCovey of the San Francisco Giants became the fourth batter in history to hit two round-trippers in the same All-Star Game and Johnny Bench of the Cincinnati Reds hit a home run in his first All-Star at bat. However, the real hero of the day, as far as the fans were concerned, was Frank Howard of the Washington Senators, who hit a solo homer in the second inning off the right center field mezzanine. The ball was estimated to have traveled 458 feet. Howard became the 10th slugger to hit a home run in his own ballpark in an All-Star Game. The only homer in the 1970 game at Cincinnati's Riverfront Stadium was hit by Dick Dietz of the San Francisco Giants in his first All-Star at bat. This game lasted 15 innings and ended when Pete Rose scored from second base by running through catcher Ray Fosse, using his left forearm and shoulder to flatten the backstop, who dropped the ball.

The 1971 contest, played at Tiger Stadium in Detroit, featured six round-trippers, the third time for that record total and the second time in this ballpark. Reggie Jackson of the Oakland Athletics pinch hit in the third inning and blasted the ball over the right field roof and off the light tower to score the first two runs of the day for the American League. Later in the inning, Frank Robinson of the Baltimore Orioles also hit a two-run clout to right field, which put the Junior Circuit ahead to stay, as they won the contest, 6-4. Robinson, who had homered in the 1959 All-Star Game for the National League, became the first and only batter to slug home runs for each league in the Midsummer Classic. Roberto Clemente of the Pittsburgh Pirates hit his only All-Star home run in his last career All-Star at bat in the eighth inning and both Clemente and Robinson also clouted four-baggers in the 1971 World Series. In the 1972 game, played at Atlanta Stadium, Braves slugger Hank Aaron hit a two-run homer in the sixth inning to put the National League ahead, 2-1, in his own ballpark. In the eighth inning, Cookie Rojas of the Kansas City Royals pinch hit and smacked a two-run homer that put the American League ahead briefly, as the National Leaguers tied the game in the bottom of the ninth and won it in the bottom of the 10th inning, 4-3. Willie Davis of the Los Angeles Dodgers hit a two-run, sixth-inning home run as a pinch hitter in the 1973 game played in Kansas City on the 40th anniversary of the first game.

In 1975, the game returned to Milwaukee's County Stadium, where it had been played 20 years earlier. In 1955, the stadium housed the National League Braves but now was the home of the American League Brewers. In the top of the second inning, Los Angeles Dodgers teammates Steve Garvey and Jim Wynn hit back-to-back solo homers to give the National League an early lead in a game they eventually won with three runs in the ninth inning. They became the third pair of batters to hit consecutive blasts in an All-Star Game and the first teammates to accomplish the feat. In the bottom of the sixth inning, Carl Yastrzemski of the Boston Red Sox hit his only All-Star home run, a three-run, pinch-hit homer to tie the score. Joe Morgan led off the 1977 game played at Yankee Stadium by hitting the 3-2 pitch for a homer to right field to become the fourth player to hit a leadoff homer in an All-Star Game.

The 1979 game at Seattle's Kingdome did not live up to the pre-game hype that predicted many long balls to be hit in the homer-friendly indoor stadium. Each team only hit one home run, including a pinch-hit roundtripper by Lee Mazzilli of the New York Mets in his first All-Star at bat, only the second time a player accomplished that pair of feats with the same homer. The first was George Altman in 1961. Mazzilli also became the first Mets player to hit a home run in All-Star competition with this blast. In 1981, because of the 59-day player strike, the All-Star Game was played on the latest date ever, August 9, and on a Sunday, making it the only time the game has been played on a weekend. The National League won the close contest at Cleveland's Municipal Stadium, 5-4, on the power of four home runs. Gary Carter of the Montreal Expos hit two to become the fifth and most recent player to hit multiple homers in one All-Star Game. Mike Schmidt's two-run home run in the eighth inning gave the National squad their winning margin.

On July 6, 1983, the 50th anniversary of the All-Star Game was celebrated at Comiskey Park in Chicago, the site of the first contest in 1933. Fred Lynn became the first Angel to hit an All-Star homer when he connected with the bases loaded in the third inning. This homer, hit off Atlee Hammaker of the San Francisco Giants, is the only grand slam in All-Star history. The American League scored seven runs in that inning off Hammaker on its way to a 13-3 drubbing of the National League. In the 1986 game, played at Houston's Astrodome, Lou Whitaker of the Detroit Tigers hit a two-run homer in the second inning to give the American League an early lead. In the seventh inning, Frank White of the Kansas City Royals pinch hit for Whitaker and socked a solo homer, thus both players in the eighth spot in the lineup hit home runs that drove in all three runs in the 3-2 American League victory. The 1988 American League starting catcher, Terry

Steinbach of the Oakland Athletics, benefited from ballot-box stuffing in Oakland, and his election was ridiculed by the media because of his first-half performance. However, in the top of the second inning, Steinbach hit a solo homer for the first run of the game, and in the third inning, he drove in another run with a sacrifice fly, as the American League won, 2-1. Steinbach's home run was on his first All-Star at bat and he is the only player to hit a home run in both his first Major League and first All-Star at bat. His two runs batted in earned him the Most Valuable Player award for the 1988 All-Star Game.

On July 11, 1989, Bo Jackson, well-known as a Heisman Trophy-winning running back, played in his only All-Star Game as a member of the Kansas City Royals. Jackson, the first batter of the game for the host American League, hit the 1-0 pitch an estimated 450 feet over the centerfield wall at Anaheim Stadium. The ball struck a television camera beyond the wall, denting the metal casing. Wade Boggs of the Boston Red Sox, not known as a power hitter in his career, followed Jackson with another homer. Jackson and Boggs became the only pair of batters to hit consecutive homers to start the first inning of an All-Star Game. In 1992 Ken Griffey Jr. of the Seattle Mariners hit a solo home run in the third inning of an American League romp in San Diego, as they won, 13-6. Junior's dad, Ken Sr., hit a homer in the 1980 game while representing the Cincinnati Reds, making them the first father and son to each hit a home run in All-Star competition. On July 12, 1994, Fred McGriff of the Atlanta Braves hit a pinch-hit, two-run, ninth-inning home run to tie the game, which the National League won in 10 innings, 8-7. The Senior Circuit had won all nine extra-inning All-Star contests to this point.

In the fourth inning of the 1995 game, Frank Thomas of the Chicago White Sox hit a two-run homer to become the first member of the Pale Hose to hit an All-Star four-bagger, unusual for a team that had been represented at all 65 previous games. In the eighth inning, Jeff Conine of the Florida Marlins pinch hit to make his first All-Star appearance, and he hit the 1-0 pitch into the left field seats to put the National League ahead to stay, 3-2. Conine later stated that he went to the plate hoping not to embarrass himself, and he did a good job avoiding any embarrassment. Although Javy Lopez of the Atlanta Braves hit a homer in his first All-Star at bat in the 1997 game, the night belonged to the Alomar family. Brothers Roberto and Sandy each played for the American League and Sandy, of the Cleveland Indians, entered the game at Cleveland's Jacobs Field in the sixth inning as a defensive replacement behind the plate. In the seventh inning, he hit a two-run home run to put the American League ahead to stay and make the Alomars the second pair of brothers to each homer in the All-Star Game, as Roberto had homered in the 1993 game. Sandy hit the blast in his home ballpark and also hit two round-trippers in that fall's World Series.

Chipper Jones of the Atlanta Braves joined Sandy Alomar on the list of players who have hit Midsummer Classic home runs in their own ballparks by hitting a solo shot in the third inning of the 2000 game played at Turner Field.

On July 10, 2001, Derek Jeter of the New York Yankees and Magglio Ordonez of the Chicago White Sox hit back-to-back home runs in the sixth inning, only the fifth set of consecutive homers in All-Star competition. These blasts came off Jon Lieber of the Chicago Cubs by the first two batters Lieber faced in an All-Star Game. Jeter also hit a homer in that year's World Series. Cal Ripken Jr. of the Baltimore Orioles, playing in his 18th and final All-Star Game, hit a solo homer in the third inning to give the American League a lead that they never surrendered in a 4-1 win at Seattle's Safeco Field. The 2002 game at Miller Park in Milwaukee ended in an 11-inning tie but featured the bat of Barry Bonds one year after he set a new single-season home run record. In the first inning, Bonds hit a fly ball to deep right center field that appeared to be headed over the wall. However, Torii Hunter of the Minnesota Twins caught the ball with a spectacular leap and stretch over the top of the wall to bring the ball back into the park. In the third inning, Bonds hit a 3-0 pitch to right field that struck the facing of the upper deck for a homer but was not hit as far as the out in the first inning. Barry joined his dad, Bobby, to become the second father/son pair to each homer in the All-Star Game, and Barry also hit four home runs in the 2002 World Series.

> **Steve Garvey hit a solo homer** in the third inning of the 1977 All-Star Game and then in October homered in the World Series, both at Yankee Stadium. Garvey is the only player in history to hit a home run in the same ballpark in the same season in both the All-Star Game and the World Series.

Hank Blalock of the Texas Rangers hit an eighth-inning home run that drove in two runs and put the American League ahead to stay in a 7-6 victory in the 2003 game in Chicago. Blalock became the fourth player to hit a pinch homer on his first All-Star at bat and the first American Leaguer to perform the feat. Jason Giambi, who had hit a home run in the seventh inning, also hit a four-bagger in that fall's World Series. In 2004 both Manny Ramirez and David Ortiz of the Boston Red Sox homered in both the All-Star Game, won by the American League, and the World Series, won by the BoSox, to become the only teammates to perform this pair of feats in the same year.

◆ ◆ ◆

Home Run Derby, first version: In December 1959 filming began at Wrigley Field in Los Angeles for a series of 30-minute television shows called "Home Run Derby." This show, the brainchild of sportscaster Mark Scott, featured 19 players competing for cash prizes by hitting home runs off batting practice pitchers out of the relatively small, homer-friendly park. The group of hitters included seven who would eventually join the 500 Home Run Club. The contest followed a basic set of rules: two batters faced each other for nine innings with the batter who hit more home runs declared the winner. Each hitter had three outs in each inning, and any batted ball that was not a home run was an out, as was a called strike. The winner of each competition earned $2,000 and went on to the next show, while his opponent received $1,000. Any player who hit three consecutive homers received a $500 bonus and a fourth consecutive blast garnered another $500 for the batter. A batter who hit any consecutive homers after the fourth received a $1,000 bonus. All 26 episodes were filmed in three weeks and were shown starting in the summer of 1960. During the competition, the player who was not batting would sit with Mark Scott and talk about the game. Some batters who lost their first match came back later to face another opponent.

Only four hitters earned bonus money for consecutive home runs. Mickey Mantle hit three in a row twice, as did Dick Stuart. Rocky Colavito hit three consecutive homers in one of his matches, and Jackie Jensen hit five in a row once to earn a $2,000 bonus. Hank Aaron won more matches than any other slugger, coming out on top six of seven times, and earned the most money, $13,500. However, many batters slugged home runs at a higher rate than "Hammerin' Hank," who hit nine homers in his first match but never hit more than six after that.

This show was an exhibition tailored to help the batters hit a lot of baseballs out of the park. The pitchers, who alternated innings, were paid bonus money for surrendering more homers, and they threw easy pitches in the strike zone to allow the hitters to whack the ball as far as they could. Table 11.1 shows the record for each batter in the one-on-one matchups, the homers hit, and the money earned. The information comes from David Gough's fine article on the Derby in *The National Pastime*, published by the Society for American Baseball Research (SABR) in 1997. The third

Table 11.1 – Home Run Derby (1959) Results

Batter	HR	HR/500	W-L	Dollars Earned
Mickey Mantle	44	122.9	4-1	10,000
Ernie Banks	25	117.3	1-2	4,500
Jackie Jensen	29	105.8	2-2	8,500
Willie Mays	35	102.9	3-2	8,000
Wally Post	16	101.3	1-1	3,000
Frank Robinson	13	97.0	1-1	3,500
Gil Hodges	13	97.0	1-1	3,000
Dick Stuart	21	94.6	2-1	6,000
Bob Cerv	11	84.6	1-1	3,000
Harmon Killebrew	23	82.1	2-2	6,000
Hank Aaron	34	76.2	6-1	13,500
Ken Boyer	9	71.4	1-1	3,000
Jim Lemon	7	57.4	0-2	2,000
Bob Allison	9	50.0	1-2	4,000
Rocky Colavito	7	50.0	0-2	2,500
Eddie Mathews	3	50.0	0-1	1,000
Al Kaline	1	17.9	0-1	1,000
Duke Snider	1	17.9	0-1	1,000
Gus Triandos	1	17.9	0-1	1,000

column shows the number of home runs each batter hit per 500 plate appearances in the Derby, which here is defined as all the outs made plus the home runs hit. Babe Ruth in his career hit 33.6 home runs per 500 plate appearances, under game conditions. Most sluggers in the Derby, under conditions set to help them, hit many more home runs per opportunity, as shown in the chart. Mickey Mantle had the highest production rate, and that is reflected in his 4-1 game record. However, Ernie Banks, with the second highest rate, had a tougher time beating his opponents. Jackie Jensen beat Banks, 14-11, in the highest scoring game of the series, and Banks hit another 11 homers when he beat Gil Hodges.

The series creator, Mark Scott, died in July 1960, and the concept died with him but these matches can be seen occasionally on cable television. There is no home video version of the series.

◆ ◆ ◆

Home Run Derby, second version: The modern version of the Home Run Derby, held each year on the day before the All-Star Game, has become one of the highlights of the Midsummer Classic. Fans fill the ballpark to watch the top sluggers in the major leagues battle in much the same conditions as the 1959 version of the event. This modern version perhaps was inspired by a workout-day exhibition in 1979. The day before that year's All-Star Game in Seattle, 10,000 fans attended the workout day to watch batting practice and witnessed a slugging show in the Kingdome.

An event named "Home Run Derby" was held for the first time in 1985, as fans paid an admission fee to watch the workout day. The two leagues competed with five players per side at the Metrodome in Minneapolis in a contest won by the American League. Dave Parker of the Cincinnati Reds hit six homers to lead all batters. Each year since then (except 1988 when it was cancelled because of rain), a home run contest has been held, although the rules have changed a few times. In 1991 the number of outs allowed per batter was raised from five to ten and Baltimore's Cal Ripken set a new individual standard by hitting 12 home runs in 22 swings. No team, let alone an individual, had hit that many long balls since the first year of the competition. Three of Ripken's homers landed in the third through fifth decks in Skydome's left field. The next year in San Diego, Mark

McGwire of the Oakland Athletics matched Ripken's total of 12, including home runs on seven consecutive swings. In 1993 at Oriole Park at Camden Yards, Seattle's Ken Griffey Jr. hit one ball completely over the right field patio area and the walkway behind it, striking the warehouse building on the fly. This was the first time that any batter had hit the building on the fly since the park opened in 1992. Juan Gonzalez of the Texas Rangers hit one ball into the left field upper deck, an estimated 473 feet from home plate. Ken Griffey Jr. won the contest held in 1994 at Three Rivers Stadium in Pittsburgh, and Frank Thomas of the Chicago White Sox hit a homer estimated at 519 feet.

The Derby changed from a team contest to an individual one in 1995. Albert Belle of the Cleveland Indians hit 16 total homers in the three rounds of the event but placed second to Frank Thomas, who out-homered Belle in the last round, 3-2. Belle set a new single-derby mark for most homers, however. Barry Bonds and Mark McGwire battled in the final round of the 1996 Derby, held at Philadelphia's Veterans' Stadium, with Bonds achieving the top overall total of 17 and out-homering McGwire in the third round to win the contest. In 1998 at Coors Field in Denver, many people expected a high-scoring, exciting Derby owing to the homer-friendly atmosphere of the park. Ken Griffey Jr. announced he would not participate in the contest but changed his mind after many people, including Hall of Famer Frank Robinson, spoke to him about being in the contest. Griffey went on to win the Derby, beating Jim Thome of the Cleveland Indians in the final round. Mark McGwire put on a show in the first round by hitting many balls farther than any other player, and he continued to shine in the 1999 Derby at Fenway Park in Boston as many of his homers cleared the left field wall and the screen on top of it. A few actually landed across the street from the park.

Sammy Sosa won the 2000 Derby held at Turner Field in Atlanta by hitting 26 homers to set a new single-derby record. He hit one over the camera area in center field an estimated 508 feet. The next year at Safeco Field in Seattle, Jason Giambi of the Oakland Athletics hit 14 home runs in the first round to set a new single-round record, but Luis Gonzalez of the Arizona Diamondbacks won the contest.

The 2004 Derby held at Minute Maid Park in Houston was billed as a tribute to the 500 Home Run Club, and all 14 living members of the club were present for the event. Miguel Tejada of the Baltimore Orioles, a last-minute replacement in the Derby, set a new single-round mark of 15 and for one Derby with 26, beating Lance Berkman of the Houston Astros in the final round. In 2005, Detroit's Comerica Park, not known as a homer-friendly environment, hosted the event and some people joked about a "Warning Track Derby" before the event. Bobby Abreu of the Philadelphia Phillies hit 24 homers in the first round, smashing the record set the previous year, and nearly topping the Derby record at the same time. Abreu won the contest and hit a total of 41 long balls in the event, nearly double the previous Derby record and 17 more than he hit during the entire 2005 season. Through 2005, Ken Griffey Jr. has hit the most career homers in the Derby with 70, with Jason Giambi a close second at 68.

12

THE ULTIMATE WEAPON

In the mid-1990s, the style of baseball changed dramatically, as the home run became the most prominent event in the game. The striking rise in the home run production rate is seen clearly in Figure 1.1 (chapter 1), with the rate hovering around 10.3 from 1977 through 1993, with the exception of the 1987 aberration, which was possibly caused by unintended changes in the physical ball. The years 1994 through 2005 have a production rate centering around 13.9, as shown in Figure 12.1, with the peak from 1999 through 2001. The production rate shows no general increase or

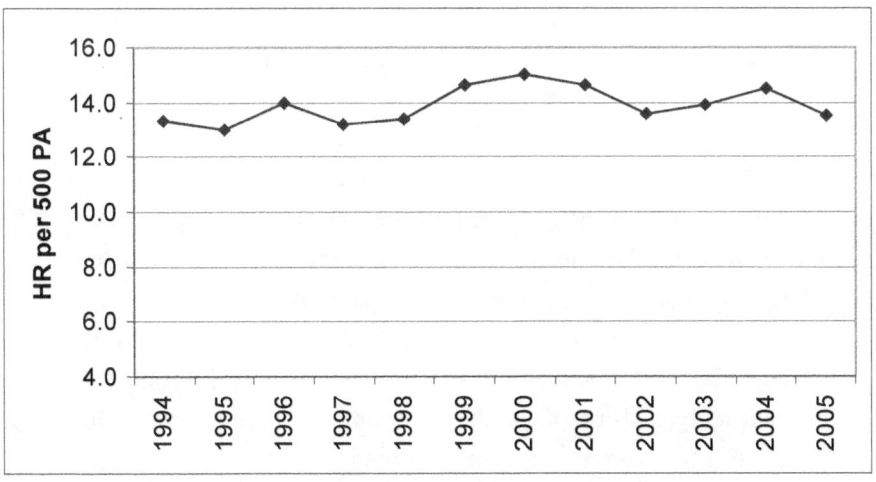

Figure 12.1 – Home Run Production Rate (1994–2005)

decrease but remains constant for the period covered in the figure, with little deviation in either direction, and the 2000 rate of 15.0 is the highest ever in the major leagues. The sudden, large increase in production starting in 1994 mirrors, to a certain extent, the increase that took place in the early 1920s, when a change in the ball was similarly followed by a change in the style of play. The level of offense in the last few years of the twentieth century reflects another change in the style of play and is closer in style to the 1950s than any decade between then and 1990.

From 1996 through 2005, batters hit at least 40 home runs in a season 119 times, which represents 43 percent of all 275 seasons of 40 or more homers through 2005. Of those 119 instances, 18 of them topped 50 home runs, a clear change in season home run totals for batters since, before 1996, there had been 19 seasons of 50 homers. Clearly, production among the top sluggers had increased dramatically, to the point that the list of "top" sluggers had grown considerably.

The reason for the late twentieth century increase is not so clear, as many factors might have affected the home run production rate in the 1990s and it is impossible to determine how much each of these items might have changed the production rate, if at all. They are listed below in no particular order:

1. **Strike zone.** Many people around the game have talked about the changes in the strike zone through the years. Gradual changes over decades have lowered the zone in general and made it shorter and wider. Since a letter-high fastball is generally harder to hit than one below the belt, this lowering of the zone has helped batters. At the same time, the zone got wider, with some pitches two to three inches off the plate being called strikes by many umpires. In the past, the American League had a higher strike zone than the National League, owing to the balloon chest protector that used to be worn by American League umpires. In recent years, Major League Baseball has made an effort to make the strike zone consistent among all umpires, changing umpire training so that the younger arbiters are all using the same methods. As more of the veterans retire, this effort should start showing fruit, and the strike zone

should be more consistent, while remaining lower than it was decades ago. The general lowering effect has helped the batters.

2. ***Ballparks.*** Another factor that may have contributed to the dramatic rise in home run production is the surge in ballpark construction that started in the early part of the 1990s. Most of the new parks favor hitters. In four years starting with 1991, four teams moved into new homes, followed by 10 more in the next 10 years, and this does not consider the four new teams that came into existence because of the two rounds of expansion in the decade. Although the size of parks at the league level has not changed dramatically as a result of this recent construction (in other words, the ballparks, overall, are not physically smaller), the effect of the new structures in most cases has helped increase offense. Many large, multipurpose stadiums have been replaced by new versions of old-style parks. While the retro look and feel is intended for the fans, the general configuration of the field has affected the game itself. The multipurpose stadium generally features a completely enclosed playing area, which prevents wind effects from changing the distance the batted ball travels. The newer parks, however, are more open, usually with a large section of the outfield area unblocked by double-level seating areas. This openness allows wind effects to prolong the flight of the ball and is a probable partial cause of the increase in offense during the last part of the twentieth century.

3. ***Earlier and better baseball training.*** Young adults coming into the game in the 1990s are products of a different sports environment than that experienced by previous generations. Today's youth sports programs are better organized, are better equipped, and use better training techniques. In the past many kids primarily played pick-up games, while today's youngsters spend most of their sports time in organized leagues. This training at an earlier age helps more players develop better skills and creates a larger pool of gifted athletes. In addition to having better skills (including hitting

mechanics), this new generation of hitters trains to hit for power rather than for average.

4. ***Body armor.*** Many hitters in the mid- to late 1990s started wearing elbow guards, wrist guards, and other armor to protect themselves against the negative effect of being struck by pitched and batted balls. Barry Bonds was one of the more prominent users of a large, protective guard on his front elbow, but many other hitters did likewise. Possibly, this was a reaction to the widened strike zone, as hitters needed to lean over the plate to get good swings at those outside pitches, but pitchers claimed that the guard gave the hitters an unfair advantage because the hitters could now lean over without fear of being struck and injured. (This is another example of the continual shifting of balance between batters and pitchers talked about earlier in the book: outside strikes shifted the balance toward the pitchers and elbow guards shifted it back.)

5. ***Video rooms.*** One of the newer methods of training is using videos of games to learn your opponents' tendencies. Batters watch pitchers and pitches to find trends in order to improve their chances the next time against that hurler. Video even comes in handy during games, as players can watch and re-watch their previous at bats to learn what happened and change the outcome in their next plate appearance. Such sophisticated training produces better batters.

6. ***New surgical procedures.*** The most famous sports-related surgical procedure of all time is named after a pitcher: Tommy John surgery. However, many advanced medical techniques help batters by repairing broken body parts with less-invasive surgery and allowing the slugger to get back on the field sooner than before—and perhaps, in many cases, to get back on the field at all. More playing time for a slugger will often translate to more home runs.

7. ***Less "small-ball."*** Many ways of scoring runs have almost disappeared from the big leagues in favor of home runs. Stolen bases

and sacrifice bunts, formerly major parts of a team's offensive arsenal, are now on the endangered species list, as more batters go to the plate looking for a pitch to drive out of the park. In fact, some players of this era have home run totals that nearly match the total of the rest of their hits combined during a season. One key example is Mark McGwire, who in 1995 hit 39 homers and had only 48 other hits. This pattern continued in 1998 (70 and 82) and 2000 (32 and 40), and he finally exceeded his other hits total in 2001 with 29 homers and 27 other hits. As a side effect of this new trend, there has been an increase in strikeouts. When Babe Ruth retired, he had struck out more than any other player in history, but after the 2005 season, he is 78th on the all-time list.

8. *Lively baseball.* Many observers have talked about the "fact" that the ball got juiced before the 1993 season—or perhaps it was the 1994 season (it depends on the commentator). There is no evidence of a change in the manufacturing process or in the materials used. And there is no evidence that Major League Baseball dictated a change to the ball at that time. However, that does not mean that one of these events did not happen. More offense means more fans buying tickets, food, and souvenirs at the ballpark and consequently more money for the owners; thus, many people see conspiracies in every front office meant to increase the owners' profits—and the "rabbit ball" is a primary example of a conspiracy theory.

9. *Changes in wood used in bats.* Many batters now use bats made of maple rather than the traditional ash. There is no scientific evidence as of this writing that maple causes the ball to fly farther. Maple is a denser wood with a harder surface than ash, and the maple grain makes the bat surface feel more like a laminated product than a simple raw wood. Because of the increase in density, maple bats are slightly smaller in diameter than ash bats. According to Alan Nathan, Professor of Physics at the University of Illinois, the smaller barrel diameter of a maple bat might cause slightly more backspin on the ball, which could result in longer distance on a fly ball.

10. ***General increase in human body size.*** In the 100 years from the beginning of the twentieth century to the beginning of the twenty-first century, the average male born in the United States has grown about three inches in height (as has the average major league player), and as the athletes get taller, their ability to hit the ball farther increases. Taller players have a larger arc to their swing, which increases the speed of the bat through the hitting zone. Players born in the 1960s are, on average, about one inch taller than those born in the 1930s, but the average height has not changed much for people born in the 1960s and 1970s compared with those born in the 1950s. Increases in body size can translate into improved athletic performance in many sports, including baseball.

11. ***Better nutrition.*** Advances in science have caused an increase in the quality of the nutritional value of the food consumed in the latter half of the twentieth century. Better nutrition at an early age stimulates muscle development and overall growth in a child, the most important period for physical development. This good nutrition also translates into healthier adults who suffer fewer injuries and heal faster, both important factors for athletes.

12. ***Weaker pitching because of expansion.*** Many people claim that league expansion has contributed to a rise in weaker pitchers without any facts to support the premise. A statistical study conducted in 1999 and published on the Retrosheet website (www.retrosheet.org) showed that this is not true. In fact, the rookie batters who played in the years immediately after expansion fared worse than did the rookie pitchers.

13. ***Competition for jobs.*** In 1901 athletes competed for 250 major league jobs. The white, male U.S. population, which made up the pool of available ballplayers at the time, according to the 1900 census was 34.2 million. (In 1901, 371 different people played in the major leagues, and over 95 percent of them were born in the United States.) In 1960 with 400 major league jobs available, the U.S.

male population, according to the census, was 88.3 million. That is a 158 percent increase in the available pool of players competing for jobs that increased by 60 percent. In addition, 10 percent of the 575 people who played in the majors in 1960 were foreign-born, meaning that the 1960 players were chosen on a much more selective basis than the 1901 players. The probability of a player getting to the major leagues became much smaller in 60 years. In 1990 there were 650 jobs on 26 Major League Baseball teams, and the male population in the United States was 119.1 million. By this time, however, nearly 14 percent of all major league players were born in other countries. This means that in the 1990s, a major league job was even harder to acquire than in 1960 and the talent level in the big leagues was proportionally higher than before. (In 2005 foreign-born players accounted for 24 percent of all major leaguers. This increase was largely caused by the influx of Caribbean-area players, who accounted for about 8 percent of the major league players in 1960 but in 2005 are almost the entire 24 percent of the foreign-born players.)

14. *Weight training.* The rise in weight training for athletes is clearly visible in many sports. Baseball players in the 1950s did not have large rooms at the stadium available to them for this purpose, but every team now provides such facilities. Weight training helps players build muscle and thus strength. Additional strength is said to allow players to hit the ball farther. However, an increase in bulk and muscle makes an athlete less flexible; muscles are slower to react to stimuli. The primary objective for a hitter is to achieve a high bat speed through the hitting zone. To help increase swing speed, empty cups have been cut at the top of the barrel and bat handles have been shaved to the size of large toothpicks through the years; less weight in the bat other than in the barrel allows a bat to be swung faster. However, slower muscles seem to contradict this process. Bat speed may be lost thanks to slowly reacting muscle, but it also may be gained via extra strength. Weight training may actually help pitchers more than hitters, since bulk

is more important in throwing than swinging. More study on this topic is necessary as the effects are not yet fully understood.

15. *Year-round training.* Most professional athletes in the 1990s, regardless of their sport, worked out all year to keep in top shape. Decades ago, they would go home in the off-season and work another job. Keeping fit was not usually an option or desire during that time. Now the pay scale is such that an athlete can take time off without worry about income, thus leaving time (and desire because of the large pay check) to keep in shape.

16. *Over-the-counter supplements.* Anyone can walk into their local shopping mall and purchase dietary supplements that purport to add muscle mass when used as part of a training regimen. These products are being used at younger ages by athletes who want to emulate the professionals in order to become one themselves. Many of these products didn't become prevalent until the 1980s and 1990s; thus any effects from them could be a possible partial cause in the increased home run production rate in the mid-1990s. A type of supplement that probably had a bigger effect for sluggers is the group that helps a body recover more quickly from the recurring stress and trauma of lifting weights, allowing them to return to the weight room sooner.

17. *Steroids.* The primary reason cited for the large increase in home run production in the last years of the twentieth century is steroid use among players. In 1991 Commissioner Fay Vincent added steroids to baseball's banned substance list, but no testing was implemented to enforce this ruling. The first MLB drug tests for illegal steroids were administered in 2003, but the first effective tests were not given until 2005. Since players have tested positive, there is no doubt that some players have used illegal steroids. How many have used illegal substances is not known, although many people in and around the game have come up with various wild guesses about the actual number. *When* players started using

steroids and *how long* they used them is also not known. But, most important, the connection between steroid use and the home run increase has yet to be made by any scientific study. Most studies in sports medicine journals have looked only at the negative side effects of the drugs, but those that have looked at benefits have concluded the following: (a) taking steroids likely—but not definitely—increases one's muscle mass and (b) there is no reliable evidence that any increased muscle mass enhances athletic performance, except in the case of weight lifters. The evidence of "enhanced performance" is anecdotal and almost entirely self-reported by athletes themselves. The uncritical use of the term "performance-enhancing drugs" by many people is misleading and helps fuel the fire of controversy. Even if there is found to be a connection scientifically, the sudden jump in the production rate could not be caused solely by steroids usage. Players did not suddenly—in one off-season—get much larger; steroid use could have caused only a gradual increase in the production rate. As we have seen, the rate jumped to the new baseline level in 1994 and has remained fairly constant (with normal, expected fluctuations) for 10 years. The sudden surge in home run totals by individual players also has been cited as a result of steroid use. However, long before steroids became a problem, players had unexplainable surges in home runs totals. Davey Johnson hit 43 in 1973, which is 25 more than any other year in his career. Roger Maris never hit more than 39 homers in one season before or after 1961, a difference of 22 from his record total. Did these batters (and others like them) take steroids? In a parallel to steroids usage, the use of amphetamines, a drug that has been in baseball clubhouses for decades, is seen by some as beneficial to those who take them, but with no physical (as opposed to psychological) evidence of effect, just like steroids. Major League Baseball added amphetamines to the banned substance list for the 2006 season, and the testing procedure was revised to include amphetamine testing. None of this is to say that taking a drug deemed illegal by the U.S. government's Food and Drug Administration with proven negative side effects on the human body is all right. There is abundant scientific evidence that these drugs cause severe liver damage after long-term use. They should not be used in an attempt to improve athletic abilities, but the moral indignation of the pundits and politicians who have ignored the facts is overblown and not productive.

Trying to assign weights to each factor that influenced the home run production rate is an impossible task. Saying that factor X caused a certain percentage of the increase in homers is a fool's errand, since the individual factors cannot be filtered out. The best that can be said is that many factors caused the production rate increase in the 1990s, but some of the commonly quoted reasons have had little or no effect. Home run production has increased gradually through the twentieth century. The production of the 1950s is significantly higher than that of the 1920s and 1930s (with the aberration caused by World War II in between). The production of the 1990s is significantly higher than that of the 1970s and 1980s, but the increase is not more than the 1950s jump in production.

After the player strike that cancelled the 1994 season (including the World Series) early and delayed the start of the 1995 season, many fans turned away from the game with declarations such as "I'll never watch a game again." The increase in offense in general, and home runs in particular, reenergized baseball in much the same way as the increased offense in the early 1920s had. Home runs and home run sluggers were the number one topic in baseball in the last half of the 1990s—the backlash would come later.

◆　　◆　　◆

After the August 11, 1994, games, the players struck, forcing the league to start cancelling games. A few weeks after the strike began, the rest of the season, including the post-season, was cancelled by Major League Baseball. Considering the fact that only 70 percent of the season had been played at that time, the home run totals for individual players that season are outstanding. Matt Williams of the San Francisco Giants led the National League with 43 homers and Jeff Bagwell hit 39 for the

Houston Astros. In the American League, Ken Griffey Jr. of the Seattle Mariners led with 40 and Frank Thomas of the Chicago White Sox hit 38 round-trippers. Both Williams and Griffey had hit 33 home runs by the All-Star break, and Thomas had 32 at that time. There had never been three players with 30 homers at the break before, and although the strike seemed inevitable at the time of the All-Star Game, it looked to be a great home run chase shaping up for the season's second half, which was not completed after the players walked out in August.

The 1995 season started late (with the first game played on April 25), but many players still piled up impressive numbers of home runs. Albert Belle of the Cleveland Indians led the American League with 50, although he started the year slowly. At the end of July, Belle had hit only 19 round-trippers, but he whacked 14 in August and 17 in September (matching Babe Ruth's September 1927 total) to reach the half-century milestone on September 30 off Melvin Bunch of the Kansas City Royals in Cleveland. (Refer to Appendix B for details of each home run number 50 in history.) Both Jay Buhner of the Seattle Mariners and Frank Thomas of the White Sox hit 40 to place second in the American League, while, in the National League, Dante Bichette of the Colorado Rockies led with 40 homers. The Rockies had joined the league as an expansion team in 1993, and Bichette would be the first of three consecutive Rockies to lead the league in home runs. Colorado had moved into their new home, Coors Field, in 1995, and the park increased offense in the league by a large percentage, thus helping three different Rockies players to top the league in the individual home run total, and the team to lead the National League for three consecutive seasons in runs and homers.

> **On September 18, 1995,** Albert Belle hit two homers at Comiskey Park. The next night, Belle clouted another one on the first pitch he saw in the top of the sixth inning. Then in the eighth, he faced Scott Radinsky, who had just come into the game for the White Sox. Belle whacked Radinsky's first pitch for a home run to center field. In the ninth, Belle again started the inning by facing a new pitcher, this time Rod Bolton. Belle deposited the fourth pitch over the center field seats for his third round-tripper of the night and fifth in two days.

In 1995 Robin Ventura of the Chicago White Sox hit two of his 18 career grand slams—and they both came in the same game. On September 4 the left-handed swinging Ventura hit his first slam in the fourth inning off lefty Dennis Cook of the Rangers at The Ballpark in Arlington. In the fifth inning Ventura hit his second slam in as many at bats off right-hander Danny Darwin, as the Pale Hose romped, 14-3. It had been 25 years since a batter had hit two grand slams in the same game.

Dave Winfield played his final game on October 1, 1995, and retired with 465 home runs and 3,110 hits in his career. In 1993 he became the fifth player to hit 400 homers and collect 3,000 hits, and he hit 59 home runs after his 40th birthday, the third most in that category after Carlton Fisk and Darrell Evans. Winfield never led a league in round-trippers for a season and never hit 40 in any one season, and his career total places him in the top five for both hitting the most homers without leading a league and hitting the most homers without hitting 40 in a season. However, he hit 20 homers 15 times in his career and more than 100 for two different clubs, with 154 for the San Diego Padres and 205 for the New York Yankees. Winfield played the first eight years of his career in the National League with the Padres to accumulate the 154 home runs but spent most of his career in the Junior Circuit, hitting 311 there.

In 1996 the home run production rate climbed higher than it had ever been before, reaching 14.0 per 500 plate appearances, beating the previous high mark of 13.8 in 1987. Mark McGwire of the Oakland Athletics hit 52 home runs to lead the American League, the first of four 50-plus seasons for McGwire. Andres Galarraga of the Colorado Rockies hit 47 clouts to lead the National League, with Barry Bonds of the San Francisco Giants and Gary Sheffield of the Florida Marlins tied for second with 42 each. Brady Anderson of the Baltimore Orioles hit 50 to place second in the league with only 19 of those blasts at home. Anderson never hit more than 24 homers in any other season, which is the biggest difference for any batter between his top two season totals. Anderson's manager with the Orioles that season, Davey Johnson, had held the previous high total in this category, having hit 43 in 1972 and 18 in 1971, a difference of 25. Luis Gonzalez of the Arizona Diamondbacks tied Anderson for this dubious honor when he hit 57 home runs in 2001, since his second highest total, in 2000, was 31. Two players had not hit 50 home runs in one season since

1961, when Roger Maris and Mickey Mantle each topped the half-century mark. (Refer to Appendix B for details of each home run number 50 in history.) Barry Bonds became the second player to achieve a 40/40 season as he hit 42 homers and stole 40 bases in 1996. As part of his 50-homer season, Brady Anderson led off 12 games with a home run, breaking Bobby Bonds's record of 11 set in 1973. Anderson led off four consecutive games with a home run from April 18 through 21, also a record.

Forty-three players hit at least 30 home runs in 1996, a record-high total, beating the 1987 total of 28 players. Seventeen of those 1996 sluggers hit 40 home runs, more than double the previous high number of 40-homer hitters of eight in 1961. Three teams broke the single-season record for a club set in 1961 by the Yankees. The Orioles hit 257, the Seattle Mariners hit 245, and the Oakland Athletics slugged 243. The Mariners set the current record in 1997 with 264 round-trippers. Also in 1996 two teams topped the record for most home runs surrendered in a season as the Detroit Tigers gave up 241 homers (still the record) and the Minnesota Twins surrendered 233 to beat the old mark of 226 set in 1987 by the Orioles.

Barry Bonds in his first year with the San Francisco Giants (1993); Bonds topped Mark McGwire's single-season homer record on October 5, 2001. *National Baseball Hall of Fame Library, Cooperstown, New York*

On August 16, 1996, the San Diego Padres hosted the first of three games in Monterrey, Mexico, against the New York Mets. Mexico native Fernando Valenzuela started for the Padres in the first game, pitched six innings and won the game. The first home run in the series was hit by Steve Finley, the third batter in the bottom of the first inning, who hit a two-run clout to right field and became the first player in history to hit a major league home run in three different countries, since Finley had already homered in the United States and Canada. Later in the game Ken Caminiti, John Flaherty, and Greg Vaughn also homered to accomplish the three-country feat. Andy Tomberlin hit the only four-bagger for the Mets that night, but the eight previous major league home runs that Tomberlin had hit had all been in the United States, and he never hit one in Canada in his career; thus he missed on the trifecta. Two days later Ken Caminiti clouted two homers in the third game of the series, and pitcher Joey Hamilton of the Padres hit the first of his four career home runs. Brian Johnson also socked a four-bagger in the game, joining Tomberlin and Hamilton with career home runs in the United States and Mexico, but not Canada.

◆ ◆ ◆

On September 6, 1996, Eddie Murray of the Baltimore Orioles hit his 500th career home run in the seventh inning of a game at Oriole Park at Camden Yards to become the 15th slugger to join the 500 Home Run Club. The start of the game, one year to the day since Cal Ripken had broken Lou Gehrig's consecutive games played record (in the same park), had been delayed two hours and 20 minutes by rain from the remnants of Hurricane Fran, which moved through the mid-Atlantic area that day and prevented some people from going to the ballpark. Murray joined Hank Aaron and Willie Mays as the only players with 500 homers and 3,000 hits. Murray was the first player to hit number 500 since Mike Schmidt in 1987 and only the fourth since 1972. Murray took more plate appearances than any other hitter to reach the 500 plateau, was the second oldest to get there, and had never hit more than 33 home runs in one season, which coincidentally matched the number on his uniform. Murray's 504 career home runs total is the most by a player who never hit 40 in one season, but Murray hit at least 10 homers in 20 consecutive seasons, the second best string in history. He clouted at least 20 in 16 seasons, including 13 of his first 14 years in the majors. Murray, the second switch-hitter to hit 500 home runs, holds the record for most games in which he hit a homer both right-handed and left-handed with 11, having topped Mickey's Mantle's record of 10 in a career. (Chili Davis tied Murray in 1997.) For the decade 1981 through 1990, only Dale Murphy hit more home runs than Murray, 299 to 268, and Murray retired with the second-most grand slams in history, with 19 to Lou Gehrig's 23, although Manny Ramirez has since passed Murray. He had started his career with the Orioles but played for three other clubs before Baltimore completed a trade with the Cleveland Indians to bring Murray back to Baltimore on July 21, 1996, just in time to reach the 500 milestone.

At the end of the 1996 season, Andre Dawson retired with 438 home runs. He had hit at least one homer in 20 consecutive seasons and 260 from 1981 through 1990, the fourth-best total for the decade. Dawson hit more than 100 for both the Montreal Expos (225) and Chicago Cubs (174). He also stole 314 bases in his career, making him the third player to combine 300 home runs and 300 steals, along with Willie Mays and Bobby Bonds.

In 1997 Ken Griffey Jr. of the Seattle Mariners led the American League with 56 home runs while Larry Walker, with 49 homers, became the third consecutive member of the Colorado Rockies to lead the National League. Mark McGwire hit 34 round-trippers for the Oakland Athletics before he was traded on July 31 to the St. Louis Cardinals,

> *On April 19–20, 1997, the San Diego Padres hosted three games with the St. Louis Cardinals at Aloha Stadium in Honolulu. Only one home run was hit in the series, on April 20 by Ron Gant of the Cardinals. Gant's drive went to the warning track in left center field and Rickey Henderson, patrolling center for the Padres, ran into the wall attempting to catch the ball. When Henderson did not get up immediately, Gant raced around the bases for an inside-the-park homer in the Aloha State.*

for whom he hit 24 home runs. Thus, McGwire hit 58 homers during the season, more than any other player, but did not lead either league since he split his season between the two circuits. Matt Williams of the Cleveland Indians evidently did not appreciate Jacobs Field as a power-hitter's ballpark in his first season in the American League as he hit only seven of his 32 homers in Cleveland, the lowest percentage of any hitter with at least 30 for a season.

In many ways 1998 seemed like the biggest year in home run history, with the nation's attention focused on home run hitters most of the season. The overall production rate that year, 13.4, was the third highest at the time, but that was not the reason for the attention. The fact that major league hitters slugged more than 5,000 home runs for the first time that season (5,064) also was not the reason. (Major league hitters have slugged over 5,000 home runs every year from 1998 through 2006.) At the All-Star break that summer, four batters had hit at least 30 home runs: Mark McGwire of the St. Louis Cardinals (37), Ken Griffey Jr. of the Seattle Mariners (35), Sammy Sosa of the Chicago Cubs (33), and Greg Vaughn of the San Diego Padres (30). These four topped the previous total of three batters in 1994. Most of the baseball talk at the time centered on the chances of someone breaking the single-season homer mark set by Roger Maris in 1961. McGwire had tied Mickey Mantle for the most homers in May with 16 and Sosa had hit 20 clouts in June to set a new record for a single calendar month, topping the previous mark of 18 set by Rudy York in August 1937. That spectacular month had placed Sosa in the race to catch Maris, and even though Griffey had the second-most homers at the break, he failed to maintain that pace in the second half of the season. McGwire had hit three homers in one game twice by May 19, and many of his first half four-baggers had drawn big crowd reactions because of the distance they flew. In fact, teams started opening their gates earlier when the Cardinals visited to allow thousands of people to watch batting practice and see McGwire hit tape-measure drives off his regular batting practice pitcher, Dave McKay. McGwire hit his 50th four-bagger of the season in the first game on August 20 off Willie Blair of the Mets in New York (only Roger Maris had previously reached 50 in August, smacking his number 50 on the 22nd), to become the first National League batter to hit 50 since George Foster in 1977 and only the third in 42 years. As with the 1927 and 1961 races, the player who eventually ended second, Sosa, stayed with the leader late into the season.

Figure 12.2 shows how the race between the sluggers progressed. Sosa hit his 50th of the year three days after McGwire, on August 23, off Jose Lima of the Houston Astros at Wrigley Field. On August 31 Sosa tied McGwire at 55 homers each, but McGwire hit four in the next two days to pull ahead for the last time. McGwire's two home runs on September 1 off Florida Marlins pitchers in Miami tied and passed Hack Wilson's 1930 National League record 56 homers, but McGwire was not done setting new marks.

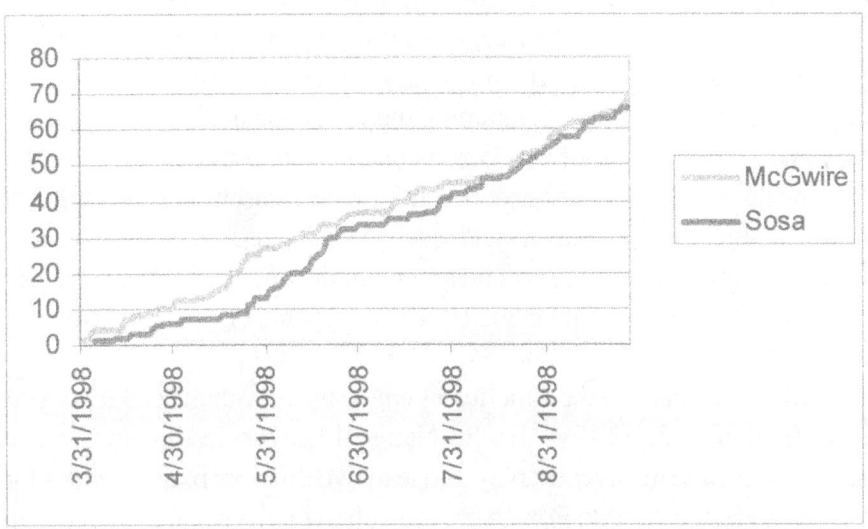

Figure 12.2 – The 1998 Home Run Race

On September 5 he became the third player (and first National Leaguer) to hit 60 homers in a season when he smacked a 2-0 pitch from Dennys Reyes of the Cincinnati Reds over the Busch Stadium left field wall in the bottom of the first inning. Two days later, on September 7, with Sosa and the Cubs in town, McGwire tied Maris in the first inning with a solo homer on a 1-1 pitch from Mike Morgan, the first of three solo home runs by the Redbirds in a 3-2 victory. The next night, with a packed stadium, including Roger Maris's wife and children, and a national television audience watching, the Cubs scored two runs in the first inning. In the bottom of the frame, McGwire grounded out to end the inning, but in the fourth, on Steve Trachsel's first pitch, he hit a line drive to left field that cleared the Busch Stadium fence and was estimated as one of the shortest home runs of the season for McGwire. This drive, hit at 8:18 p.m. CDT, gave the single-season record to McGwire, and the ensuing celebration lasted 11 minutes, thus delaying the game. Roger Maris had hit 61 in '61, and McGwire's numbers were equally easy to remember, as he hit number 62 on 9/8/98. Sosa also topped the previous record by hitting 66 for the year, the most for a batter in one year without leading the league. His 60th blast came off Valerio de los Santos of the Milwaukee Brewers in Chicago on September 12. Ken Griffey Jr. hit 56 to lead the American League, hitting his 50th on September 7 in Seattle with a grand slam off Jimmy Key of the Baltimore Orioles, while Greg Vaughn ended with 50, attaining the milestone on the last day of the season off Aaron Small of the Arizona Diamondbacks in Phoenix. Vaughn became the first San Diego player to hit 50 in one season. This was the first time in history that four players had reached the 50 mark in one season, and Griffey's slam was only the second among 50th homers (Jimmie Foxx had hit a slam in 1938 for number 50). (Refer to Appendix B for details of each home run numbers 50, 60, and 70 in history.)

McGwire had led the American League twice with the Oakland Athletics (including 52 in 1996), so his National League–leading total made him the sixth and most recent player to lead two different major leagues for a season. He and Jimmie Foxx were the only two players to hit at least 50 home runs in a season for two different teams. Foxx had hit his for the 1932 Philadelphia Athletics and the 1938 Boston Red Sox. McGwire also hit 38 of his 1998 home runs at home, the second most for a player in one season in one ballpark; only Hank Greenberg's 1938 total of 39 at Tiger Stadium tops McGwire. McGwire ended the season with five home runs in the last three days to seemingly put the record out of reach with the jaw-dropping total of 70, hitting that milestone on his last plate appearance of the season off Carl Pavano of the Montreal Expos.

On August 14, 1998, Chris Hoiles of the Baltimore Orioles hit two grand slams in one game at Cleveland's Jacobs Field. Hoiles was the ninth player to accomplish the feat, and all nine had been on the road. Alex Rodriguez of the Seattle Mariners hit 42 home runs and stole 46 bases to become the third player with a 40/40 season.

Baseball, still basking in the glow from the previous September, saw a new high mark in home run production in 1999, as batters hit 14.6 long balls for every 500 plate appearances that season. As part of that production rate, 45 batters hit at least 30 for the season, topping the old mark of 43 batters set in 1996. Mark McGwire approached his newly minted single-season record by hitting 65 homers to lead the National League again. He was the first player to lead the Senior Circuit in two consecutive years since Dale Murphy in 1984–85. Sammy Sosa hit 63 to take second place in the league, but because he hit his 60th on September 18—eight days before McGwire—off Jason Bere of the Milwaukee Brewers, Sosa became the first player to hit 60 in multiple seasons. McGwire reached 60 for the second time on September 26 off Scott Sullivan of the Cincinnati Reds. This was the fourth consecutive year that at least two players had hit 50 home runs, which caused some observers to say that 50 was the new 40 for a season total and others to wonder where it might all end. Ken Griffey Jr. led the American League for the third consecutive season by hitting 48 homers, with Rafael Palmeiro of the Texas Rangers right behind him at 47.

The San Diego Padres opened their 1999 season with one game in Monterrey, Mexico, on April 4. Dante Bichette of the Colorado Rockies hit the only home run in the contest, thus joining the list of players who had hit round-trippers in three countries. Two batters hit two grand slams in one game in 1999. On April 23 Fernando Tatis of the St. Louis Cardinals hit both of his in the third inning at Dodger Stadium, as the Cardinals scored 11 runs off Chan Ho Park. Tatis is the only player to hit two grand slams in the same inning, and unbelievably, they came off the same pitcher (no other batter with two slams in one game has ever hit both off the same hurler). Tatis was only the second National Leaguer to hit two slams in one game. On May 10 Nomar Garciaparra of the Boston Red Sox hit three homers in the game, with a grand slam in the first inning and one in the eighth inning, to become the first player with two slams to perform the feat in his own ballpark, after 10 consecutive times by players on the road.

On August 5, Mark McGwire hit his 500th career homer in the third inning off Andy Ashby of the San Diego Padres at Busch Stadium. In the eighth inning, he hit a second clout to join Harmon Killebrew as the only batters to have a multi-homer game in the game they hit number 500. McGwire had hit 363 home runs for the Oakland Athletics in the American League and finished with 220 for the National League Cardinals. He became the second player to hit at least 200 for each of two teams, along with Jimmie Foxx, and the second with at least 200 in each league, following Frank Robinson. McGwire is first on the all-time home run list for the Athletics franchise and fourth on the Cardinals franchise list. He is the only Cardinal batter to slug 50 home runs in a season, and he performed the feat twice with the Redbirds, topping 60 both times. McGwire reached the 500

Home Run Club in the fewest plate appearances of any member, and his career home run production rate of 38.1 per 500 plate appearances is the highest of any player with 300 home runs. He led the American and National Leagues in home runs for a season twice each, in addition to the strange 1997 feat of leading the majors without leading either league. His 135 homers in 1998–99 are the most in two consecutive years for any player, and he holds the records for most homers in three (193 in 1997–99) and four (245 in 1996–99) consecutive seasons. When he retired he held the marks for most in one season and in two through six consecutive years. He hit at least 50 home runs in four consecutive years from 1996 through 1999, which ties for the longest streak in history with Sammy Sosa. His 398 homers from 1991 through 2000 are two less than the leader, Ken Griffey Jr., and he hit four-baggers in 39 different ballparks, including 17 in 1997. McGwire moved into the list of top-five home run sluggers on August 11, 2001, when he hit his 574th clout off Glendon Rusch of the New York Mets to pass Harmon Killebrew on the all-time list. The makeup of the top-five list had not changed since April 8, 1974, when Hank Aaron passed Babe Ruth for the top spot. There had been many changes from 1965 through 1974, but since that day, the list had been Aaron, Ruth, Willie Mays, Frank Robinson, and Killebrew.

In 2000 home run production set another new high, as batters stroked four-baggers at the rate of 15.0 for every 500 plate appearances. This mark is still the record in the major leagues. Forty-seven different players hit at least 30 for the year, setting the current record in that category. Sammy Sosa led the National League for the first time by hitting 50 home runs, a large drop from his previous two season totals of 66 and 63. Sosa hit number 50 on September 16 off Garrett Stephenson of the Cardinals in St. Louis. Barry Bonds of the San Francisco Giants hit 49, and Jeff Bagwell of the Houston Astros placed third with 47. In the American League, Troy Glaus of the Anaheim Angels hit 47 to lead the circuit. The season started with two games in Japan as Major League Baseball continued their effort to market the game in other countries. On March 29 the Chicago Cubs and the New York Mets played at Tokyo Dome, and Shane Andrews of the Cubs hit the first major league home run in Japan off Dennis Cook, thus joining the list of batters who have slugged round-trippers in three countries. Mark Grace of the Cubs and Mike Piazza of the Mets also homered that day to join the Three Country Club. The next day Benny Agbayani of the Mets hit a grand slam in the 11th inning for the only extra-inning homer and the only slam outside North America. Agbayani had not hit a home run in Canada at this time but hit his first in Montreal in April 2001 to join the list of batters who have homered in three countries.

Three pitchers made home run news in 2000, but not with events they want to remember. The Benes brothers of the St. Louis Cardinals, Andy and Alan, each surrendered a home run to Lance Berkman of the Houston Astros at Enron Field (later called Astros Field and then Minute Maid Park) in a game on July 23. Andy actually gave up four blasts that day with Berkman taking him deep in the second inning. Alan watched Berkman circle the bases in the seventh inning of a game won by the Astros, 15-7. The Benes brothers became the third pair to surrender home runs to the same batter in the same game and the first since 1976. Jose Lima of the Astros gave up 48 gopher balls during the season to set a new National League record in that category by topping the 46 given up by Robin Roberts in 1956.

◆   ◆   ◆

The record-high home run production levels continued in 2001 as batters slugged 14.6 long balls per 500 plate appearances, thus matching the second highest rate set in 1999. The season started on April 1 in San Juan, Puerto Rico, as the Toronto Blue Jays hosted the Texas Rangers at Estadio Hiram Bithorn and won, 8-1, behind the pitching of Esteban Loaiza. Two Blue Jays hit home runs that day, with Shannon Stewart claiming the honors for the first major league home run hit in the Caribbean with his third-inning solo shot off Rick Helling. Tony Batista hit a two-run home run in the fourth inning to put Toronto ahead to stay in the contest. Major League Baseball returned to the island in 2003. Sammy Sosa hit three home runs in one game three times during the 2001 season, the only time this has been accomplished by one batter.

On April 17, 2001, Barry Bonds of the San Francisco Giants hit his 500th career homer, a two-run shot off Terry Adams of the Dodgers at Pacific Bell Park (later called SBC Park and AT&T Park) to become the 17th batter to join that club, but he did not stop with that milestone.

Bonds hit 11 homers in April, 17 in May (more than any other batter in May), and another 11 in June but did not homer from June 24 through the All-Star break. His May assault included 10 clouts in a seven-day span to tie Frank Howard's record for a week. He set a new record for most home runs at the All-Star break with 39 but hit only six in July. In August Bonds hit 12 round-trippers, including his 50th on August 11 (the earliest date ever for number 50) off Joe Borowski of the Cubs at Chicago's Wrigley Field and reached 57 by the end of the month. He hit number 60 on September 6 off Albie Lopez of the Arizona Diamondbacks in San Francisco to become the fifth different slugger to attain that milestone, and the oldest by over a year. Bonds hit three home runs on September 9 at Coors Field in Denver, before baseball shut down for a week on September 11 because of the terrorist attacks on the U.S. East Coast, making Bonds wait to complete his chase to Mark McGwire's record. Bonds hit another six before the end of September for his second consecutive month of 12 homers. The postponed week was moved to the end of the season, and Bonds hit his 70th homer of the season on October 4 off Wilfredo Rodriguez into the upper deck in right field at Enron Field in Houston to tie Mark McGwire's three-year-old record. The next day he hit two more off Chan Ho Park of the Los Angeles Dodgers at San Francisco's Pacific Bell Park to break the record, and then, on the last day of the season, he hit his 73rd and final clout of the year off Dennis Springer of the Dodgers to establish a new single-season mark. Bonds hit number 70 on his 654th plate appearance of the season, 27 fewer than McGwire's 681 in 1998, a remarkable feat, but this was the only year that Bonds hit more than 49 home runs. Bonds teamed with Rich Aurilia, who hit 37 homers in 2001, to hit a combined total of 110 to place second on the all-time list for two teammates, behind the 115 clouted by Roger Maris and Mickey Mantle in 1961.

Sammy Sosa hit 64 the same year, the third time in four seasons that he had topped the 60 mark—and in those three years he never led the National League in home runs. Sosa hit 17 in August to tie Rudy York in 1943 and Willie Mays in 1965 for the second highest total in August behind York's 18 in 1937. Luis Gonzalez of the Arizona Diamondbacks hit 57 to place third (third with 57!) in the National League. Alex "ARod" Rodriguez, in his first year with the Texas Rangers, led the American League with 52 homers, while Jim Thome of the Cleveland Indians hit 49 and ARod's teammate, Rafael Palmeiro, hit 47. Four players hit at least 50 home runs in one season for the second time in 2001 during the run to a new single-season record, just as four had hit 50 in 1998 in the midst of the first run to a new record. (Refer to Appendix B for details of each home run numbers 50, 60, and 70 in history.)

Two players with 400 career home runs retired at the end of the 2001 season. Cal Ripken hit 431 homers in his career with the Baltimore Orioles and collected 3,184 hits to become the seventh player to reach the 400/3,000 double milestone. He is the career leader in home runs for the Orioles and smacked at least 10 homers in 20 consecutive seasons, tied for second behind Hank Aaron's 23 years. He never hit more than 34 in any one season but had 10 consecutive years with 20 or more. Ripken spent most of his career at shortstop, and 345 of his home runs were hit at that position, the career record. The other 400 slugger to retire in 2001 was Jose Canseco, who hit 462 with seven different teams. Canseco led the American League twice, hit 40 homers three times, and 30 home runs in eight different years.

In 2002 the home run production rate dropped a point from the previous year, still within the production level of the period. Alex Rodriguez of the Texas Rangers led the American League for the second consecutive year with 57 home runs, and Jim Thome of the Cleveland Indians hit 52 to place second. Sammy Sosa led the National League for the second time with 49 homers, and Barry Bonds finished second with 46. Sosa had led the Senior Circuit twice in a five-year period from 1998 through 2002 by hitting 50 and 49 homers, yet in the three years he placed second, he hit over 60 home runs each year.

On May 2 the Seattle Mariners beat the Chicago White Sox at Comiskey Park, 15-4, and the game was never a contest as the Mariners scored 10 runs in the top of the first inning. Ichiro Suzuki was hit with the first pitch of the game, and Bret Boone followed with a home run on the next pitch. Former White Sox outfielder Mike Cameron followed with a second consecutive home run to make the score 3-0 after six pitches. The Mariners batted around, and when Boone came to the plate for the second time, the score was 6-0. He hit his second homer of the inning to right field, thus becoming the second batter in history and the first in the American League to clout two home runs in the first inning. Cameron strode to the plate for the second time in the inning and hit the 3-2 pitch over the center field wall for his second homer of the frame. Boone and Cameron became the first pair of batters to hit back-to-back home runs twice in the same inning. Two innings later, Cameron hit his third home run in three innings, only the second player to do this after Carl Reynolds of the White Sox on July 2, 1930. In the bottom of the third inning, Magglio Ordonez of the Pale Hose batted with the bases loaded and two out. He hit a fly ball that appeared to be a grand slam but Cameron scaled the wall and caught the ball over the fence, thus stealing a slam from his former teammate. In the fifth inning, Cameron hit his fourth consecutive home run to become the 13th player to smash four in one game and the fifth to hit them in consecutive at bats. In the seventh inning Cameron was hit by a pitch and the Chicago fans booed their own pitcher. He came to bat again in the top of the ninth inning but hit a line drive to right field for an out. All four of his circuit drives were solo shots, and thus he became the only four-homer hitter to collect only four runs batted in on his round-trippers. He tied the American League record for total bases in one game with 16. Bret Boone's brother, Aaron, hit three home runs in one game on August 9, including two in the first inning. Thus, only four batters have hit two homers in the first inning of a game, and two of them are in the Boone family.

Three weeks after Mike Cameron's big day, Shawn Green of the Los Angeles Dodgers hit four homers in one game 97 miles north of Comiskey Park at Miller Park in Milwaukee. On May 23, 2002, Green doubled in the first inning; homered in the second, fourth, and fifth; singled in the eighth; and homered again in the ninth inning. His 19 total bases set a new major league record for one game as he became the 14th player to hit four homers in one game. Green's third homer of the four was his 200th career blast. He hit a home run the next day and two the following day to smack seven in three games, breaking the previous record for most homers in three consecutive games of six held by many players. Also in this span, Green hit 10 homers in seven days starting on May 21 to tie Frank Howard and Barry Bonds for the most in one week.

Barry Bonds moved into fifth place on the all-time home run list on May 25, 2002, by hitting home run number 584 off Denny Neagle of the Rockies at Coors Field, thus passing Mark McGwire. Eleven days later, on June 5, he passed Frank Robinson to claim fourth place on the list by hitting a grand slam in the third inning off Dennis Tankersley of the Padres at San Diego's Qualcomm Stadium. The names of the top four sluggers had not changed since August 17, 1973, when Robinson moved ahead of Harmon Killebrew into fourth place. Bonds became the fourth player and third National Leaguer to hit 600 major league homers on August 9, 2002, when he smacked the 2-1 pitch from Kip Wells over the center field wall at Pacific Bell Park against his former team, the Pittsburgh Pirates.

On June 5, 2002, Juan Gonzalez of the Texas Rangers hit his 400th career home run, a solo shot in Anaheim off Jarrod Washburn. JuanGon, who led the American League in 1992 and 1993, hit 40 homers five times, and his 357 from 1991 through 2000 placed sixth for the 10-year span. Gonzalez is the career leader for the Texas Rangers franchise with 372 for that club and his 434 homers place him 36th on the career list through 2006.

Jim Thome of the Cleveland Indians hit a home run in seven consecutive games from June 25 through July 3, 2002. A strange note related to this feat is that, through 2005, all three batters holding the record of eight (Dale Long, Don Mattingly, and Ken Griffey Jr.), as well as Thome, are left-handed sluggers.

In 2003, for the first time since 1994 when the season ended early, no player hit 50 home runs, breaking a string of eight years. Alex Rodriguez of the Texas Rangers led the American League for the third consecutive year by hitting 47 homers, and Frank Thomas of the Chicago White Sox and Carlos Delgado of the Toronto Blue Jays tied for second place with 42. In the National League, Jim Thome, in his first season with the Philadelphia Phillies, hit 47, with Barry Bonds of the Giants and Richie Sexson of the Milwaukee Brewers tied with 45. So, in 2003 both league leaders hit 47 and the runnersup in each league tied for that honor. On May 28 the first three Atlanta Braves batters, in the bottom of the first inning, each hit a home run against the Cincinnati Reds. The blasts by Rafael Furcal, Mark DeRosa, and Gary Sheffield started the Braves on the way to a 15-3 victory and matched the feat performed by the 1987 San Diego Padres. On July 29 Bill Mueller of the Boston Red Sox hit three home runs in one game, including two grand slams in consecutive innings. Mueller hit one slam right-handed and one left-handed to become the only player to accomplish that feat. Mueller is the most recent batter to hit two slams in the same game.

On July 18, 2003, Rickey Henderson of the Los Angeles Dodgers hit his 296th career home run, a solo shot off Brett Tomko of the St. Louis Cardinals at Dodger Stadium. This home run gave Henderson at least one homer in 25 consecutive seasons, breaking his tie for the record with Ty Cobb. It is interesting that two players known primarily for their base-running, not slugging, have hit homers in more consecutive seasons than any other batter. Henderson's next round-tripper, the last of his career, came, appropriately enough, as the leadoff batter for the Dodgers on July 20. Henderson holds the record for most home runs leading off the game, with 81. Through 2006, second place on the list belongs to Craig Biggio with 50.

◆ ◆ ◆

Two batters joined the 500 Home Run Club in 2003, the first time that two had hit number 500 in the same season since 1971, and coincidentally, they were the first two players born outside the United States to reach that plateau. On April 4 Sammy Sosa of the Chicago Cubs hit his first homer of the season in the seventh inning at Great American Ballpark in Cincinnati off Scott Sullivan. Sosa, from the Dominican Republic, had hit 40 home runs seven times and 50 or more homers in four consecutive seasons from 1998 through 2000 (tied with Mark McGwire for the record). Sosa hit 60 in three of those four years, which is the most seasons hitting 60 or more in history. His total of six consecutive seasons with 40 home runs from 1998 through 2003 is tied for the second-longest streak with Alex Rodriguez's and one behind Babe Ruth's seven straight years. He led the National League twice and holds the record for most homers in any calendar month with 20 in June 1998. He and Richie Sexson each hit five in October 2001, when the season was delayed a week, to claim the top spot for regular season homers in one October. Sosa holds three of the top five places for the most home runs in one season by a right-handed batter, with his 66 in 1998 being the most ever hit by a batter in one season who did not lead his league for the year. He holds the record for most home runs in five through 10 consecutive seasons and is tied for the record for most consecutive years of hitting 60 (two) with McGwire. Sosa is third on the career list for right-handed sluggers behind Hank Aaron and Willie Mays. Sosa is tied with Johnny Mize with six three-homer games in his career and is third on the career list with 68 career multi-homer games. His 11 multi-homer games in 1998 tied Hank Greenberg's 1938 total for the most in one season, and he is also tied with five other players for the next highest total with 10 in 2001. He hit home runs in 42 ballparks in his career, including a record 18 in 1998 (a record tied by Mike Piazza of the New York Mets in 2000). His 293 homers at Chicago's Wrigley Field are the most by any batter. He holds the record for the most by a visitor at Dolphins Stadium (also known as Joe Robbie Stadium and Pro Player Stadium) with 12 and at Minute Maid Park (also known as Enron Field and Astros Field) with 15. His career home run production rate is the third highest for players with 300 homers, at 31.1 per 500 plate appearances. On June 3, 2003, Sosa was ejected from a game in the first inning when his bat broke on a ground out and the umpires discovered cork inside the barrel of the bat. Major League Baseball suspended him for eight games, which was reduced to seven because of his quick and penitent statements after the contest. Many people, including players, questioned Sosa's explanation at the time that he mistakenly used a bat with cork in it. No other bats were discovered to have been tampered with, but the incident tarnished Sosa's image in the minds of many fans. There is no evidence that corking the bat actually adds distance to a batted ball, even though players believe it. The umpire crew chief in that game, Tim McClelland, had been the plate umpire in George Brett's 1983 "pine-tar" game.

On May 11, 2003, Rafael Palmeiro of the Texas Rangers, who was born in Cuba, joined Sosa by hitting his 500th home run in a game against the Cleveland Indians at The Ballpark in Arlington (also known as Ameriquest Field) off David Elder. Palmeiro had hit his first home run as a member of the Cubs team and his 500th with the Rangers, while Sosa had hit his first home run as a Ranger and his 500th as a Cub. Palmeiro hit 569 home runs to place ninth all-time and third on the career list for left-handed batters, and that total is the most for a batter who never led the league in any season. His 544 American League blasts place him fourth in the Junior Circuit. Palmeiro hit 210 round-trippers after his 35th birthday, one of three players to top 200 at that age (Hank Aaron and Barry Bonds are the other two). He hit more than 200 homers for two different teams, with 321 for the Rangers and 223 for the Baltimore Orioles, one of three batters to accomplish this. These totals place him second on the Rangers all-time franchise list and fifth on the Orioles list. Palmeiro never hit 50 in one season, reaching his peak of 47 twice. He has hit the most home runs at Oriole Park at Camden Yards with 124 and the most at Ameriquest Field with 130. Palmeiro has clouted the most home runs as a visitor at two parks: Network Associates Coliseum in Oakland (20) and Safeco Field in Seattle (17). On July 15, 2005, Palmeiro collected his 3,000th career hit to become the fourth batter with 500 home runs and 3,000 hits. Just 16 days later, on August 1, Major League Baseball suspended Palmeiro for 10 games because he failed a drug test, but officials would not say when the test had been administered. He became the highest-profile player to fail a test for banned substances through the 2006 season.

National League baseball came to the Caribbean in 2003 as the Montreal Expos played 22 of their "home" games at Estadio Hiram Bithorn in San Juan, Puerto Rico, the same park in which the Toronto Blue Jays and Texas Rangers played one game in 2001. The Expos' first game in their "home away from home" was played on April 11 against the New York Mets, and Brian Schneider of the Expos hit the first National League home run in Puerto Rico in the third inning off David Cone. Brad Wilkerson and Jose Vidro also homered in the game for the Expos, who also played 21 games in San Juan in 2004.

On July 20, 2003, Jeff Bagwell hit his 400th career home run, a solo shot off Danny Graves of the Reds, to become the 35th player to reach that milestone. Through 2005 Bagwell had hit 40 homers in one season three times and 30 for eight consecutive years from 1996 through 2003. Although he never led the National League, he hit 310 homers from 1991 through 2000, good for ninth place in the majors during that period. He spent most of that time playing his home games at Houston's Astrodome, which had a negative effect on home runs, thus making his achievement greater.

Carlos Delgado of the Toronto Blue Jays became the 15th and most recent batter to slug four home runs in one game on September 25, 2003, against the Tampa Bay Devil Rays at Skydome (later known as Rogers Centre). The Blue Jays won the contest, 10-8, with three tallies in the bottom of the eighth inning. Delgado hit his quartet in consecutive at bats, only the sixth to perform that feat. His first homer of the day was his 300th career round-tripper. On April 4, 1994, he had hit his first major league home run, his only four-bagger of the day. On September 17, 1998, Delgado hit two in the game, the first of which was career home run number 100. Then on April 20, 2001, he slugged three in a game, the third being home run number 200. So on each milestone homer of his career to this point, Delgado had hit one more on the day than the last time: one for number 1, two for number 100, three for number 200, and four for number 300.

Adrian Beltre of the Los Angeles Dodgers led the National League with 48 home runs in 2004, while Adam Dunn of the Cincinnati Reds and Albert Pujols of the St. Louis Cardinals tied for second place with 46 homers. Barry Bonds finished fourth with 45. In the American League, Manny Ramirez of the World Series champion Boston Red Sox led by hitting 43 home runs, and his teammate David Ortiz and Paul Konerko of the Chicago White Sox tied for second with 41 round-trippers. The major league season started on March 30 at Tokyo Dome, where the Tampa Bay Devil Rays and New York Yankees split a two-game series. In the first game Jason Giambi of the New York Yankees hit the first American League homer in Japan in the first inning off Victor Zambrano, to join the list of players who had hit home runs in three countries. Jose Cruz Jr. and Tino Martinez each homered for the Devil Rays, thus joining the same list. On March 31 Tony Clark hit a home run for the Yankees and Jorge Posada whacked two. The other four-bagger in the game was hit by the Yankee left fielder and Japanese native, Hideki Matsui. Matsui, in his second year playing in the major leagues, had not yet hit a major league home run outside the United States but did join the three country list in August 2004, when he homered in Toronto.

Barry Bonds of the San Francisco Giants hit his 661st major league home run on April 13, 2004, off Ben Ford of the Milwaukee Brewers to pass Willie Mays, who had also played for the Giants, and take the third spot on the all-time homer list. Mays had been either second or third on the list since June 27, 1966, when he passed Ted Williams, and had held second place from August 17, 1966, through June 9, 1972. In the first of two games on June 12, 2004, at Baltimore's Camden Yards, Bonds, with 674 home runs coming into the game, hit a four-bagger in the top of the third inning. Rafael Palmeiro of the Orioles, who had hit 535 career homers before this day, clouted one in the bottom of the same inning, to mark the third time in history that two batters with at least 500 home runs had each hit one in the same game. All three occasions had involved the Giants as Mays and Ernie Banks of the Cubs had performed the accomplishment on June 17, 1970, and Mays and Hank Aaron had repeated the feat on May 8, 1971.

Ken Griffey Jr. of the Cincinnati Reds became the 20th and most recent batter to join the 500 Home Run Club on June 20, 2004, at Busch Stadium in St. Louis when he hit a sixth inning solo homer off Matt Morris. Griffey became the fifth player to hit number 500 since August 1999, and only the seven in a six-year period from 1965 through 1971 tops this number. Through 2005 Griffey had led the American League four times, including three consecutive years, hit 50 twice and 40 seven times, including 40 in five consecutive seasons. He hit 16 before his 20th birthday, the third-most home runs for a teenager, behind Tony Conigliaro and Mel Ott.

> **The Ken Griffeys** *(Senior and Junior) became the only father and son to homer in the same game on September 14, 1990 at Anaheim Stadium (later known as Edison Field and Angel Stadium of Anaheim). In the top of the first inning, dad hit a two-run homer to left-center field off Kirk McCaskill of the Angels. Junior walked to the plate and hit the 3-0 pitch to the same spot for a father-son, back-to-back homer-fest.*

From 1991 through 2000, Griffey hit more homers than any other player with 400, thus becoming the fourth player to smack 400 homers in a decade. He has hit home runs in 41 different ballparks through 2005, the third highest total all-time. In April 1997 Griffey hit 13 home runs to set a new record for the month of April, since tied by Luis Gonzalez in 2001. His 56 home runs in 1996 and 1997 are the sixth highest total for a lefty in one season. The Griffeys have combined for the second-most home runs in history for a father/son pair, with 688 through 2005.

On September 17, 2004, Barry Bonds hit his 700th home run, a solo shot off Jake Peavy of the San Diego Padres in San Francisco, to become the third slugger to reach that milestone. In May 2001 Bonds had hit 17 homers to set a new record for the month of May. He has the fourth highest home run production rate for players with 300 career round-trippers at 30.4 per 500 plate appearances. Bonds clouted 30 home runs for 13 consecutive seasons from 1992 through 2004, the highest total of any batter. He hit 40 homers eight times, including five consecutive years. He only topped 50 once, when he set the single-season record at 73, and led the National League twice. His 377 round-trippers are the third most for the decade from 1991 through 2000 and his 708 through 2005 are the second-most all-time in the National League but the most by a left-handed hitter in the league. (See chapter 14 for a 2006 update to this and other Bonds's notes.) Bonds is fourth on the career home run list for the Pittsburgh Pirates and second for the Giants franchise. Through 2005 Bonds hit 286 home runs after his 35th birthday, topping the record in this category set by Hank Aaron of 245. Bonds has 68 multi-homer games, tied for second with Sammy Sosa behind Babe Ruth. As a visitor, he is the leader at three ballparks with his 27 at Dodger Stadium, 24 at Coors Field, and 17 at Chase Field (also known as Bank One Ballpark). He is one of four players with 300 home runs and 300 stolen bases, along with Willie Mays, Andre Dawson, and his dad, Bobby. Bobby and Barry have combined for the most home runs in history for a father/son pair, with 1,040 through 2005.

Fred McGriff played his last game on July 15, 2004, ending his career with 493 home runs, tied with Lou Gehrig in 21st place on the all-time list. McGriff had led both the American and National Leagues in homers for a season, one of six players to lead multiple leagues for a campaign. He is one of three players to hit at least 200 home runs in each league, by hitting 224 in the American League and 269 in the National to join Frank Robinson and Mark McGwire on this very exclusive list. McGriff hit 10 or more homers for 17 consecutive years, and his career total is the second highest without ever hitting 40 in one season (only Eddie Murray hit more). McGriff set a record by hitting at least 30 for five different clubs: the Blue Jays (three times), Padres (twice), Braves (once), Devil Rays (once), and Cubs (once), but fellow Tampa native Gary Sheffield tied McGriff's mark in 2004. Having played in both leagues at a time when many new ballparks were constructed, McGriff hit homers in 43 different parks, the record. Ken Griffey Jr. tied this mark in 2006.

In 2005 the home run production rate dropped one point from the previous year to 13.5 per 500 plate appearances. During the season, the commissioner proclaimed that the newly installed program to test for banned substances worked because home runs were down. However, as can be seen from the figures used throughout this book to show the yearly production rate, seasonal deviations are the norm. The 2005 rate falls within the range of rates from 1994 through 2004 and, in fact, is almost identical to the rates for 1998 (when single-season record fell) and 2004. The statement by the commissioner also relies on the unproven supposition that steroid use among hitters actually caused the increase in the first place.

Andruw Jones of Atlanta became the first slugger in Braves franchise history to hit 50 home runs in a season when he led the National League with 51 in 2005. The 50-homer season by Jones was the first in the majors since 2002, the 37th time a batter had reached that milestone, and the 19th time since 1995—just over half of the 50-homer seasons have occurred in an 11-year period. Jones clouted number 50 on September 14 off Geoff Geary of the Phillies in Philadelphia. Derrek Lee of the Chicago Cubs placed second in the league with 46. Alex Rodriguez of the New York Yankees led the American League with 48 home runs and a pair of sluggers for the Boston Red Sox finished second and third, as David Ortiz hit 47 clouts, while Manny Ramirez hit 45. ARod led the American League for three years while playing for the Texas Rangers and, after 2005, had led the league four of five years.

Sammy Sosa joined Rafael Palmeiro on the Baltimore Orioles roster in 2005, the first time that two sluggers each with over 500 home runs played for the same team in one year. Neither had good years, as Sosa hit 14 round-trippers and Palmeiro clouted 18 in a year that saw both of them play less than a full season. They did not homer in the same game during the season. On June 12, 2005, the Cincinnati Reds hosted the Orioles at Great American Ballpark. Sosa, who came into the day with 580 career homers, hit two in consecutive at bats in the second and third innings. Cincinnati's Ken Griffey Jr., who had hit 511 and was tied with Mel Ott, smashed a home run in the fifth inning in a game won by the Reds, 10-6. This was the fourth and most recent time that two members of the 500 Home Run Club hit four-baggers in the same game, and the first that did not involve the San Francisco Giants. The third instance had been exactly one year earlier at Baltimore's Camden Yards. On July 27 Sosa hit his 587th home run, a solo clout off Chris Young of the Texas Rangers, to pass Frank Robinson and move into fifth place on the all-time home run list. Robinson had been in the top five since 1973.

After all the celebrations of home runs in the late 1990s, a backlash arose concerning the supposed "cheating" by some players who used illegal substances in an attempt to gain an advantage over their competitors. This terminology was also applied to players who approached and broke long-standing records. With some historical perspective gained only by the passing of years and more scientific studies on the effects of known factors, the emotional responses should cool so that sound reasoning and civilized discourse can explain what happened. One year's decrease in production is not enough to prove that steroids caused the inflated numbers of the late 1990s and that Major League Baseball's testing program is making the home run production rate drop. The production rate over the next few years will be interesting to watch.

The game of baseball has withstood crises and negative reactions in the past because of a variety of events: labor wars, internal politics, world events, and on-the-field scandals. The game has survived those critical times, and it will survive this time.

13
CONCLUSION

Our nineteenth-century ancestors might not recognize the style of the game played by Major League Baseball in the twenty-first century, as players now rely on the home run as the key weapon in their offensive arsenal. The home run can change the complexion of a game in an instant by plating up to four runs with one swing of the bat, thus turning a closely contested game into one-sided contest or vice versa. Sluggers also tend to make more money than other hitters, a fact noted by Ralph Kiner, one of the best home run hitters of all-time, when he said, "Cadillacs are down at the end of the bat."

The home run has grown from a minor factor in the game to a major event, and this change is popular with fans, since most would rather see the big boppers swing for the fences than a pitching duel. Therefore, the high-octane offense has drawn more people to the park, and the income of the team owners interested in making money (this is a business to them) is boosted by this increased interest of fans.

One on-the-field result of the increased reliance on home runs is the percentage of runs scored from round-trippers. This figure reached 20 percent for the first time in 1937 (20.1 percent) and 30 percent in 1955 (32.1 percent). In 1987 a new high was set when 35.3 percent of all runs were scored on four-baggers and the 35 percent level has been topped every year from 1999 through 2005.

Taking a very broad look at Figure 1.1 (chapter 1), one might split the history of baseball into the following home run periods:

Nineteenth century
Deadball Era
1920s and 1930s
World War II
Late 1940s to late 1960s
Late 1960s to early 1990s
Early 1990s to 2006

World War II caused a large downturn in the home run rate that can be viewed as nothing more than a temporary aberration in the general increase in production from 1920 through the early 1960s. The 1970s through the early 1990s saw a decrease in the production rate from the previous period, part of the natural ebb and flow between batters and pitchers, but that was reversed in the mid-1990s. During the 1970s and 1980s, the production rate stayed about the same for two decades, although there were many deviations from year to year. In the 11-year stretch starting in the mid-1990s, the production rate, although higher than in the past, remained approximately the same. An increase in single-season totals for individual batters is a natural result of the increase in the production rate. Yearly deviations in the home run production rate are a normal occurrence and have varied from the largest increase of 3.7 (from 1976 to 1977) to the largest decrease of 3.8 (from 1987 to 1988). A change by as much as one home run per 500 plate appearances (for example, from 2004 to 2005) is common.

The rate of home run production has varied through the years, with periods of higher rates following periods of lower rates. Figure 1.1 clearly shows these pendulum-like swings between higher and lower offense: pitchers will dominate the game for a time and then batters will dominate for a time. These swings are the result of many factors. Rule changes might be considered the largest single contributing factor to the changes in production rate through the years, but many other factors that are internal to baseball (such as changes in ballparks) and external to the game (such as world wars) have also had their effects.

Figure 13.1 adds a trend line to Figure 1.1, illustrating the steady increase in home run production from the beginning of the National League in 1876 through 2005. The movement of the rate line around the trend line documents the pendulum effect of the production through the years. It is also clear that the production rate of the late 1990s is closer to the trend line than was the rate during the 1950s. The emotional statements regarding the supposed correlation between home run production and illegal drug use at the beginning of the twenty-first century are overblown and misleading: they are not based on factual evidence but rather on conjecture and are more inflammatory than informative. Emotionally charged words like "cheater" and phrases like "performance-enhancing drugs" should be given a moratorium until there is evidence to support them. Figure 13.1 shows that the home run production rate of the late 1990s was not an aberration but merely an extension of a trend that has existed in baseball for 130 years. As we have seen in previous chapters, every player who has broken a home run record has been met with a negative reaction. In most cases, that reaction was concurrent with the record but for Mark McGwire and Barry Bonds that reaction took a few years to surface.

Many individuals have stood out through the years as home run sluggers. These players have come from many backgrounds and, more recently, many countries. They have clouted major league round-trippers in 26 states and the District of Columbia; Canada, Mexico, Puerto Rico, and Japan; indoors and outdoors; in daylight and under the lights; in the sunshine, rain,

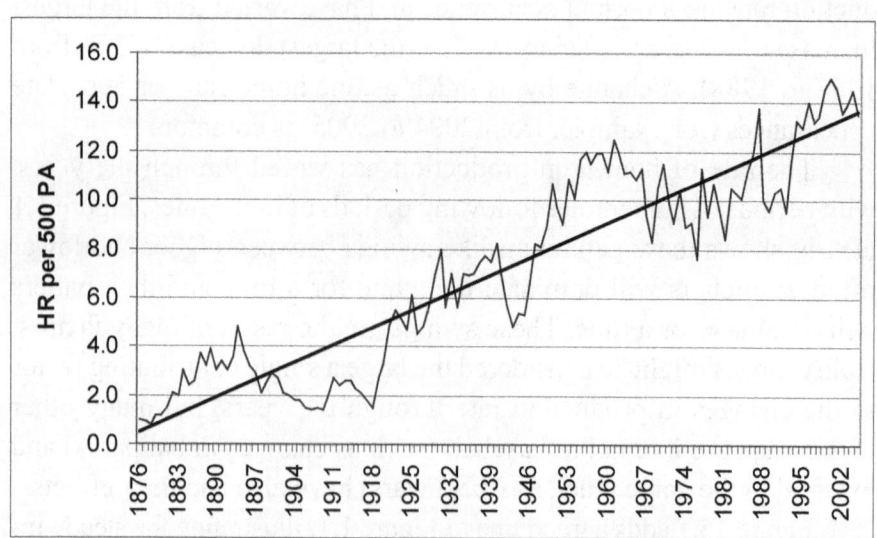

Figure 13.1 – Home Run Production Rate with Trend Line (1876–2005)

CONCLUSION

and snow; inside the park and out; over, through, and under walls, fences, hedges, scoreboards, fountains, and carriages. They have hit four in a game, 70 in a season, and 700 in a career. From Harry Stovey to Babe Ruth to Hank Aaron to Barry Bonds, we have traced the evolution of the home run and its fascination in the sporting world and beyond. The television commercial stated, "Chicks dig the long ball," but the scope of a four-bagger's power is really much wider than that—with the exception of pitchers, everyone loves the long ball!

14

POSTSCRIPT:
THE 2006 SEASON

The 2006 season provided many home run highlights for fans to enjoy. Both individuals and teams combined to create many fan-friendly homer moments. The home run production rate of 14.4 per 500 plate appearances in 2006, the second highest rate in five years, represented an increase of almost one homer per 500 plate appearances over the previous season. This rate remains in line with all seasons since 1994 and provides additional evidence that the attention to steroid use by batters was overblown. The drug-testing program instituted by Major League Baseball has not reduced the home run rate, contrary to statements made by various officials.

Both league leaders topped the 50 homer mark in 2006, the first time since 2001 that both league leaders clouted over 50 home runs. Sophomore Ryan Howard of the Philadelphia Phillies led all sluggers with 58 dingers for the season, while Boston's David Ortiz led the American League by hitting 54 four-baggers. Howard set a new standard for second-year players with his 58 clouts, topping the old mark set by Ralph Kiner when he smacked 51 in 1947. Ortiz broke the Red Sox single-season record of 50 held by Jimmie Foxx since 1938, while Howard easily broke the Phillies single-season record of 48, set by Mike Schmidt in 1980. Ortiz hit 47 of his clouts as a designated hitter, thus breaking his own record for that position during one season, set in 2005. Albert Pujols of the St. Louis Cardinals placed second in the National League with 49 homers.

Kevin Mench of the Texas Rangers had the first home run highlight of 2006 when he homered in seven consecutive games, starting on April 21, thus missing the record of eight by one game. Mench became the first right-handed batter to hit a home run in at least seven consecutive games, joining four lefties. Albert Pujols smacked 14 homers in the month of April, setting a new mark for that month.

On April 20 Julio Franco of the New York Mets hit a homer at the age of 47 years 240 days to top pitcher Jack Quinn as the oldest player to hit a major league home run. Quinn set his record in 1930, just eight days short of his 47th birthday. Franco homered again on September 30 at RFK Stadium at the age of 48 years 38 days. Thus, Franco is the only player to homer at the age of 47 and also the only one to homer as a 48 year old.

Another over-40 player, San Francisco Giant Barry Bonds, also made news as a slugger during the season. On May 28 Bonds whacked the 715th homer of his career, passing Babe Ruth for second place on the all-time list. Bonds also became the all-time leader among left-handed batters with this clout. The last four-bagger of the year for Bonds was number 734, which set a new career record for National League sluggers. Hank Aaron had held that mark since 1974 (as shown in Table 1.5, chapter 1). Bonds also had one multi-homer game, the 69th of his career, during the season to move into second place on the career list behind Babe Ruth's 72 multi-home run games. Bonds also increased his leading totals as a visitor in three ballparks: 28 at Dodger Stadium, 25 at Coors Field, and 18 at Chase Field in Phoenix, formerly known as Bank One Ballpark. Bonds and his dad, Bobby, have combined for 1,066 home runs through 2006, the most of any father/son pair. The Ken Griffeys (Sr. and Jr.) are second with 715. Barry Bonds has hit 312 home runs after his 35th birthday through the 2006 season, thus extending his own record. Bonds has hit 558 circuit clouts as a San Francisco Giant, the most for the California version of the club. Through 2006, Bonds had hit at least one home run off 434 different pitchers and he is the only slugger to have victimized more than 400 hurlers. Rafael Palmeiro homered off 364 pitchers, good for second place behind Bonds. As a comparison of how baseball has changed, Babe Ruth swatted his 714 homers off only 216 different pitchers, while Jimmie Foxx, the second batter to join the 500 Home Run Club, homered off 173 pitchers.

Alfonso Soriano of the Washington Nationals hit many newsworthy home runs in 2006. Soriano, in his first season playing in the National League, whacked nine leadoff home runs during the season, thus tying the fifth highest total for one campaign (and second-highest total in the NL history) and moving into eighth place on the career chart for leadoff four-baggers. Soriano ended the season with 46 total long balls and 41 stolen bases, the fourth time that he had topped the 30/30 mark in those two statistics. Only two other players have had four 30/30 seasons, and they are both named Bonds—Bobby and son Barry. In addition, Soriano's combination made him the fourth player in history to have a 40/40 season, joining Jose Canseco, Barry Bonds, and Alex Rodriguez.

◆ ◆ ◆

A number of sluggers achieved career milestones during the 2006 season. Both Reggie Sanders and Steve Finley hit their 300th home runs and, having each already collected 300 stolen bases, became the fifth and sixth members of the 300/300 Club, along with Willie Mays, Bobby Bonds, Andre Dawson, and Barry Bonds. It is interesting that the number of players with both 300 homers and steals grew by half in one season. In April Frank Thomas blasted his 200th home run as a designated hitter. He ended the season with 236 as a DH to go with the 249 he smacked as a first baseman. Thomas is the third slugger to hit at least 200 homers at each of two positions. Babe Ruth hit 354 as a right fielder and 313 as a left fielder while Ernie Banks clouted 277 at shortstop and 210 at first base. Alex Rodriguez became the youngest player to hit 450 homers on July 21, six days before his 31st birthday. He beat the record held by his former teammate, Ken Griffey Jr., who hit number 450 at 31 years 261 days.

Mike Piazza of the San Diego Padres joined the 400 Homer Club on April 26 and ended the season with 419 four-baggers. Of that total, 396 had been hit as a catcher, the most ever by a backstop. Piazza hit at least 30 home runs for eight consecutive years from 1995 through 2002 and hit 14 as a visitor at Atlanta's Turner Field, the highest visitor total for that stadium.

On August 22 Carlos Delgado of the New York Mets joined the 400 Homer Club. (Delgado's exploits when hitting a milestone home run were discussed in chapter 12.) Delgado hit "only" two homers in the August 22 game, but he achieved his milestone with a grand slam, the first time in history that any player has hit a slam as an even-hundred homer, 300 or higher. Delgado is the career home run leader (336) for the Toronto Blue Jays, the club with which he started his career, and the all-time leader at Rogers Centre (formerly Skydome) with 175 long balls. He is tied with Tino Martinez for the most homers hit as a visitor at Ameriquest Field (formerly The Ballpark in Arlington) with 19. From 1997 through 2006, Delgado hit at least 30 home runs each season.

Forty-three-year-old pitcher Jamie Moyer of the Seattle Mariners surrendered five home runs on July 21 against the Boston Red Sox. The first of these, by David Ortiz, made Moyer the ninth hurler to surender 400 gopher balls in his career.

Travis Hafner hit six grand slams between May 1 and August 13 to tie Don Mattingly's 1987 single-season record. Richie Sexson of the Seattle Mariners hit five during the season. Only five players in history have hit as many as five slams in one season, and two of them achieved the feat in 2006. Pitcher Carlos Zambrano of the Chicago Cubs slashed six homers during the season, the most for a hurler since Mike Hampton's seven in 2001. The record for moundsmen is nine by Wes Ferrell in 1931. On September 2 Kevin Kouzmanoff of the Cleveland Indians hit the first major league pitch he saw for a grand slam; he is the first batter to perform this feat in big league history.

Ken Griffey Jr. homered for the first time at Detroit's Comerica Park and the new Busch Stadium in St. Louis during the 2006 season. Thus, Griffey has now homered in 43 different ballparks to tie Fred McGriff for the career record of most parks in which at least one home run has been hit by a slugger.

On September 18 the Los Angeles Dodgers trailed the San Diego Padres, 9-5, in the middle of the ninth inning. Pitcher Jon Adkins entered the game for the Padres, and each of the first two batters he faced, Jeff Kent and J. D. Drew, homered. Trevor Hoffman, the Padres extraordinary closer, relieved Adkins and surrendered two homers on the first two pitches he threw in the contest to Russell Martin and Marlon Anderson. Thus, the Dodgers became the fourth team to hit four consecutive home runs, joining the Braves, Indians, and Twins. Three of these came on three consecutive pitches off two hurlers who surrendered a total of nine homers in the entire 2006 season; therefore, the two pitchers surrendered a total of five homers in all other games they pitched in 2006. The quartet of four-baggers by Los Angeles tied the game at nine runs apiece, but then the Dodgers won the contest when Nomar Garciaparra hit a two-run shot in the bottom of the 10th inning.

During the 2006 Home Run Derby, held at PNC Park in Pittsburgh, left-handed batters took aim at the Allegheny River. David Ortiz plunked eight balls into the water. Ryan Howard won the derby, hitting 23 four-baggers, while David Wright had the best single round with 16 in the first frame. In the game the next night, Wright homered on his first All-Star at bat.

In the National League Championship Series, Carlos Beltran of the New York Mets continued to terrorize the St. Louis pitching staff with his post-season slugging. In 2004, while a member of the Houston Astros, Beltran had belted four home runs in 32 plate appearances in the NLCS, and in 2006 he nearly matched the output by hitting three in 31 plate appearances. His home run production rate for the two series is 55.6 per 500 plate appearances, an incredible number for a batter, although the results may have been skewed by his relatively low number of plate appearances. In the American League Championship Series, Detroit's Magglio Ordonez hit a solo homer in the bottom of the sixth inning to tie the contest, 3-3. With two outs in the ninth inning, Ordonez hit a three-run shot to win the game and the series, thus propelling the Tigers into the World Series. Ordonez was the first batter to tie a post-season game with a four-bagger and then end the same game with a home run.

◆ ◆ ◆

The 2006 season ended with Barry Bonds approaching Hank Aaron's career record and four sluggers in sight of the 500 Home Run Club (Frank Thomas, Jim Thome, Manny Ramirez, and Alex Rodriguez). At least one major league homer has been hit by 6,796 of 16,639 total major league players, with a grand total of 240,730 hit from 1876 through 2006.

It will be fun to watch as future batters add their names to the list of historic sluggers. With every game, there is a chance that a unique event, often involving a home run, will occur. Keep watching!

APPENDIX A

CAREER HOME RUN MILESTONES

Details of Home Run Number 500

Date	Batter	Team (League)	Opponent	*Age
08/11/29	Babe Ruth	New York (AL)	@Cleveland	34.186
09/24/40	Jimmie Foxx	Boston (AL)	@Philadelphia	32.337
08/01/45	Mel Ott	New York (NL)	Boston	36.152
06/17/60	Ted Williams	Boston (AL)	@Cleveland	41.291
09/13/65	Willie Mays	San Francisco (NL)	@Houston	34.130
05/14/67	Mickey Mantle	New York (AL)	Baltimore	35.206
07/14/67	Eddie Mathews	Houston (NL)	@San Francisco	35.274
07/14/68	Hank Aaron	Atlanta (NL)	San Francisco	34.159
05/12/70	Ernie Banks	Chicago (NL)	Atlanta	39.101
08/10/71	Harmon Killebrew	Minnesota (AL)	Baltimore	35.042
09/13/71	Frank Robinson	Baltimore (AL)	Detroit	36.013
06/30/78	Willie McCovey	San Francisco (NL)	@Atlanta	40.171
09/17/84	Reggie Jackson	California (AL)	Kansas City	38.122
04/18/87	Mike Schmidt	Philadelphia (NL)	@Pittsburgh	37.203
09/06/96	Eddie Murray	Baltimore (AL)	Detroit	40.194
08/05/99	Mark McGwire	St. Louis (NL)	San Diego	35.308
04/17/01	Barry Bonds	San Francisco (NL)	Los Angeles	36.267
04/04/03	Sammy Sosa	Chicago (NL)	@Cincinnati	34.143
05/11/03	Rafael Palmeiro	Texas (AL)	Cleveland	38.229
06/20/04	Ken Griffey Jr.	Cincinnati (NL)	@St. Louis	34.212

Details of Home Run Number 600

Date	Batter	Team (League)	Opponent	*Age
08/21/31	Babe Ruth	New York (AL)	@St. Louis	36.196
09/22/69	Willie Mays	San Francisco (NL)	@San Diego	38.139
04/27/71	Hank Aaron	Atlanta (NL)	San Francisco	37.081
08/09/02	Barry Bonds	San Francisco (NL)	Pittsburgh	38.016

Details of Home Run Number 700

Date	Batter	Team (League)	Opponent	*Age
07/13/34	Babe Ruth	New York (AL)	@Detroit	39.157
07/21/73	Hank Aaron	Atlanta (NL)	Philadelphia	39.166
09/17/04	Barry Bonds	San Francisco (NL)	San Diego	40.056

*Age: years and days format

APPENDIX B

SINGLE-SEASON HOME RUN MILESTONES

Details of Home Run Number 50

Date	Batter	Team (League)	Opponent	*Age	HR
09/24/20	Babe Ruth	New York (AL)	Washington	25.230	54
09/03/21	Babe Ruth	New York (AL)	Washington	26.209	59
09/11/27	Babe Ruth	New York (AL)	St. Louis	32.217	60
09/15/28	Babe Ruth	New York (AL)	@St. Louis	33.221	54
09/15/30	Hack Wilson	Chicago (NL)	@Philadelphia	30.142	56
09/03/32	Jimmie Foxx	Philadelphia (AL)	Boston	24.316	58
09/12/38	Hank Greenberg	Detroit (AL)	Chicago	27.254	58
10/01/38	Jimmie Foxx	Boston (AL)	New York	30.344	50
09/18/47	Ralph Kiner	Pittsburgh (NL)	Brooklyn	24.326	51
09/20/47	Johnny Mize	New York (NL)	Philadelphia	34.256	51
09/19/49	Ralph Kiner	Pittsburgh (NL)	New York	26.327	54
09/20/55	Willie Mays	New York (NL)	Pittsburgh	24.137	51
09/18/56	Mickey Mantle	New York (AL)	@Chicago	24.333	52
08/22/61	Roger Maris	New York (AL)	@Los Angeles	26.346	61
09/03/61	Mickey Mantle	New York (AL)	Detroit	29.318	54
09/25/65	Willie Mays	San Francisco (NL)	Milwaukee	34.142	52
09/23/77	George Foster	Cincinnati (NL)	@Atlanta	28.296	52
10/03/90	Cecil Fielder	Detroit (AL)	@New York	27.012	51
09/30/95	Albert Belle	Cleveland (AL)	Kansas City	29.036	50
09/14/96	Mark McGwire	Oakland (AL)	@Cleveland	32.348	52
09/29/96	Brady Anderson	Baltimore (AL)	@Toronto	32.254	50
09/07/97	Ken Griffey Jr.	Seattle (AL)	@Minnesota	27.290	56

Number 50 (continued)

Date	Batter	Team (League)	Opponent	*Age	HR
09/10/97	Mark McGwire	St. Louis** (NL)	@San Francisco	33.344	58
08/20/98	Mark McGwire	St. Louis (NL)	@New York	34.323	70
08/23/98	Sammy Sosa	Chicago (NL)	Houston	29.284	66
09/07/98	Ken Griffey Jr.	Seattle (AL)	Baltimore	28.290	56
09/27/98	Greg Vaughn	San Diego (NL)	@Arizona	33.086	50
08/21/99	Sammy Sosa	Chicago (NL)	Colorado	30.282	63
08/22/99	Mark McGwire	St. Louis (NL)	@New York	35.325	65
09/16/00	Sammy Sosa	Chicago (NL)	@St. Louis	31.308	50
08/11/01	Barry Bonds	San Francisco (NL)	@Chicago	37.018	73
08/26/01	Sammy Sosa	Chicago (NL)	St. Louis	32.287	64
08/29/01	Luis Gonzalez	Arizona (NL)	San Francisco	33.360	57
09/28/01	Alex Rodríguez	Texas (AL)	@Anaheim	26.063	52
09/05/02	Alex Rodríguez	Texas (AL)	@Baltimore	27.040	57
09/25/02	Jim Thome	Cleveland (AL)	@Minnesota	32.029	52
09/14/05	Andruw Jones	Atlanta (NL)	@Philadelphia	28.144	51
09/03/06	Ryan Howard	Philadelphia (NL)	Atlanta	26.288	58
09/20/06	David Ortiz	Boston (AL)	Minnesota	30.306	54

Details of Home Run Number 60

Date	Batter	Team (League)	Opponent	*Age	HR
09/30/27	Babe Ruth	New York (AL)	Washington	32.236	60
09/26/61	Roger Maris	New York (AL)	Baltimore	27.016	61
09/05/98	Mark McGwire	St. Louis (NL)	Cincinnati	34.339	70
09/12/98	Sammy Sosa	Chicago (NL)	Milwaukee	29.304	66
09/18/99	Sammy Sosa	Chicago (NL)	Milwaukee	30.310	63
09/26/99	Mark McGwire	St. Louis (NL)	@Cincinnati	35.360	65
09/06/01	Barry Bonds	San Francisco (NL)	Arizona	37.044	73
10/02/01	Sammy Sosa	Chicago (NL)	Cincinnati	32.324	64

Details of Home Run Number 70

Date	Batter	Team (League)	Opponent	*Age	HR
09/27/98	Mark McGwire	St. Louis (NL)	Montreal	34.361	70
10/04/01	Barry Bonds	San Francisco (NL)	@Houston	37.072	73

HR: total home runs for the season
* Age: years and days format
** McGwire hit 38 for Oakland and 28 for St. Louis in 1997.

APPENDIX C

SINGLE-GAME HOME RUN MILESTONES

Details of Four Home Run Games

Date	Batter	Team (League)	Opponent	*Age	RBI /Pit	HR /THR
5/30/1894	B. Lowe	Boston (NL)	Cincinnati	28.324	6 /1	28/71
7/13/1896	E. Delahanty	Philadelphia (NL)	@Chicago	28.256	7 /1	53/101
06/03/32	L. Gehrig	New York (AL)	@Philadelphia	28.349	5 /2	240/493
07/10/36	C. Klein	Philadelphia (NL)	@Pittsburgh	31.276	6 /3	242/300
07/18/48	P. Seerey	Chicago (AL)	@Philadelphia	25.123	7 /3	74/86
08/31/50	G. Hodges	Brooklyn (NL)	Boston	26.149	9 /4	54/370
07/31/54	J. Adcock	Milwaukee (NL)	@Brooklyn	26.274	7 /4	64/336
06/10/59	R. Colavito	Cleveland (AL)	@Baltimore	25.304	6 /3	101/374
04/30/61	W. Mays	San Francisco (NL)	@Milwaukee	29.359	8 /3	281/660
04/17/76	M. Schmidt	Philadelphia (NL)	@Chicago	26.202	8/3	94/548
07/06/86	B. Horner	Atlanta (NL)	Montreal	28.334	6 /2	201/218
09/07/93	M. Whiten	St. Louis (NL)	@Cincinnati	26.286	12/3	38 /105
05/02/02	M. Cameron	Seattle (AL)	@Chicago	29.114	4/2	93 /195**
05/23/02	S. Green	Los Angeles (NL)	@Milwaukee	29.194	6/3	197/318**
09/25/03	C. Delgado	Toronto (AL)	Tampa Bay	31.092	6/3	299/407**

*Age: years and days format
** active in 2006

RBI: runs batted in from the home runs
Pit: number of pitchers victimized
HR: career home runs before hitting four in game
THR: total career home runs

APPENDIX D

YEARLY HOME RUN LEADERS BY LEAGUE

Bold print indicates new major league record.
Italic print indicates new American or National League record.

Year	League	Player	Team	HR
1876	NL	**George Hall**	**Philadelphia**	5
1877	NL	Lip Pike	Cincinnati	4
1878	NL	Paul Hines	Providence	4
1879	NL	**Charley Jones**	**Boston**	9
1880	NL	Jim O'Rourke	Boston	6
		Harry Stovey	Worcester	6
1881	NL	Dan Brouthers	Buffalo	8
1882	AA	Oscar Walker	St. Louis	7
	NL	George Wood	Detroit	7
1883	AA	**Harry Stovey**	**Philadelphia**	14
	NL	*Buck Ewing*	*New York*	10
1884	AA	John Reilly	Cincinnati	11
	NL	**Ned Williamson**	**Chicago**	27
	UA	Fred Dunlap	St. Louis	13
1885	AA	Harry Stovey	Philadelphia	13
	NL	Abner Dalrymple	Chicago	11
1886	AA	Bid McPhee	Cincinnati	8
	NL	Dan Brouthers	Detroit	11
		Hardy Richardson	Detroit	11
1887	AA	Tip O'Neill	St. Louis	14
	NL	Billy O'Brien	Washington	19

Year	League	Player	Team	HR
1888	AA	John Reilly	Cincinnati	13
	NL	Jimmy Ryan	Chicago	16
1889	AA	Bug Holliday	Cincinnati	19
		Harry Stovey	Philadelphia	19
	NL	Sam Thompson	Philadelphia	20
1890	AA	Count Campau	St. Louis	9
	NL	Oyster Burns	Brooklyn	13
		Mike Tiernan	New York	13
		Walt Wilmot	Chicago	13
	PL	Roger Connor	New York	14
1891	AA	Duke Farrell	Boston	12
	NL	Harry Stovey	Boston	16
		Mike Tiernan	New York	16
1892	NL	Bug Holliday	Cincinnati	13
1893	NL	Ed Delahanty	Philadelphia	19
1894	NL	Hugh Duffy	Boston	18
1895	NL	Sam Thompson	Philadelphia	18
1896	NL	Ed Delahanty	Philadelphia	13
		Bill Joyce	Washington/NY	13
1897	NL	Hugh Duffy	Boston	11
1898	NL	Jimmy Collins	Boston	15
1899	NL	Buck Freeman	Washington	25
1900	NL	Herman Long	Boston	12
1901	AL	*Nap Lajoie*	*Philadelphia*	*14*
	NL	Sam Crawford	Cincinnati	16
1902	AL	*Socks Seybold*	*Philadelphia*	*16*
	NL	Tommy Leach	Pittsburgh	6
1903	AL	Buck Freeman	Boston	13
	NL	Jimmy Sheckard	Brooklyn	9
1904	AL	Harry Davis	Philadelphia	10
	NL	Harry Lumley	Brooklyn	9
1905	AL	Harry Davis	Philadelphia	8
	NL	Fred Odwell	Cincinnati	9
1906	AL	Harry Davis	Philadelphia	12
	NL	Tim Jordan	Brooklyn	12
1907	AL	Harry Davis	Philadelphia	8
	NL	Dave Brain	Boston	10

YEARLY HOME RUN LEADERS BY LEAGUE

Year	League	Player	Team	HR
1908	AL	Sam Crawford	Detroit	7
	NL	Tim Jordan	Brooklyn	12
1909	AL	Ty Cobb	Detroit	9
	NL	Red Murray	New York	7
1910	AL	Jake Stahl	Boston	10
	NL	Fred Beck	Boston	10
		Frank Schulte	Chicago	10
1911	AL	Home Run Baker	Philadelphia	11
	NL	Frank Schulte	Chicago	21
1912	AL	Home Run Baker	Philadelphia	10
		Tris Speaker	Boston	10
	NL	Heinie Zimmerman	Chicago	14
1913	AL	Home Run Baker	Philadelphia	12
	NL	Gavvy Cravath	Philadelphia	19
1914	AL	Home Run Baker	Philadelphia	9
	FL	Dutch Zwilling	Chicago	16
	NL	Gavvy Cravath	Philadelphia	19
1915	AL	Braggo Roth	Chicago/Cleveland	7
	FL	Hal Chase	Buffalo	17
	NL	Gavvy Cravath	Philadelphia	24
1916	AL	Wally Pipp	New York	12
	NL	Dave Robertson	New York	12
		Cy Williams	Chicago	12
1917	AL	Wally Pipp	New York	9
	NL	Gavvy Cravath	Philadelphia	12
		Dave Robertson	New York	12
1918	AL	Babe Ruth	Boston	11
		Tilly Walker	Philadelphia	11
	NL	Gavvy Cravath	Philadelphia	8
1919	AL	*Babe Ruth*	*Boston*	*29*
	NL	Gavvy Cravath	Philadelphia	12
1920	AL	*Babe Ruth*	*New York*	*54*
	NL	Cy Williams	Philadelphia	15
1921	AL	*Babe Ruth*	*New York*	*59*
	NL	High Pockets Kelly	New York	23
1922	AL	Ken Williams	St. Louis	39
	NL	*Rogers Hornsby*	*St. Louis*	*42*

Year	League	Player	Team	HR
1923	AL	Babe Ruth	New York	41
	NL	Cy Williams	Philadelphia	41
1924	AL	Babe Ruth	New York	46
	NL	Jack Fournier	Brooklyn	27
1925	AL	Bob Meusel	New York	33
	NL	Rogers Hornsby	St. Louis	39
1926	AL	Babe Ruth	New York	47
	NL	Hack Wilson	Chicago	21
1927	AL	*Babe Ruth*	*New York*	*60*
	NL	Cy Williams	Philadelphia	30
		Hack Wilson	Chicago	30
1928	AL	Babe Ruth	New York	54
	NL	Jim Bottomley	St. Louis	31
		Hack Wilson	Chicago	31
1929	AL	Babe Ruth	New York	46
	NL	*Chuck Klein*	*Philadelphia*	*43*
1930	AL	Babe Ruth	New York	49
	NL	*Hack Wilson*	*Chicago*	*56*
1931	AL	Lou Gehrig	New York	46
		Babe Ruth	New York	46
	NL	Chuck Klein	Philadelphia	31
1932	AL	Jimmie Foxx	Philadelphia	58
	NL	Chuck Klein	Philadelphia	38
		Mel Ott	New York	38
1933	AL	Jimmie Foxx	Philadelphia	48
	NL	Chuck Klein	Philadelphia	28
1934	AL	Lou Gehrig	New York	49
	NL	Ripper Collins	St. Louis	35
		Mel Ott	New York	35
1935	AL	Jimmie Foxx	Philadelphia	36
		Hank Greenberg	Detroit	36
	NL	Wally Berger	Boston	34
1936	AL	Lou Gehrig	New York	49
	NL	Mel Ott	New York	33
1937	AL	Joe DiMaggio	New York	46
	NL	Joe Medwick	St. Louis	31
		Mel Ott	New York	31

YEARLY HOME RUN LEADERS BY LEAGUE

Year	League	Player	Team	HR
1938	AL	Hank Greenberg	Detroit	58
	NL	Mel Ott	New York	36
1939	AL	Jimmie Foxx	Boston	35
	NL	Johnny Mize	St. Louis	28
1940	AL	Hank Greenberg	Detroit	41
	NL	Johnny Mize	St. Louis	43
1941	AL	Ted Williams	Boston	37
	NL	Dolph Camilli	Brooklyn	34
1942	AL	Ted Williams	Boston	36
	NL	Mel Ott	New York	30
1943	AL	Rudy York	Detroit	34
	NL	Bill Nicholson	Chicago	29
1944	AL	Nick Etten	New York	22
	NL	Bill Nicholson	Chicago	33
1945	AL	Vern Stephens	St. Louis	24
	NL	Tommy Holmes	Boston	28
1946	AL	Hank Greenberg	Detroit	44
	NL	Ralph Kiner	Pittsburgh	23
1947	AL	Ted Williams	Boston	32
	NL	Ralph Kiner	Pittsburgh	51
		Johnny Mize	New York	51
1948	AL	Joe DiMaggio	New York	39
	NL	Ralph Kiner	Pittsburgh	40
		Johnny Mize	New York	40
1949	AL	Ted Williams	Boston	43
	NL	Ralph Kiner	Pittsburgh	54
1950	AL	Al Rosen	Cleveland	37
	NL	Ralph Kiner	Pittsburgh	47
1951	AL	Gus Zernial	Philadelphia	33
	NL	Ralph Kiner	Pittsburgh	42
1952	AL	Larry Doby	Cleveland	32
	NL	Ralph Kiner	Pittsburgh	37
		Hank Sauer	Chicago	37
1953	AL	Al Rosen	Cleveland	43
	NL	Eddie Mathews	Milwaukee	47
1954	AL	Larry Doby	Cleveland	32
	NL	Ted Kluszewski	Cincinnati	49

Year	League	Player	Team	HR
1955	AL	Mickey Mantle	New York	37
	NL	Willie Mays	New York	51
1956	AL	Mickey Mantle	New York	52
	NL	Duke Snider	Brooklyn	43
1957	AL	Roy Sievers	Washington	42
	NL	Hank Aaron	Milwaukee	44
1958	AL	Mickey Mantle	New York	42
	NL	Ernie Banks	Chicago	47
1959	AL	Rocky Colavito	Cleveland	42
		Harmon Killebrew	Washington	42
	NL	Eddie Mathews	Milwaukee	46
1960	AL	Mickey Mantle	New York	40
	NL	Ernie Banks	Chicago	41
1961	AL	***Roger Maris***	***New York***	***61***
	NL	Orlando Cepeda	San Francisco	46
1962	AL	Harmon Killebrew	Minnesota	48
	NL	Willie Mays	San Francisco	49
1963	AL	Harmon Killebrew	Minnesota	45
	NL	Hank Aaron	Milwaukee	44
		Willie McCovey	San Francisco	44
1964	AL	Harmon Killebrew	Minnesota	49
	NL	Willie Mays	San Francisco	47
1965	AL	Tony Conigliaro	Boston	32
	NL	Willie Mays	San Francisco	52
1966	AL	Frank Robinson	Baltimore	49
	NL	Hank Aaron	Atlanta	44
1967	AL	Harmon Killebrew	Minnesota	44
		Carl Yastrzemski	Boston	44
	NL	Hank Aaron	Atlanta	39
1968	AL	Frank Howard	Washington	44
	NL	Willie McCovey	San Francisco	36
1969	AL	Harmon Killebrew	Minnesota	49
	NL	Willie McCovey	San Francisco	45
1970	AL	Frank Howard	Washington	44
	NL	Johnny Bench	Cincinnati	45
1971	AL	Bill Melton	Chicago	33
	NL	Willie Stargell	Pittsburgh	48

YEARLY HOME RUN LEADERS BY LEAGUE

Year	League	Player	Team	HR
1972	AL	Dick Allen	Chicago	37
	NL	Johnny Bench	Cincinnati	40
1973	AL	Reggie Jackson	Oakland	32
	NL	Willie Stargell	Pittsburgh	44
1974	AL	Dick Allen	Chicago	32
	NL	Mike Schmidt	Philadelphia	36
1975	AL	Reggie Jackson	Oakland	36
		George Scott	Milwaukee	36
	NL	Mike Schmidt	Philadelphia	38
1976	AL	Graig Nettles	New York	32
	NL	Mike Schmidt	Philadelphia	38
1977	AL	Jim Rice	Boston	39
	NL	George Foster	Cincinnati	52
1978	AL	Jim Rice	Boston	46
	NL	George Foster	Cincinnati	40
1979	AL	Gorman Thomas	Milwaukee	45
	NL	Dave Kingman	Chicago	48
1980	AL	Reggie Jackson	New York	41
		Ben Oglivie	Milwaukee	41
	NL	Mike Schmidt	Philadelphia	48
1981	AL	Tony Armas	Oakland	22
		Dwight Evans	Boston	22
		Bobby Grich	California	22
		Eddie Murray	Baltimore	22
	NL	Mike Schmidt	Philadelphia	31
1982	AL	Reggie Jackson	California	39
		Gorman Thomas	Milwaukee	39
	NL	Dave Kingman	New York	37
1983	AL	Jim Rice	Boston	39
	NL	Mike Schmidt	Philadelphia	40
1984	AL	Tony Armas	Boston	43
	NL	Dale Murphy	Atlanta	36
		Mike Schmidt	Philadelphia	36
1985	AL	Darrell Evans	Detroit	40
	NL	Dale Murphy	Atlanta	37
1986	AL	Jesse Barfield	Toronto	40
	NL	Mike Schmidt	Philadelphia	37

Year	League	Player	Team	HR
1987	AL	Mark McGwire	Oakland	49
	NL	Andre Dawson	Chicago	49
1988	AL	Jose Canseco	Oakland	42
	NL	Darryl Strawberry	New York	39
1989	AL	Fred McGriff	Toronto	36
	NL	Kevin Mitchell	San Francisco	47
1990	AL	Cecil Fielder	Detroit	51
	NL	Ryne Sandberg	Chicago	40
1991	AL	Jose Canseco	Oakland	44
		Cecil Fielder	Detroit	44
	NL	Howard Johnson	New York	38
1992	AL	Juan Gonzalez	Texas	43
	NL	Fred McGriff	San Diego	35
1993	AL	Juan Gonzalez	Texas	46
	NL	Barry Bonds	San Francisco	46
1994	AL	Ken Griffey	Seattle	40
	NL	Matt Williams	San Francisco	43
1995	AL	Albert Belle	Cleveland	50
	NL	Dante Bichette	Colorado	40
1996	AL	Mark McGwire	Oakland	52
	NL	Andres Galarraga	Colorado	47
1997	AL	Ken Griffey	Seattle	56
	NL	Larry Walker	Colorado	49
1998	AL	Ken Griffey	Seattle	56
	NL	***Mark McGwire***	***St. Louis***	***70***
1999	AL	Ken Griffey	Seattle	48
	NL	Mark McGwire	St. Louis	65
2000	AL	Troy Glaus	Anaheim	47
	NL	Sammy Sosa	Chicago	50
2001	AL	Alex Rodriguez	Texas	52
	NL	***Barry Bonds***	***San Francisco***	***73***
2002	AL	Alex Rodriguez	Texas	57
	NL	Sammy Sosa	Chicago	49
2003	AL	Alex Rodriguez	Texas	47
	NL	Jim Thome	Philadelphia	47
2004	AL	Manny Ramirez	Boston	43
	NL	Adrian Beltre	Los Angeles	48

YEARLY HOME RUN LEADERS BY LEAGUE

Year	League	Player	Team	HR
2005	AL	Alex Rodriguez	New York	48
	NL	Andruw Jones	Atlanta	51
2006	AL	David Ortiz	Boston	54
	NL	Ryan Howard	Philadelphia	58

APPENDIX E

HOLLYWOOD HOMERS

After talking about all those real-life home runs, let's discuss a few imaginary ones. Here are some fun home run moments in movies. This is not intended to be a ranked list or an all-inclusive list but rather a collection of classic cinematic circuit clouts.

The Natural: In the climatic moment of this 1984 film, Roy Hobbs (Robert Redford) wins a league championship for his team, the New York Knights, by smacking a home run that strikes the lights above the right field grandstand, breaking many bulbs, and causing a shower of glass. Hobbs performed the feat after breaking his "magical" bat and while bleeding through his shirt at the plate, evidently from an old gunshot wound. Of course, the ending was different in Bernard Malamud's novel, but Hollywood loves a happy ending.

Bull Durham: After his pitcher, Ebby Calvin "Nuke" LaLoosh (Tim Robbins), keeps shaking off catcher "Crash" Davis (Kevin Costner), Davis tells an opposing batter that a fastball is coming. The batter clouts the ball over the right field fence, hitting the bull. LaLoosh says that the batter hit it as if he knew LaLoosh was going to throw a fastball, to which Davis replies, "He did know. I told him." Later in the film, LaLoosh starts shaking Davis off again, so Davis tells the batter that a curve ball is next. This batter hits the ball even farther than the first batter had, off the building behind the bull. Davis tells LaLoosh, "Anything that travels that far ought to have a stewardess on it."

Bull Durham: Near the end of this 1988 film, "Crash" Davis hits his 247th career minor league home run, supposedly setting a new record for the minors, and then quits playing to return to Annie Savoy (Susan Sarandon). The real minor league record is held by Hector Espino, who hit 484 home runs, mostly in the Mexican League, and who had completed his career before this movie was released.

A League of Their Own: In the climatic moment of this 1992 film, the Racine Belles and Rockford Peaches battle for the championship in the first year of the All-American Girls Professional Baseball League, and the game comes down to the bottom of the ninth inning with Rockford ahead by a run. Kit Keller (Lori Petty), formerly a Peaches player but now with the Belles, bats with one runner on base and hits the ball past the outfielders. After the tying run scores, Keller runs through her coach's stop sign at third base and attempts to score on a inside-the-park home run. She runs into the catcher, Dottie Hinson (Geena Davis), who also happens to be her sister, and knocks the ball out of Hinson's hand to score the championship-winning run. Racine did win the first league championship in 1943.

Major League: Rookie pitcher Rick "Wild Thing" Vaughn (Charlie Sheen) makes his big league debut by facing the previous year's American League home run champion, Clue Haywood of the Yankees, in this 1989 movie. Vaughn had walked the bases loaded on 12 pitches, and Haywood smashes the first pitch he sees for a grand slam. The inside joke here is that Haywood is played by 1982 American League Cy Young Award winner Pete Vuckovich, who never homered in 208 big league at bats. Near the end of the movie, Vaughn gets his revenge as he strikes out the slugger in the key moment of the final game of the season.

Mr. Destiny: Larry Burrows (Jim Belushi) fails to get the big hit in a high school championship game and, on his 35th birthday, bemoans the state of his life. A mysterious bartender (Michael Caine) gives Larry the chance to change his life: he hits the game-winning home run (breaking lights on the scoreboard in imitation of *The Natural*), marries the boss's daughter (Rene Russo), and becomes president of the company. But when he realizes that this new life is not as good as what he had, he begs to go back to his original life in this 1990 comedy.

Taking Care of Business: Jim Belushi made two movies released in 1990 that have baseball as part of the storyline. In this comedy, Jimmy Dworski (Belushi) escapes from jail to go to game six of the World Series between the Chicago Cubs and the California Angels at Anaheim Stadium with tickets he won on a radio trivia contest. In the game, Mark Grace of the Cubs hits a home run off Bert Blyleven into the right field seats and Dworski leaps onto a railing and makes a circus catch of the ball. The Cubs win the game and the Series—well, it *is* Hollywood!

The Slugger's Wife: Darryl Palmer (Michael O'Keefe) of the Atlanta Braves is mired in a slump when he meets a singer, Debby Huston (Rebecca De Mornay), in this 1985 film.

He climbs out of the slump as their relationship develops. They eventually marry, and he bats well enough to threaten Roger Maris's single-season home run record. He breaks the record but loses the girl, as she returns to her singing career at the end of the story.

BIBLIOGRAPHY

Benson, Michael. *Ballparks of North America*. Jefferson, NC: McFarland, 1989.
Boston Globe. Various issues.
Chicago Tribune. Various issues.
Dickson, Paul. *Dickson Baseball Dictionary*. New York: Facts On File, 1989.
Gough, David. "Home Run Derby," *The National Pastime*, 1997.
Koppett, Leonard. *Koppett's Concise History of Major League Baseball*. New York: Carroll & Graf, 2004.
Lane, F. C. "Has the 'Lively' Ball Revolutionized the Game?" *Baseball Magazine*, September 1921.
Los Angeles Times. Various Issues.
Lowry, Philip J. *Green Cathedrals*. New York: Addison-Wesley, 1992.
McConnell, Bob. *Going for the Fences: The Minor League Home Run Record Book.* Cleveland: SABR, 1997.
McConnell, Bob, and David Vincent. *SABR Presents the Home Run Encyclopedia*. New York: Macmillan, 1996.
New York Times. Various Issues.
Smith, David W. "Expansion: Does It Add Muscle or Fat?" 1999. http://www.retrosheet.org/Research/SmithD/Expansion.pdf.
Sporting News, The. St. Louis. Various Issues.
Vincent, David, Lyle Spatz, and David W. Smith. *The Midsummer Classic: The Complete History of Baseball's All-Star Game*. Lincoln, NE: Bison Books, 2001.

INDEX

3Com Park (San Francisco). *See* Candlestick Park
40 home runs and 40 stolen bases, 178, 209, 214, 236
200 home runs
    at each of two positions, 130
    for each of two leagues, 133, 215, 227
    for each of two teams, 85, 215, 224
300 home runs and 300 stolen bases, 227, 236
400 home runs surrendered, 116, 119, 169, 172, 175, 177, 179, 237
500 Home Run Club, 53, 84, 87, 106, 120, 124–6, 129, 132–3, 167, 172, 176, 210, 215, 217, 222, 223, 226
    three or more active players, 125, 127, 129, 133
500 home runs and 3000 hits, 129, 210, 224
500 home runs surrendered, 122
600 Home Run Club, 54, 128, 131, 221
    two active players, 131
700 Home Run Club, 54, 162, 226

Aaron, Hank, 55, 66, 85, 102–3, 106, 109, 115–7, 120–2, 124–31, 134, 162–4, 168, 170, 172, 176, 188, 192–3, 210, 216, 219, 223, 226–7, 235, 238
    career summary, 163–4
Aaron, Tommie, 66
Abreu, Bobby, 196
Acosta, Jose, 50
Adams, Terry, 217
Adcock, Joe, 99–100, 115, 118
Adkins, Jon, 237
Agbayani, Benny, 217
Agee, Tommie, 146
Aikens, Willie, 149–50
Alexander, Grover Cleveland "Pete," 17, 70
Allen, Dick, 119, 121, 134, 164, 187
Allison, Bob, 118, 133
All-Star Game home runs, 182–196
    brothers, 184, 190–1
    extra inning, 184

father and son, 190–1
first, 54
first back-to-back, 185
for both leagues, 133, 188
game ending, 184–5, 187
grand slam, 189
multiple in one game, 183–5, 187, 189
Aloha Stadium (Honolulu), 211
Alomar, Roberto, 154, 190–1
Alomar, Sandy, 154, 190–1
Alou, Felipe, 115
Altman, George, 186, 189
Amalfitano, Joey, 115
American League, first home run, 23
Ameriquest Field (Arlington, TX). *See* Ballpark in Arlington
Anaheim Angels, 108, 121, 126, 189
Anaheim Stadium (Anaheim, CA), 172, 175, 187, 190, 226
Anderson, Brady, 30, 100, 162, 208–9
Anderson, Marlon, 237
Andrews, Shane, 216
Anson, Cap, 9, 29
Arlett, Buzz, 77
Armas, Tony, 169, 171
Ashby, Alan, 150, 215
Astrodome (Houston), 119–20, 224
Astros Field (Houston). *See* Minute Maid Park
AT&T Park. *See* Pacific Bell Park
Atlanta Braves, 121, 154, 162–3, 176, 221. *See also* Boston Braves; Milwaukee Braves

Atlanta-Fulton County Stadium (Atlanta), 162–163, 170, 174
Aurilia, Rich, 114, 218
Ausmus, Brad, 157
Avenue Grounds (Cincinnati), 4
Averill, Earl, 74, 135

Bagby, Jim, 50, 138
Bagwell, Jeff, 206, 216, 224
    career summary, 224
Baines, Harold, 117, 171–2
Bakely, Jersey, 13
Baker Bowl (Philadelphia), 30, 63
Baker, Dusty, 148
Baker, Frank "Home Run," 27–28, 30, 32–33, 75, 89, 137–8
ball
    change to, 29, 61, 73, 165, 174, 201
    price of historic, 53
    rubbing before game, 60
ballpark changes, 199
Ballpark in Arlington, The (Arlington, TX), 223–4, 237
Baltimore Orioles, 98–99, 102, 114–5, 121, 175, 209, 224, 228. *See also* St. Louis Browns
Bando, Sal, 147
Bank One Ballpark (Phoenix), 227, 235
Banks, Ernie, 56, 104–6, 116, 120, 127, 129–30, 134, 194, 226, 236
    career summary, 129–30
Barfield, Jesse, 174
Barnes, Jesse, 62, 165, 180
Barnes, Ross, 4, 6

INDEX

Barnes, Virgil, 62, 165, 180
Barrow, Ed, 44
base on balls, changes to, 1
Batista, Tony, 217
bats, wood used for, 201
Bauer, Hank, 143
Baylor, Don, 151
Bayne, Bill, 51
Beck, Erve, 23
Bell, Buddy, 167
Bell, David, 167
Bell, George, 175
Bell, Gus, 167, 185
Bell, Mike, 167
Belle, Albert, 80, 195, 207
Beltran, Carlos, 157, 238
Beltre, Adrian, 89, 225
Bench, Johnny, 129, 134, 147, 187
Benes, Alan, 217
Benes, Andy, 217
Bere, Jason, 214
Berger, Wally, 71, 77–78, 175
Berkman, Lance, 196, 217
Berra, Yogi, 97, 141–2, 144, 156, 186
Bichette, Dante, 207, 215
Bierbauer, Lou, 7
Biggio, Craig, 222
Blaeholder, George, 54, 70, 83
Blair, Paul, 145, 153
Blair, Willie, 212
Blalock, Hank, 192
Blum, Geoff, 148, 157
Blyleven, Bert, 61, 101, 174, 179
body armor, 200
Boggs, Wade, 190
Bolton, Rod, 207
Bonds, Barry, 50–51, 110, 114, 126–8, 133, 147, 156–7, 168, 172, 178, 180, 191, 195, 208–9, 216–21, 223, 225–7, 232, 235–6, 238
  career summary, 226–227
Bonds, Bobby, 128, 162, 177, 191, 209, 211, 227, 236
Boone, Aaron, 148, 156, 167, 220
Boone, Bob, 156, 167
Boone, Bret, 156, 167, 219–20
Boone, Ray, 167, 185
Booth, Amos, 6
Borden, Joe, 6
Borowski, Joe, 218
Boston Braves (Beaneaters, Bees, Red Caps), 6, 9, 38, 163. *See also* Atlanta Braves; Milwaukee Braves
Boston Red Sox, 123–4, 163, 225
Bottenfield, Kent, 180
Bottomley, Jim, 68, 181
Boudreau, Lou, 184
bounce home run, 21, 66, 72–73
Bowerman, Frank, 39
Boyer, Clete, 68, 144–5
Boyer, Ken, 68, 144, 186–7
Bradley, George, 7
Branca, Ralph, 95–96, 184
Braves Field (Boston), 33, 85, 97
Breeden, Hal, 86, 162
Brett, George, 149, 156, 170–1, 223
Bridges, Tommy, 54
Briggs Stadium. *See* Tiger Stadium
Brinkman, Joe, 170
Brooklyn Dodgers, 89, 97, 99, 100, 108. *See also* Los Angeles Dodgers

Brother Matthias, 43
brothers
    home run, same game, 66
    surrender home run to same batter, same game, 62, 165, 217
Brouthers, Dan, 7, 14, 18
Brown, Larry, 118
Brown, Tommy, 88
Bruce, Bob, 119
Bruton, Bill, 98, 143
Buffalo Bisons, 9
Buffinton, Charlie, 14
Buford, Don, 146
Buhner, Jay, 207
Bunch, Melvin, 207
Burdette, Lew, 143, 145
Burke, Chris, 157
Burroughs, Jeff, 166
Burwell, Bill, 49
Busch Stadium (St. Louis, opened 1966), 128, 167, 176, 213, 215, 226
Busch Stadium (St. Louis, opened 2006), 237
Bush, Guy, 80

Calderon, Ivan, 175
California Angels. *See* Anaheim Angels
Callison, Johnny, 187
Cameron, Mike, 219–20
Camilli, Dolph, 85
Caminiti, Ken, 210
Camp, Rick, 173
Campanella, Roy, 97
Campaneris, Bert, 147, 171

Candlestick Park (San Francisco), 121, 125, 186
Canseco, Jose, 178–9, 219, 236
    career summary, 219
Carbo, Bernie, 147–148
Carlton, Steve, 177
Carroll, Clay, 132
Carter, Gary, 189
Carter, Joe, 144, 153, 177–8
Cartwright, Ed, 7
Carty, Rico, 125
Cash, Norm, 115–6, 130, 162
Caster, George, 84
Cepeda, Orlando, 115, 120, 125, 161
Cey, Ron, 148
Chamberlain, Ice Box, 17
Chambliss, Chris, 148
Chase Field (Phoenix). *See* Bank One Ballpark
Chase, Hal, 31–32
Chicago Cubs (White Stockings), 8–9, 11, 66, 78, 92, 104, 150, 156, 211, 216, 223
Chicago White Sox, 87, 104, 130, 190
Cincinnati Reds, 9, 82, 87, 99, 102, 109, 114–6, 118, 121, 123, 140
Cinergy Field (Cincinnati). *See* Riverfront Stadium
Clark, Tony, 225
Clark, Will, 152
Clarkson, John, 9, 15, 17, 70
Clemente, Roberto, 188
Clendenon, Donn, 131
Cleveland Indians, 94, 99, 115, 118, 133, 238

Cleveland Stadium (Cleveland). *See* Municipal Stadium
Cloninger, Tony, 122
Cobb, Ty, 26, 222
Colavito, Rocky, 105, 115–6, 170, 186, 192
Colbert, Nate, 99, 134–5
Cole, Bert, 51
Coleman, Gordy, 118
Coleman, Joe, 130
Coleman, John, 11
Collins, Eddie, 28
Collins, Harry "Rip," 77
Collins, Hub, 15
Collins, James "Ripper," 77, 101
Collins, Jimmy, 38
Collins, Phil, 11, 70
Colorado Rockies, 115, 162, 180, 207
Columbia Park (Philadelphia), 25
Columbus Colts, 9
Comerica Park (Detroit), 237
Comiskey Park (Chicago, opened 1910), 135, 171, 182
Comiskey Park (Chicago, opened 1991). *See* U.S. Cellular Field
Comiskey, Charles, 31
Concepcion, Dave, 132
Cone, David, 224
Congress Street Grounds (Boston), 13–14, 17
Conigliaro, Tony, 74, 120, 226
Conine, Jeff, 190
Connie Mack Stadium (Philadelphia). *See* Shibe Park
Connor, Roger, 13–15, 18, 51, 59
Cook, Dennis, 208, 216

Cooney, James Edward "Jimmy," 63
Cooney, James Joseph "Jimmy," 63
Cooney, Johnny, 63
Cooper, Walker, 92, 100
Coors Field (Denver), 207, 227, 235
Corcoran, Larry, 11, 93
Corkins, Mike, 128
County Stadium (Milwaukee), 98, 109, 119, 129, 188
Courtney, Clint, 98
Courtney, Harry, 51
Cravath, Clifford "Gavvy," 30–31, 44–45, 50–51, 56, 58–59, 85, 88–89, 93
Crawford, Sam, 24, 26, 33
Cronin, Joe, 84, 86, 162
Crosetti, Frank, 82
Crosley Field (Cincinnati), 66, 78, 115, 123
Cruz, Jose Jr., 225
Cuellar, Mike, 132, 146
Curtright, Guy, 87
Cutshaw, George, 32
Cuyler, Hazen "Kiki," 140

Dahlgren, Babe, 82
Dalrymple, Abner, 9, 29
Daly, Tom, 15
Danning, Harry, 81
Darwin, Danny, 208
Daubert, Jake, 39
Daulton, Darren, 154
Dauss, Hooks, 50
Davenport, Jim, 115
Davis, Chili, 210
Davis, Eric, 177
Davis, George, 24

Davis, Glenn, 150
Davis, Harry, 25, 33, 89
Davis, Willie, 188
Dawson, Andre, 128, 168, 175, 211, 227, 236
   career summary, 211
Day, Boots, 162
de los Santos, Valerio, 213–4
Dean, Tommy, 125
DeCinces, Doug, 103, 169
Delahanty, Ed, 17–18, 76, 79, 94, 174
Delgado, Carlos, 221, 224, 237
Demaree, Frank, 82
Demeter, Don, 116
Dempsey, Rick, 117, 178
Dent, Bucky, 168
DeRosa, Mark, 176, 221
designated hitter
   definition, 158
   first home run by, 160
Detroit Tigers, 116, 123, 209
Dickey, Bill, 82, 141
Dickshot, Johnny, 87
Dickson, Murry, 11, 83, 92, 102
Dietz, Dick, 188
DiMaggio, Joe, 64, 77–79, 82, 85, 88, 92, 94, 106, 141, 144, 156, 182, 184
DiMaggio, Vince, 184
Doby, Larry, 97, 99, 126, 185
Dodger Stadium (Los Angeles), 116, 227, 235
Doerr, Bobby, 84
Dolphins Stadium (Miami), 223
Dougherty, Patsy, 136–7
Downing, Al, 163

Doyle, Larry, 137
Dragnet, 56
Drew, J. D., 156, 237
Drysdale, Don, 104, 164
Duffy, Hugh, 17–18, 39
Dunlap, Fred, 11
Dunn Park (Cleveland). *See* League Park
Dunn, Adam, 225
Dunn, Jack, 43–44
Durante, Sal, 114
Durocher, Leo, 88
Durst, Cedric, 140
Dwyer, Frank, 14
Dwyer, Jim, 177
Dykstra, Lenny, 152–3

Easter, Luke, 97
Ebbets Field (Brooklyn), 32, 79, 88, 94, 97, 99
Eckersley, Dennis, 151
Eephus pitch, 184
Eisenreich, Jim, 154
Elder, David, 223
Eller, Hod, 39
Elliott, Bob, 185
Emslie, Bob, 24, 34
Ennis, Del, 92–93
Enron Field (Houston). *See* Minute Maid Park
epidemic of home runs, 69
equipment changes, 2
Essegian, Chuck, 143, 148
Estadio Hiram Bithorn (San Juan, Puerto Rico). *See* Hiram Bithorn Stadium
Etton, Nick, 87

INDEX

Evans, Darrell, 162, 172, 174, 178, 208
    career summary, 178
Evans, Dwight, 147, 169
Evers, Hoot, 184
Evers, Johnny, 61
Ewing, Buck, 7
expansion, 108–36, 166, 180, 202
Expansion: Does It Add Muscle or Fat?, 109
extra innings
    first home run, 6
    two home runs in same game, 86, 117, 123, 131, 177

Fairly, Ron, 167
father-son home runs, 63, 226–7
Feller, Bob, 80
Fenway Park (Boston), 2, 45, 47–49, 52, 65, 67, 80, 86, 105, 137, 184
Fernandez, Tony, 154
Ferrara, Al, 125
Ferrell, Rick, 67, 85
Ferrell, Wes, 67, 85, 119, 132, 237
Fielder, Cecil, 179
Finley, Steve, 209, 236
Fishel, Robert, 148
Fisher, Cherokee, 4
Fisher, Eddie, 135
Fisher, Jack, 112, 120
Fisk, Carlton, 107, 148, 157, 178, 208
Flaherty, John, 210
Florida Marlins, 180
Forbes Field (Pittsburgh), 34, 55, 79, 100, 102, 104

Ford, Ben, 225
Fosse, Ray, 188
Foster, George, 100, 128, 166–7, 179, 212
Fournier, Jack, 63
Foxx, Jimmie, 74–80, 84–85, 87–89, 91, 106, 110, 114, 120–1, 124–5, 128–9, 133, 135, 163, 214–5, 234, 236
    career summary, 84–85
Foytack, Paul, 118
Franco, Julio, 235
Francona, Tito, 118
Frazee, Harry, 48–49
Frazier, George, 171
Freeman, Buck, 10, 18, 24–25, 29, 46
Frick, Ford, 110–2
Friday, Joe (Sgt.), 56
Frisch, Frankie, 182–3
Fryman, Woodie, 135
Fulton County Stadium (Atlanta). *See* Atlanta-Fulton County Stadium
Furcal, Rafael, 176, 221

Gaetti, Gary, 151
Galarraga, Andres, 208
Gamble, Oscar, 162
game
    eight consecutive with home run, 102, 177, 180
    eight home runs by team, 82
    four home runs, 17, 18, 76, 93, 94, 99, 105, 109, 164, 174, 181, 219–20, 224
    two grand slams, 78, 82, 89,

110, 122, 126, 130, 207–8, 214–5, 221–2
game-ending hit, 38–40
Gant, Ron, 211
Garciaparra, Nomar, 215, 238
Gardner, Larry, 137–8
Garr, Ralph, 131, 177
Garvey, Steve, 188, 191
Geary, Geoff, 228
Gehrig, Lou, 51–52, 55, 64–66, 68, 71, 74, 76–79, 82, 88, 92–94, 100, 102, 106, 114, 120, 125, 139–43, 150, 168, 182, 186, 210–11, 227
    career summary, 76–77
Gentile, Jim, 110, 115, 126
Giambi, Jason, 67, 192, 195–6, 225
Giambi, Jeremy, 67
Gibson, Bob, 126, 145–6
Gibson, Kirk, 151–2
Gillenwater, Carden, 88
Gilliam, Jim, 186
Gladden, Dan, 151
Glaus, Troy, 146, 216
Gonzalez, Alex, 157
Gonzalez, Juan, 154, 179–80, 195, 221
    career summary, 221
Gonzalez, Luis, 195, 208, 218, 226
Gonzalez, Tony, 146
Goodman, Ival, 79
Gordon, Joe, 82, 141
Goslin, Leon "Goose," 139
Gossage, Rich, 170
Gough, David, 193
Gowdy, Hank, 137
Grace, Mark, 216

Grady, Mike, 98
Graves, Danny, 224
Gray, Dick, 104
Great American Ballpark (Cincinnati), 222, 228
Green Cathedrals, 8
Green, Shawn, 126, 220
Greenberg, Hank, 77, 79–81, 84, 88–89, 91, 94, 114, 214, 223
Grich, Bobby, 169
Griffey, Ken Jr., 89, 102, 127, 153–4, 180, 190, 195–6, 207, 211–2, 214–6, 221, 226–8, 235–7
    career summary, 226
Griffey, Ken Sr., 190, 226, 235
Griffith Stadium (Washington), 47, 64, 87, 98
Grimes, Burleigh, 41
Grimsley, Jason, 180
Grimsley, Ross, 132
Groom, Bob, 30
ground rule, 8, 12, 21–22
Grzenda, Joe, 130
Guerrero, Vlad, 67
Guerrero, Wilton, 67
Guidry, Ron, 171
Gullett, Don, 147
Gwynn, Tony, 176

Haas, Mule, 136
Hafner, Travis, 237
Hall, George, 6
Hall, Jimmie, 118–9, 122
Hallahan, Bill, 182
Hamilton, Joey, 210
Hammaker, Atlee, 189
Hampton, Mike, 237

INDEX

Hanlan's Point (Toronto), 44
Harper, Terry, 173
Harper, Tommy, 129
Harris, Joe, 139
Hatcher, Billy, 151, 157
Hauser, Joe, 63
Hayes, Von, 173
Heading Home, 48
Hecker, Guy, 12, 86
Held, Woodie, 118
Helling, Rick, 217
Henderson, Dave, 151–2
Henderson, Hardie, 14
Henderson, Rickey, 26, 30, 152, 211, 222
Henderson, Steve, 169
Henrich, Tommy, 82, 141
Herman, Babe, 78
Hernandez, Keith, 173
Heydler, John, 35–38, 46, 110
High, Andy, 40
Hiller, Chuck, 144
Hines, Paul, 6–7, 17
Hiram Bithorn Stadium (San Juan, Puerto Rico), 217, 224
Hodges, Gil, 94–95, 100, 118, 185, 194
Hoffman, Trevor, 237
Hoiles, Chris, 214
Holliday, James "Bug," 12, 15, 17, 25
Holmes, Tommy, 87, 130
Holtzman, Ken, 147
home run
  Derby, 192, 194
  epidemic of, 69
  production rate, definition, 3

Hooper, Harry, 30
Horner, Bob, 169–70, 174
Hornsby, Rogers, 15, 58, 61–63, 65, 68–70, 76, 79–80, 85, 91, 165
Horton, Willie, 126
Hough, Charlie, 180
Houston Astros (Colt .45s), 108, 116, 119, 153, 157
Howard, Frank, 126, 128–9, 134, 187–8, 218, 220
Howard, Ryan, 234, 238
Howser, Dick, 170
Hrbek, Kent, 151, 179
Hubbell, Carl, 55, 182
Hudlin, Willis, 53
Huggins, Miller, 52, 69
Hughes, Dick, 139, 145
Hughson, Tex, 86
Hunter, Catfish, 160
Hunter, Torii, 191
Huntington Avenue Baseball Grounds (Boston), 136

inning
  five home runs (team), 115, 122
  three home runs surrendered, 8
  two home runs (first time), 7
Irwin, Arthur, 18

Jack Murphy Stadium (San Diego). *See* Qualcomm Stadium
Jackson, Bo, 190
Jackson, Grant, 128
Jackson, Reggie, 15, 52, 124, 128, 130–1, 138, 142, 149, 162, 164, 167–9, 172, 178, 186

career summary, 172
Jackson, "Shoeless" Joe, 31
Jacobs Field (Cleveland), 211
Jarry Park (Montreal), 127
Jarvis, Pat, 129
Javier, Julian, 155
Javier, Stan, 155
Jay, Joey, 115
Jefferson Street Grounds (Philadelphia), 6, 17
Jenkins, Fergie, 169, 172
Jensen, Jackie, 192, 194
Jeter, Derek, 154, 191
Joe Robbie Stadium (Miami). *See* Dolphins Stadium
Johnson, Brian, 210
Johnson, Davey, 162, 208
Johnson, Hank, 67
Johnson, Howard, 173, 177, 179
Johnson, Si, 85
Johnson, Walter, 30
Jones, Andruw, 100, 147, 154, 228
Jones, Charley, 4, 6–7, 10, 14
Jones, Davy, 137
Jones, Larry "Chipper," 191
Jones, Mack, 125, 127
Jones, Willie, 93
Joost, Eddie, 133
Joyce, Bill, 18, 31
Justice, David, 153

Kaline, Al, 147
Kansas City Athletics, 98–99, 119, 126, 176. *See also* Oakland Athletics; Philadelphia Athletics
Kansas City Royals, 127
Kauff, Benny, 32
Kell, George, 185
Keller, Charlie, 140
Kelly, George "High Pockets," 58, 60, 62, 74, 92, 100
Kelly, King, 98
Kennedy, Adam, 156
Kent, Jeff, 237
Kenworthy, Duke, 31
Kerr, Dickie, 49
Key, Jimmy, 214
Killebrew, Harmon, 103, 105, 115–20, 122, 123, 127–9, 132–5, 162, 186–7, 215–6, 221
  career summary, 132–3
Kiner, Ralph, 79, 88–89, 91–95, 97, 100, 103, 114, 120, 126, 133, 164, 174, 184–5, 230, 234
Kingdome (Seattle), 166, 173, 189
Kingman, Dave, 164, 166, 168–9, 173–4
  career summary, 173–4
Kirke, Jay, 39
Kirkland, Willie, 117
Klein, Chuck, 68–69, 71, 74, 76–79, 89, 93–94, 164
Klesko, Ryan, 153–154
Kluszewski, Ted, 79, 97–98
Knott, Jack, 81
Konerko, Paul, 225
Koppett, Leonard, 39
Kouzmanoff, Ken, 237
Kruk, John, 176
Kuenn, Harvey, 105
Kuhel, Joe, 87

INDEX

Kuhn, Bowie, 163
Lajoie, Nap, 24
Lake Front Park (Chicago), 8–9, 11, 17, 29, 46, 66
Landis, Kennesaw Mountain, 52
Lange, Bill, 18
Lary, Lin, 64
Lazzeri, Tony, 78–79, 83, 110, 140
Leach, Tommy, 88
league leader
    multiple leagues, 8, 15, 25, 26, 179, 214, 227
    playing for three teams, 15, 172
League Park (Cincinnati), 14, 53
League Park (Cleveland), 138
Lee, Derrek, 228
Leibrandt, Charlie, 152
Lemaster, Denny, 118
Lemon, Bob, 119
Lemon, Jim, 106
Leonard, Emil "Dutch," 78
Lewis, Mark, 153
Leyritz, Jim, 153
Lieber, Jon, 191
Lima, Jose, 101, 212, 217
Loaiza, Esteban, 217
Lolich, Mickey, 145
Lollar, Sherm, 141
Lonborg, Jim, 124
Long, Dale, 102, 177, 180, 221
Lopez, Albie, 218
Lopez, Javy, 190
Los Angeles Angels. *See* Anaheim Angels
Los Angeles Dodgers, 99, 103–4, 115, 126, 178, 237–8. *See also* Brooklyn Dodgers
Los Angeles Memorial Coliseum (Los Angeles), 104, 186
Louden, William "Baldy," 34
Louisville Baseball Park (Louisville), 6
Lowe, Bobby, 7, 16, 18, 79, 93–94
Lowenstein, John, 149
Lowry, Phil, 8
Lucier, Lou, 86
Luque, Dolf, 66
Lynch, Tom, 38
Lynn, Fred, 150, 189

Mack, Connie, 25, 27, 32, 75, 78, 82
Maddox, Garry, 174
Maddux, Greg, 152, 182
Magee, Sherry, 38
Maglie, Sal, 185
Majeski, Hank, 142
Malzone, Frank, 186
Manning, Jack, 9
Mantle, Mickey, 77, 98–99, 101, 104, 106, 110–1, 114, 120, 124–5, 127–8, 135, 138–9, 144, 150, 162, 179, 185–6, 192, 194, 210, 212, 218
    career summary, 124–5
Marberry, Frederick "Firpo," 66
Marichal, Juan, 115, 125
Maris, Roger, 50, 106, 110–2, 114, 144–5, 179, 208, 212–3, 218
Marquard, Rube, 28, 137
Martin, Billy, 170–1
Martin, Jerry, 149
Martin, Russell, 237
Martinez, Carlos, 179
Martinez, Dennis, 178

Martinez, Edgar, 161
Martinez, Pedro, 180
Martinez, Ramon, 180
Martinez, Tino, 225, 237
Mathews, Eddie, 74, 97, 100, 105–6, 115, 120–1, 124–7, 168–9, 186
   career summary, 125
Mathewson, Christy, 28
Matsui, Hideki, 225
Matthias, Brother, 43
Mattingly, Don, 102, 171, 177, 180, 221, 237
Maxvill, Dal, 127
Mays, Willie, 39, 62, 88, 99–100, 102–3, 109–10, 115–21, 124–5, 127–31, 133–4, 142, 163–4, 168, 170, 176–7, 185–6, 210–1, 216, 218, 223, 225–7, 236
   career summary, 128–9
Mazeroski, Bill, 144
Mazzilli, Lee, 189
McBride, Bake, 149
McCarver, Tim, 174
McCaskill, Kirk, 226
McClelland, Tim, 170, 223
McCormick, Barry, 39
McCormick, Mike, 127
McCovey, Willie, 117, 120, 126, 128, 144, 167–8, 187
   career summary, 167–8
McDougald, Gil, 143
McFarlane, Todd, 53
McGlinchy, Kevin, 155
McGraw, Frank "Tug," 150
McGraw, John, 28
McGriff, Fred, 105, 178–9, 190, 227, 237
   career summary, 227
McGwire, Mark, 50, 54, 56, 71, 75, 85, 110, 132, 135, 152, 175, 179, 195, 208, 211–6, 218, 220, 222–3, 227, 232
   career summary, 215–6
McKay, Dave, 212
McLain, Denny, 124, 126
McMillan, Roy, 116
McNally, Dave, 146
McPhail, Lee, 170–1
McQuillan, Hugh, 39
Medwick, Joe, 80, 182
Mejias, Roman, 116
Melton, Bill, 130
Memorial Stadium (Baltimore), 105, 122, 133
Mench, Kevin, 235
Metrodome (Minneapolis), 194
Metropolitan Stadium (Minneapolis), 110, 113, 132
Meusel, Bob, 52, 58, 60, 63, 66, 68, 138, 140
Meusel, Emil "Irish," 68, 138, 140
Mile High Stadium (Denver), 180
Miller Park (Milwaukee), 220
Miller, Bob, 116
Miller, Stu, 124
Milwaukee Braves, 82, 98, 109, 115, 121, 163, 238. *See also* Atlanta Braves; Boston Braves
Milwaukee Brewers, 129, 163. *See also* Seattle Pilots
Mincher, Don, 122
Minnesota Twins, 108, 115, 118, 122–3, 209, 238. *See also*

INDEX

Washington Senators
Minute Maid Park (Houston), 157, 223
Mitchell, Kevin, 178
Mize, Johnny, 55, 81, 84, 91–92, 94–95, 114, 141, 143, 169, 174, 223
Molitor, Paul, 150
Money, Don, 169
Montreal Expos, 127, 178, 211
Moore, Donnie, 151
Moore, Jo-Jo, 81–82
Morgan, Joe, 150, 189
Morgan, Mike, 213
Morris, Matt, 226
Mountain, Frank, 132
Moyer, Jamie, 237
Mueller, Bill, 221
Mumphrey, Jerry, 171
Municipal Stadium (Cleveland), 106, 117, 177
Munoz, Pedro, 117, 180
Murphy, Dale, 170–1, 174–6, 210, 214
Murphy, Johnny, 80
Murray, Eddie, 105, 125, 129, 141, 153, 156, 164, 168–9, 176, 210–1, 227
   career summary, 210–1
Musial, Stan, 55, 92, 99, 105–7, 135, 167, 170, 184–6
   career summary, 105

Nathan, Alan, 201
National League, first home run, 4
Navin Field (Detroit). *See* Tiger Stadium

Neagle, Denny, 220
Neagle, Jack, 7
Neal, Charlie, 143
Nettles, Graig, 68, 149, 164
Nettles, Jim, 68
Network Associates Coliseum (Oakland). *See* Oakland-Alameda County Coliseum
New York Giants, 9, 38, 81–82, 84, 92–93, 99–100, 102, 108, 114–6, 119. *See also* San Francisco Giants
New York Mets, 108, 116, 189, 216
New York Yankees, 9, 66, 78, 82, 92, 109, 111, 114–6, 140, 142, 153, 157, 208–9, 225
Newcombe, Don, 95, 141
Newsom, Bobo, 81
Nicholson, Bill, 87
Niekro, Joe, 125, 165
Niekro, Phil, 125, 165, 172
night game, first home run, 78
Nixon, Trot, 156
no-hitter and home run, 132
Northrup, Jim, 126
Nottebart, Don, 120
Noyes, Win, 46
nutrition, 202

O'Neill, Paul, 154
O'Neill, Tip, 8, 13, 17
Oakland Athletics, 115, 126, 140, 209, 211. *See also* Kansas City Athletics; Philadelphia Athletics
Oakland-Alameda County Coliseum, 126, 160, 224

Odwell, Fred, 25, 99
Oglivie, Ben, 169, 171
Oliva, Tony, 118–9, 122, 160
Ordonez, Magglio, 191, 220, 238
Oriole Park at Camden Yards (Baltimore), 195, 210, 224–5
Orsino, John, 115
Orth, Al, 61
Ortiz, David, 155, 157, 161, 192, 225, 228, 234, 237–8
Osteen, Claude, 121
Ott, Mel, 12, 68, 74, 76–78, 80–81, 85, 87–89, 93, 102, 106, 120–1, 124, 226, 228
   career summary, 87–88
Owen, Mickey, 184

Pacific Bell Park (San Francisco), 217, 221
Pafko, Andy, 100
Palmeiro, Rafael, 84, 105, 127, 129, 164, 172, 215, 219, 223–5, 228, 235
   career summary, 223–4
Palmer, Jim, 147
Parc Jarry. *See* Jarry Park
Park, Chan Ho, 122, 215, 218
Parker, Dave, 194
Passeau, Claude, 183
Patterson, Arthur, 98
Pavano, Carl, 214
Pavletich, Don, 118
Peavy, Jake, 226
Peckinpaugh, Roger, 40
Pelekoudas, Chris, 121
Pena, Tony, 153, 169
Pepitone, Joe, 144

Perez, Eddie, 154–5
Perez, Eduardo, 156
Perez, Tony, 129, 187
Perry, Gaylord, 131, 162, 170
Perry, Jim, 162
Petrocelli, Rico, 145
Pfeffer, Fred, 9, 29, 30
Philadelphia Athletics, 24, 78, 98. *See also* Kansas City Athletics; Oakland Athletics
Philadelphia Phillies, 93, 116, 156, 186
Phillips, Dave, 171
Piazza, Mike, 216, 223, 236
Piche, Ron, 118
pinch-hit home run, 15, 86
Pipp, Wally, 32, 40, 64
pitcher, hitting three home runs in game, 12, 86
Pittsburgh Pirates, 82, 123, 227
Plank, Eddie, 28
player strike, 206
player/manager, 12, 85
playing field, changes to, 2, 16
PNC Park (Pittsburgh), 238
Podres, Johnny, 143
Polo Grounds (New York), 24, 27–28, 40, 46–47, 49–51, 62, 74, 80–81, 87–88, 100, 116
Porter, Chuck, 171
Posada, Jorge, 225
Powell, Boog, 135
Pratt, Todd, 155
Pro Player Stadium (Miami). *See* Dolphins Stadium
Puckett, Kirby, 152
Pujols, Albert, 225, 234–5

INDEX

Putnam Grounds (Troy, NY), 7

Qualcomm Stadium (San Diego), 221

Quinn, Jack, 235

Radinsky, Scott, 207
Raines, Tim, 154
Ramirez, Manny, 157, 168, 192, 211, 225, 228, 238
Ramos, Pedro, 118
Rariden, Bill, 33
Rath, Morrie, 39
Rawlings Sporting Goods Company, 165–6, 174–5
Rawlings, Johnny, 33
Rayfield, Floyd, 177
Reach and Company, 41–42, 59
Recreation Park (Detroit), 14
Redland Field (Cincinnati). *See* Crosley Field
Reed, Jack, 116–117
reserve clause, 13
Reuschel, Paul, 164–5, 180
Reuschel, Rick, 164–5, 180
Reyes, Dennys, 213
Reynolds, Allie, 141
Reynolds, Carl, 220
Rhodes, Dusty, 142
Rhodes, Gordon, 74
Rice, Jim, 161, 166–7, 180
Richardson, Hardy, 7, 17
Rickey, Branch, 90
Ripken, Cal Jr., 182, 191, 194–5, 210, 219
  career summary, 219
Ripple, Jimmy, 140

Riverfront Stadium (Cincinnati), 132, 181
Rivers, Mickey, 168
Rizzuto, Phil, 137
Robert F. Kennedy Memorial Stadium (Washington), 130, 134
Roberts, Robin, 101–3, 116–7, 122–3, 164, 172, 174, 217
Robertson, Bob, 146, 156
Robinson, Brooks, 145, 187
Robinson, Frank, 102, 120–1, 124, 127, 130, 133–4, 145–6, 153, 161–2, 175, 188, 195, 215–6, 221, 227–9
  career summary, 133–4
Robinson, Jackie, 90, 97, 185
Robinson, Wilbert, 69–70
Robison Field (St. Louis), 14
Rodriguez, Alex, 174, 178, 214, 218–9, 221–2, 228, 236, 238
Rodriguez, Wilfredo, 218
Rogers Centre (Toronto). *See* Skydome
Rojas, Cookie, 188
Rollins, Rich, 122
Rommel, Eddie, 61
Root, Charlie, 139, 145
Rose, Pete, 133, 147, 187
Rosen, Al, 94, 97, 99, 185
Ross, Buster, 52
Roth, Robert "Braggo," 30–31
Rowe, Lynwood "Schoolboy," 93
Rudi, Joe, 166
Ruffing, Charles "Red," 70, 83, 102
rule changes, 1–2, 10, 12–13, 15, 21, 35, 38, 40, 61, 69, 72–73, 94, 104, 117, 127, 230

Runnels, Pete, 187
Ruppert, Jacob, 48
Rusch, Glendon, 216
Ruth, George H. "Babe," 15, 24, 33, 38–40, 43–66, 68, 70–71, 74–81, 84–89, 95, 97, 103, 106, 110–4, 119–20, 124–5, 129–34, 138–40, 142, 150, 163–4, 167–8, 172, 174, 182, 194, 207, 216, 222, 235–6
    breaking own record, 50–52
    career summary, 55–56,
    first home run, 44
    only minor league home run, 44
Ryba, Mike, 86

Sabo, Chris, 180
Sadecki, Ray, 122
Safeco Field (Seattle), 224
Salvo, Manny, 82
San Diego Padres, 127, 176, 208, 214–5, 221
San Diego Stadium (San Diego). *See* Qualcomm Stadium
San Francisco Giants, 82, 99, 103, 109, 115–6, 119, 126, 142, 156, 168. *See also* New York Giants
Sandberg, Ryne, 179
Sanders, Reggie, 180, 236
Santiago, Jose, 145
Santo, Ron, 165
Sauer, Hank, 97, 104, 126
SBC Park. *See* Pacific Bell Park
Scherman, Fred, 133
Schmidt, Mike, 79, 150, 164–5, 167–71, 174, 176, 189, 210, 234
    career summary, 176
Schneider, Brian, 224
Schoendienst, Red, 184
Schulte, Frank, 29–30
Scott, George, 164
Scott, Mark, 192, 194
Seals Stadium (San Francisco), 103–4
Seattle Mariners, 114, 153, 166, 209
Seattle Pilots, 127, 129. *See also* Milwaukee Brewers
Seaver, Tom, 131, 147
Sebring, Jimmy, 136
Seerey, Pat, 79, 93–94, 164
Segui, Diego, 166
Selkirk, George, 82
Seminick, Andy, 93
Sewell, Truett "Rip," 184
Sexson, Richie, 221–2, 237
Seybold, Ralph "Socks," 24
Shamsky, Art, 123
Shaw, Jim, 50
Shawkey, Bob, 47
Shea Stadium (New York), 120, 167
Sheffield, Gary, 176, 208, 221, 227
Shibe Park (Philadelphia), 28, 52, 76, 82–83, 92–93, 102, 176
Shibe, Thomas, 59
Shirley, Tex, 89
Shocker, Urban, 61
Sievers, Roy, 103
Simmons, Al, 94
Simmons, Curt, 121
Sisler, George, 50, 59, 61
Skopec, John, 24
Skowron, Bill, 142, 144
Skydome (Toronto), 224, 237
Slaughter, Enos, 142

Small, Aaron, 214
Smith, David W., 108
Smith, Elmer, 138, 140
Smith, Hal, 116
Smith, Lonnie, 152
Smith, Ozzie, 150
Smith, Reggie, 145, 149
Snider, Edwin "Duke," 97, 101, 103-4, 117–8, 123, 141–3, 150, 164
  career summary, 117–8
Snyder, Charles "Pop," 6
Soriano, Alfonso, 178, 236
Sosa, Sammy, 53, 80, 95, 127, 195, 212–9, 222–3, 227–8
  career summary, 222–3
South End Grounds (Boston), 15
South Side Park (Chicago), 24, 30
Spahn, Warren, 115–6, 119, 122, 129, 164, 186
Spalding Company, 41–42, 165–6
special rules committee (1969), 38–39
Spencer, Daryl, 104
Spikes, Charlie, 162
spitball, 40–41, 59, 62
Sportsman's Park (St. Louis), 62, 138
Springer, Dennis, 218
St. Louis Browns, 98. *See also* Baltimore Orioles
St. Louis Cardinals, 156, 211
St. Mary's Industrial School for Boys, 43
Stallard, Tracy, 113
Stanley, Bob, 168
Stargell, Willie, 123, 130–1, 162, 167, 176
  career summary, 167

Steinbach, Terry, 189
Stengel, Casey, 139
Stenzel, Jake, 7
Stephens, Vern, 86–87, 117, 177
Stephenson, Garrett, 216
steroids, 204–6
Stewart, Shannon, 217
Stobbs, Chuck, 98
Stovey, Harry, 7–8, 10, 13–16, 25, 31, 59, 85, 172
Strawberry, Darryl, 178
strike zone, 94, 117, 127, 198–9
Stuart, Dick, 117, 192
Sullivan, Scott, 215, 222
supplements, 204
surgical procedures, 200
Sutton, Don, 175
Suzuki, Ichiro, 219

Tabor, Jim, 82, 84, 110, 135
Tackett, Jeff, 179
Tampa Ray Devil Rays, 225
Tanana, Frank, 179
Tankersley, Dennis, 221
Tatis, Fernando, 122, 215
Taylor, Ron, 131
team, four consecutive home runs, 115, 118–9, 237
Tejada, Miguel, 196
Tenace, Gene, 147
Terry, Adonis, 18
Terry, Ralph, 144
Texas Rangers, 134, 217, 221, 223–4. *See also* Washington Senators
Thomas, Frank (debut 1951), 104, 115
Thomas, Frank (debut 1990), 190, 195, 207, 221, 236, 238

Thomas, Gorman, 169
Thomas, Lee, 125
Thome, Jim, 80, 195, 218–9, 221, 238
Thompson, Eugene "Junior," 139–40, 145
Thompson, Sam, 18, 29, 59, 63
Thomson, Bobby, 96, 141
Thormahlen, Hank, 46
Three Rivers Stadium (Pittsburgh), 131, 176
Tiant, Luis, 122
Tiernan, Mike, 18
Tiger Stadium (Detroit), 47, 50, 54, 81, 95, 116, 124, 135, 172, 183, 188, 214
Tinker, Joe, 137
Tobin, Jack, 40
Tobin, Jim, 12, 85, 132
Tokyo Dome (Tokyo, Japan), 216, 225
Tomberlin, Andy, 210
Tomko, Brett, 222
Toronto Blue Jays, 109, 157, 166, 217, 237
Torrez, Mike, 168
Trachsel, Steve, 213
traded, season home run champ, 18, 31, 77–78, 95
Triple Crown, 7, 13, 17, 24, 26, 61, 64, 77, 80, 85, 91–92, 101, 121, 124, 133, 170
Trosky, Hal Sr., 77–78
Turner Field (Atlanta), 237
Turner, Jim, 81
Twitchell, Wayne, 134

U.S. Cellular Field (Chicago), 207, 219–20

Valenzuela, Fernando, 209
Vaughan, Joseph "Arky," 183
Vaughn, Greg, 210, 212, 214
Ventura, Robin, 155, 207–8
Versalles, Zoilo, 122
Veterans Stadium (Philadelphia), 134
Viau, Lee, 14
video rooms, 200
Vidro, Jose, 224
Vukovich, George, 150

Wagner, Leon, 116
Walberg, George "Rube," 52
Walker, Albert "Rube," 100
Walker, Clarence "Tilly," 40, 44, 58–59
Walker, Fleetwood, 90
Walker, Greg, 172
Walker, Larry, 211
Walker, Welday, 90
Wallach, Tim, 180
Wambsganss, Bill, 138
Waner, Lloyd, 66
Waner, Paul, 66, 79
Ward, Aaron, 40, 66
Washburn, Jarrod, 221
Washington Senators, 87, 103, 108, 134. *See also* Minnesota Twins; Texas Rangers
Washington, UL, 171
Waslewski, Gary, 128
Wathan, John, 149
Watt, Frank, 74

INDEX

weight training, 203–4
Welch, Mickey, 7
Welke, Tim, 171
Wells, Kip, 221
Wertz, Vic, 185
West Side Park (Chicago), 10, 17, 29
West, Max, 183
Whitaker, Lou, 189
White, Charlie, 99
White, Frank, 189
Whitehead, Burgess, 82
Whitehill, Earl, 70
Whiten, Mark, 181
Wilkerson, Brad, 224
Williams, Bernie, 155
Williams, Billy, 129, 165, 187
    career summary, 165
Williams, Claude "Lefty," 47
Williams, Fred "Cy," 18, 53, 58–59, 63, 65
Williams, Ken, 58, 60–62, 74, 92, 100, 102, 117, 170
Williams, Matt, 141, 154–5, 196–7, 211
Williams, Mitch, 153
Williams, Ted, 45, 64, 81, 84–85, 88, 91, 94–95, 102–3, 106–7, 120–1, 125, 128, 163, 167–8, 183–6, 225
    career summary, 106–7
Williamson, Ned, 9, 18, 29, 46–47, 61, 103
Wilson, Bill, 99
Wilson, Earl, 132
Wilson, Lewis "Hack," 64–66, 68–71, 74–75, 78, 81, 89, 93–94, 212
Wine, Bobby, 119
Winfield, Dave, 97, 208
    career summary, 208
Wise, Rick, 131–132
wood used for bats, 201
wool, Australian, 42, 61
World Series home runs, 27–29, 52, 68, 125
    brothers, 140, 145
    end with, 144, 153
    first, 136
    first game ending, 141
    first grand slam, 138
    first in extra innings, 137
    first lead-off, 136
    first pinch hit, 141
    for both leagues, 142–5, 149, 152, 154
    in three decades, 141, 144, 153
    two pinch hit in same Series, 143, 148
Wright, David, 238
Wrigley Field (Chicago), 81, 122, 129, 164, 176, 223
Wrigley Field (Los Angeles), 113, 192
Wynn, Early, 119
Wynn, Jim, 165, 188
Wynne, Marvell, 176

Yankee Stadium (New York), 53, 66, 88, 105, 112, 114, 124–5, 139, 148, 170, 191
Yastrzemski, Carl, 124, 129, 145, 168, 170, 189

career summary, 170
Yawkey, Tom, 45
York, Rudy, 53, 80, 87, 89, 110, 141, 184, 212, 218
Young, Chris, 228
Young, Denton "Cy," 136
Young, Eric, 180
Young, Mike, 177

youngest player to homer, 88
youth sports programs, 199–200

Zachary, Tom, 53
Zambrano, Carlos, 237
Zambrano, Victor, 225
Zernial, Gus, 95, 97, 99
Zwilling, Edward "Dutch," 31–32

ABOUT THE AUTHOR

David Vincent is a long-time member of the Society for American Baseball Research (SABR) and was presented with the organization's highest honor, the Bob Davids Award, in 1999. He is co-author of the award-winning book, *The Midsummer Classic: The Complete History of Baseball's All-Star Game*, *SABR presents the Home Run Encyclopedia*, and *Home Runs in the Old Ballparks*. *Parade* magazine ran a feature on Vincent in 2005.

Vincent is referred to as "The Sultan of Swat Stats" by ESPN and is regularly consulted by Major League Baseball, ESPN, FOX, *USA Today*, and many other media entities on the history of the home run.

He is the founding secretary of Retrosheet and regularly lends his expertise to this and other baseball history websites. Vincent has been an official scorer in four minor leagues and is now official scorer at RFK Stadium for the Washington Nationals.

Vincent graduated from the University of Massachusetts, earned a Doctor of Musical Arts degree from the University of Miami, and is a computer systems engineer for EDS. He and his wife, JoLynne, live in Northern Virginia.

www.ingramcontent.com/pod-product-compliance
Lightning Source LLC
Chambersburg PA
CBHW022105150426
43195CB00008B/279